THE PHILOSOPHY OF ITALIAN FASCISM

THE PHILOSOPHY OF ITALIAN FASCISM

FORMATION & EVOLUTION

DMITRY MOISEEV

ARKTOS
LONDON 2024

ARKTOS

Arktos.com fb.com/Arktos arktosmedia arktosjournal

ISBN

978-1-915755-40-7 (Paperback)
978-1-915755-41-4 (Hardback)
978-1-915755-42-1 (Ebook)

Translation

Harko Sked

Editing

Constantin von Hoffmeister

Layout & Cover

Tor Westman

CONTENTS

'Ideas always rule the world; political actions come in their wake — however well these actions may be planned, financed, or executed.'

Tomislav Sunic

'Fascism cannot be understood in many of its practical manifestations as a party organisation, as a system of education, as a discipline, unless it is seen in the light of its overall conception of life, in a spiritual way.'

Giovanni Gentile

'Only with awareness is action possible.'

Julius Evola

INTRODUCTION

Why examine Fascism today?

This work aims to reconstruct the historical and philosophical development of Italian Fascism, as well as to analyse it. The question of whether it is relevant to study the Fascist doctrine and its genesis in the historical and philosophical context is quite touchy, especially in Russia. Communist propaganda ingrained the erroneous notion in the national consciousness that Spanish Falangism, German National Socialism, and Italian Fascism were identical — political movements and their respective doctrines belonging to the same ideological pole. All European radical-right political movements in the first half of the twentieth century were branded 'Fascist'; the Sovietised explanation of the term closely parallels the position of the famous Italian neo-Hegelian Benedetto Croce, who posited that anti-Fascism is culture and Fascism is barbarism. We find a vivid illustration of this view in a famous Soviet poster, which reads: 'Fascism is the enemy of mankind. Fascism is the destruction of culture! Fascism is hunger! Fascism is prison! Fascism is war!' The assessment is extremely emotional and has a strong value judgement stemming from historical and ideological factors.

Italian Fascism should undoubtedly be considered a phenomenon of the twentieth century. In its revolutionary-modernist aspirations it belongs entirely to the era that spawned it, a period of profound social, political, and axiological crisis. It has long been the ghost of a bygone era, of which almost no trace remains. The movements commonly referred to as 'neo-Fascist' have unsuccessfully tried to turn back time, thus violating one of the guiding principles of the original Italian Fascist philosophy — that political forms should address contemporary challenges, and thus must be appropriate to their own time. One could justifiably argue that 'reviving' Fascism in the twenty-first century is not only pointless, it is technically impossible, and its contemporary apologists 'know not what they do'.

What, then, is the relevance of the question we pose? Contemporary political culture often sets too-narrow a framework of values to accommodate the diverse heritage of human thought. In today's world, with its plethora of international political institutions and the clear requirements of political order for countries that do not wish to become pariahs, turning to the radical political systems of the past might seem like a waste of time and energy. Nevertheless, these questions have not lost their relevance because history so often takes quite unexpected turns, with issues resurfacing that may have seemed long 'obsolete'.

Even if Fascism is forever a thing of the past, the values and political motives that gave rise to it, brought it to power in Europe, and secured its position of political hegemon for twenty years are still relevant today. Nor will they lose their significance in the future. A young nation in search of its own identity, endowed with a formidable historical legacy and outraged by its profound and thoroughly secondary position compared to the leading world powers, raises to political Olympus an ambitious young leader who promises change and who attempts to achieve this change by any means at his disposal. Against this backdrop of renewed political vitality, intellectual battles erupt between different schools of thought, one of which, in solidarity with the young radical political movement, becomes dominant and spawns a highly original philosophy. Soon afterwards, the leader becomes a tyrant, and the regime which promised so much delivers too little. The result is all too familiar — disaster, military defeat, decline, loss of sovereignty, and abandonment of the intellectual legacy that has been developed. For us, these are eternal themes that can be useful to examine from an intellectual and a political point of view (in terms of penetrating the essence of the events that took place and identifying their correlation and consequences). History should help us learn from the mistakes of the past. The history of philosophy, in turn, should reconstruct arguments with the greatest intellectual integrity.

This work should by no means be regarded as an apologia for Italian Fascism. While certainly a gentler and more liberal political system than its contemporaries — the bloody tyrannies of Stalin and Hitler — Mussolini's regime was far from any ideal. It was characterised by political repression (including political assassinations), a highly inefficient state and party apparatus, mass surveillance, the 'cult of the leader', the absence of any reasonable decentralisation, and many other shortcomings common to autocracies. All these facts have been extensively studied by historians and are common knowledge. At the same time, this book does not intend to reinforce and promote unscientific popular stereotypes associated with the big bad word that is 'Fascism'. Italian Fascism is too-significant a phenomenon in twentieth-century history and in the history of political teaching to be ignored for ideological, political, or ethical reasons, or to be brushed aside by ideological clichés of one sort or another. It requires no less study (both historically and historico-philosophically) than German National Socialism, which is much more 'popular' with researchers of right-wing radical regimes today.

Moreover, as this study shows, Italian Fascism had a deep philosophical tradition as its intellectual foundation. In addition to the fact that the Fascist leader himself was no stranger to intellectual pursuits, he also contributed to the doctrinal development of the regime's intellectual foundations by favouring thinkers of academic standing (Giovanni Gentile, Alfredo Rocco) who had significant academic reputations. This fact demands a reflection on the Fascist doctrine and motivates an analysis of its origins, content, and development.

With all this in mind, it becomes necessary to reconstruct the political philosophy of Italian Fascism in its temporal context to understand this doctrine in the light of all the key aspects of its formation, formulation, and development. The appeal to study the Fascist legacy should not be interpreted as a political action; its motivation is purely scientific. Science, of course, does not provide definitive answers to questions of values. However, this does not mean that it provides us no insight at all. As Max Weber noted, it may be 'useful for somebody who is able to ask the right question'.[1]

What are the aims of the author and this work?

The aim of this study is to provide a comprehensive historical and philosophical reconstruction of Italian Fascist philosophy in the spirit of hermeneutic methodology, taking into account the key influences that shaped the thinking of the major Italian Fascist intellectuals, the philosophical foundations of the Fascist doctrine, the main directions of its development, and the internal contradictions that ultimately led this intellectual tradition to its demise and oblivion.

In order to achieve this goal, we need to examine the most significant layers of Italian history, philosophy, and political culture in this context. First of all, we have to identify and analyse the preconditions for Italian Fascist philosophy, namely the political situation in Italy in the second half of the nineteenth and early twentieth centuries and Italian philosophical idealism of the Risorgimento period, Revolutionary and National Syndicalism, elitism, nationalism, and Futurism. It is then necessary to consider the intellectual development of Benito Mussolini himself, the leader of Italian Fascism, and the main philosophical influences on the evolution of his ideas — while not a professional philosopher, the Duce was personally involved in the shaping of the Fascist doctrine, which is why his distinctive intellectual biography is of undoubted interest to us.

1 Max Weber, *Science as a Vocation,* (London: Unwin Hyman, 1989).

Moving on to philosophy, we will look at the key epistemological, ontological, and anthropological dimensions of the 'actual idealism' of Giovanni Gentile, the 'philosopher of Fascism', as well as his social and political philosophy, which is the foundation of the Fascist political and philosophical doctrine. Of particular importance in this context are Gentile's theoretical works: *The Theory of Mind as Pure Act*, *Genesis and Structure of Society*, *The Reform of Education*, as well as political texts such as *Manifesto of the Fascist Intellectuals* and *The Doctrine of Fascism*, in the creation of which the Italian philosopher took a very active part. Particularly relevant to the purpose of our study is a detailed analysis of *The Doctrine of Fascism*, which, as we will show, is based on the ontological and ethical foundations of the philosophy of actual idealism.

We then turn to non-actualist variations on the social philosophy of Italian Fascism, namely the ideas of Alfredo Rocco, Sergio Panunzio, Carlo Costamagna, Giuseppe Bottai, and Julius Evola. Since the intellectual horizon of Fascist Italy was not limited to Gentile, with competing ideals of social order engaged in an active intellectual debate over the future course of the country, for the sake of objectivity we have to briefly consider other models that are not derived from actualism.

It is also important to take a look at the ideas of the most important representatives of the 'Gentile school', Ugo Spirito and Camillo Pellizzi. Working in the framework of actual idealism, they proposed their own variations on Gentile's ideas. Finally, we will investigate the particular character of republican Fascism during the Italian Social Republic (Republic of Salò), whose theoretical foundations were very different from those of the *ventennio*, the 'twenty years of Fascism'.

The main subjects of our study will be works by the aforementioned authors that articulate the political philosophy of Italian Fascism, as well as various historical and biographical materials. It is important to note that the political philosophy of Fascism itself is viewed as an independent intellectual phenomenon that took place in the context of both the general European and the specifically Italian political philosophy of the nineteenth and twentieth centuries.

Existing Approaches to Explaining the Fascist Phenomenon

The history of twentieth century political thought has produced a variety of different concepts that attempt to explain Fascism.[2] However, it is only relatively recently– since the 1960s — that Fascism began to be studied as an independent political phenomenon with its own ideological content. The first theoretical studies in this field were authored by Italian and German historians. The intellectual history of Fascism has since attracted the interest of political scientists in the English-speaking world, resulting in a body of scholarly research texts.

In twentieth-century political philosophy and intellectual history, one can distinguish several distinct theories that investigated Fascism: Marxist political philosophy, the liberal theory of totalitarianism, and the conservative approach. The fundamentally different analytical perspectives of the Fascist phenomenon offered by these theories are explained by their essentially different political ontology.

The Marxist reaction to Fascism followed almost immediately after the latter came to power in Italy — in November 1922. At the Fourth Congress of the Communist International, Fascism was described as 'a tool in the hands of large landowners'.[3] Amadeo Bordiga, one of the leaders of the Italian Communist Party, pointed out that the problem is not just that the Fascist movement is a counterrevolutionary terrorist organisation, but also that Fascism is dangerous social demagogy that is rapidly gaining the support of the masses. For Communists,

2 For more detail, see: Dmitry Moiseev, 'Интеллектуальная история итальянского фашизма. Современные подходы' [An intellectual history of Italian Fascism. Contemporary approaches], *Dialogue with Time* 55 (2016): 194–207.

3 J. M. Cammett, 'Communist Theories of Fascism, 1920–1935', *Science & Society* 31, no. 2 (Spring, 1967), p. 150.

Fascism represents the interests of the conservative bourgeoisie, and the Fascists' rise to power in Italy was not a revolution but simply the consequence of the fact that the capitalists had 'changed the model of governance'.[4] For this reason, they saw Fascism as an imperialist reactionary movement inimical to socialism, democracy, and humanism. From the Communist point of view, Fascism was a bourgeois dictatorship that suppressed the revolutionary sentiments of working people; a tool of monopolistic capital directed against the working class.[5]

It was specifically this Marxist approach that Soviet thinkers adopted when they broached the topic of Italian Fascism. Hershen Berkovich Sandomierski[6] and Dmitry Igorevich Antonov[7] pioneered the Russian Marxist critique of Fascism. Their trajectory was continued by S.M. Slobodskoj,[8] who authored the first major Soviet scholarly work on Italian Fascism, which was published in 1946 by the Institute of World Economy and International Relations of the USSR Academy of Sciences. The author makes no secret of his ideological approach to the subject. From the first lines, he brands Fascism with all the propaganda clichés at his disposal. According to Slobodskoj, it is a filthy offspring of greedy imperialism, a system of total terror and violence;

4 Jane Degras, *The Communist International, 1919–1943: Documents,* (London: Oxford University Press, 1956), p. 137.

5 See: Georgi Dimitrov, 'The Fascist Offensive and the Tasks of the Communist International in the Struggle of the Working Class against Fascism', in *Selected Works in Three Volumes* (Volume 2), (Sofia Press, 1972); Walter L. Adamson, 'Gramsci's Interpretation of Fascism', *Journal of the History of Ideas* 41: no. 4 (Oct.–Dec., 1980), pp. 615–633; Robert S. *Wistrich,* 'Leon Trotsky's Theory of Fascism', *Journal of Contemporary History* 11, no. 4, Special Issue: Theories of Fascism (Oct., 1976), pp. 157–184.

6 Hershen Berkovich Sandomierski, *Фашизм* [Fascism], (Moscow, 1923); Sandomierski, *Закат фашизма* [Decline of Fascism], (Moscow, 1925); Sandomierski, *Фашизм и молодежь* [Fascism and Youth], (Moscow, 1925).

7 Dmitry Antonov, *Очерки фашизма в Италии* [Essays on Fascism in Italy], (Moscow, 1923).

8 S. M. Slobodskoj, *Социальная сущность фашизма* [The Social Nature of Fascism], (Moscow, 1928).

Mussolini is an unprincipled, conniving adventurer who despises people; Gentile is a Fascist liar.

Slobodskoj offers a simple and straightforward ideological narrative in the Marxist spirit: the unification of Italy did not improve the lives of the workers, the bourgeoisie dragged the country into World War I, after which it was swept away in a 'Fascist coup', and the country's new Fascist leadership served the interests of the financial oligarchy. These changes resulted in the impoverishment of the masses, the exacerbation of social tensions, an explosion of popular indignation, and the overthrow of Mussolini.

'The attempts of the most reactionary, adventurist groups of the bourgeoisie to impose on the Italian people the role of a ferocious imperialist predator, a strangler of other nations, have failed. These attempts, which turned Italy into an instrument of Hitler's thugs, the world's fiercest imperialists, could not but end in disaster for the country and destruction for Fascism',[9] Slobodskoj concludes. The whole ideological content of Fascism is described in his work as a 'shouting anti-capitalist demagogy, sharpened mainly against the liberal bourgeoisie'.

The Marxist ideological narrative of Fascism in Soviet scholarship was continued by the historian B.R. Lopukhov, who devoted a whole series of works, published between 1959 and 1986, to matters of Italian Fascism. Lopukhov speaks rapturously about the activities of Italian Communists Antonio Gramsci and Palmiro Togliatti, noting that their 'revolutionary work' 'provoked resistance from the bourgeoisie, which set out to organise a counter-revolutionary and anti-democratic-Fascist terror'.[10] In another book, published in 1968, commenting on Slobodskoj's work mentioned above, Lopukhov notes that 'now that

9 S. M. Slobodskoj, *Итальянский фашизм и его крах* [Italian Fascism and its Collapse], (Moscow: Gospolitizdat, 1946), p. 205.

10 B. R. Lopukhov, *Борьба рабочего класса Италии против фашизма* [The Italian Working Class Struggle against Fascism], (Moscow: USSR Academy of Sciences Publishing, 1959), p. 49.

the era of Fascism in Italy is receding ever further into the past, the essence of this historical phenomenon appears to us more and more complex. A great historical perspective opens up a new connection of phenomena and facts'.[11] In a later work, following the same approach ('imperialist interests and nationalist passions'[12] are identified as the main motives of Fascist policy), the author mentions the works of Ernst Nolte and intellectual influences on the formation of Mussolini's world view (in particular, Friedrich Nietzsche, Georges Sorel, and William James), rather than just economic statistics showing the 'impoverishment of the masses', as was done in the early Soviet studies. In his last work on the subject, published in the years of *perestroika*, the author allows himself to refer to Alceste De Ambris, Carlo Costamagna, and Antonio Rocco, but the discursive nature of the approach remains consistently Marxist.[13]

In addition to the early critiques of Fascism by Hershen Sandomierski and Dmitry Antonov, as well as the scholarly works of S.M. Slobodskoj and B.R. Lopukhov, when considering the Soviet Marxist historiography of Italian Fascism, the works of G. S. Filatov and V. I. Mikhailenko should be highlighted. The first, although adhering to a critical position invariable for Marxists, raised a new layer of intellectual material on Italian Fascism for the Soviet reader — his works contain references to Paolo Orano, Roberto Mazzetti, and Giuseppe Bottai.[14] The second, noting that 'the theme of Fascism is constantly in the midst of the ideological and political struggle between

11 Lopukhov, *Фашизм и рабочее движение в Италии* [Fascism and the Labour Movement in Italy], (Moscow: Nauka, 1968), p. 398.

12 Lopukhov, *История фашистского режима в Италии* [The History of the Fascist Regime in Italy], (Moscow: Nauka, 1977), p. 218.

13 Lopukhov, *Эволюция буржуазной власти в Италии* [The evolution of bourgeois power in Italy], (Moscow: Nauka, 1986).

14 See: G. S. Filatov, *Фашизм, неофашизм и антифашистская борьба в Италии* [Fascism, Neo-Fascism and the Anti-Fascist Struggle in Italy], (Moscow: Nauka, 1984).

Marxist-Leninist science and bourgeois historiography',[15] pays attention to the genesis of Fascist ideology, citing Enrico Corradini and Alfredo Rocco.[16] Despite the gradual movement of Soviet historians away from Marxist dogmatism towards scientific objectivity, no ideologically unbiased work on Fascism was published in Russian in the period preceding the collapse of the USSR.

Let us move on from Marxist theories regarding the examination of Fascism to other intellectual frames of reference. Liberal theorists operated in a different paradigm, radically distinct from that of Communism. Friedrich von Hayek, one of the most prominent classical liberals, equated Italian Fascism, German National Socialism, and Soviet Stalinism in his famous book *The Road to Serfdom* (1944), claiming that all of these regimes were products of the same socialist premises. In *Totalitarian Dictatorship and Autocracy* (1956)[17] Zbigniew Brzezinski and Carl Joachim Friedrich point out the essential similarity of Communist and Fascist totalitarianism, established as a result of economic and political crises in Europe. According to liberal theorists, Fascism is a kind of totalitarianism in which nationalist state ideology, repressive domestic policies, and a socialist economy play a key role. For classical liberals, Fascism is a denial of the Enlightenment (a thesis that would be questioned in later intellectual history) and one of humanity's major mistakes in the twentieth century.[18]

15 V. I. Mikhailenko, *Итальянский фашизм: основные вопросы историографии* [Italian Fascism: Main Issues of Historiography], (Sverdlovsk: Urals University Press, 1987), p. 3.

16 Ibid., pp. 134–150.

17 In this context, it should be noted that the view that there are no substantive differences between Communism and Fascism is not characteristic of all liberals, but rather of those who represent right-wing, classical liberalism. Proof of this is the so-called 'historians' dispute' of 1986–1987, during which the left-wing liberal Jürgen Habermas harshly criticised Ernst Nolte for comparing Communism and Fascism, accusing him of apologising for the latter and 'demoralising' the past.

18 See: Friedrich Hayek, *The Road to Serfdom*, (Oxfordshire: Routledge Classics, 2001); Zbigniew Brzezinski and Carl Joachim Friedrich, *Totalitarian Dictatorship and Autocracy*, (Cambridge, Massachusetts: Harvard University Press, 1956).

Special mention should be made of the theories of Fascism which can be conventionally called conservative. Eric Voegelin reasoned that linguistic vulgarity and the use of pagan symbols are proof that the true essence of Fascism is criminal barbarism. According to Ivan Solonevich, social revolution is organised by the 'biological scum of humanity', wreaking havoc and destruction. The terror organised by Fascist and Communist regimes is physical, economic, and spiritual in nature. For conservatives, Fascism is an essentially plebeian, primitive phenomenon, brought to the forefront of world history by the masses. Its language and morals are vulgar, its barbaric methods brutal, its inner content lacking any profound substance. The conservative approach assesses Fascism according to its own internal logic — elitist, hierarchical, and anti-egalitarian.[19]

All three theories of Fascism listed above present a more or less ideological perspective on the phenomenon, largely due to the fact that these thinkers and politicians were mostly contemporaries of Fascism; for many of them their political and intellectual activities in opposition to Fascism ended tragically. Bordiga was repeatedly arrested and sent into exile; Antonio Gramsci was convicted and died in prison; Arendt and Voegelin were forced to emigrate. As for Soviet historians, the same G. S. Filatov participated in the war effort and worked in Italy

---

Hannah Arendt is also frequently included among conventionally liberal theorists, which is not entirely accurate: her own interpretation of Fascism, Nazism, and Stalinism in *The Origins of Totalitarianism* (1951) was misunderstood largely due to the fact that her political thinking was closer to the political logic of such anti-liberal thinkers as Martin Heidegger and Carl Schmitt. See Hannah Arendt, *The Origins of Totalitarianism*, (San Diego: Harcourt, 1973); Arendt, *Between Past and Future*, (London: Penguin Books, 1993). However, despite her view that neither liberalism nor conservatism are capable of grasping the essence of political reality, her attitude towards Fascism and Nazism can be described as critical.

19 See: Eric Voegelin, 'The Political Religions' in *The Collected Works of Eric Voegelin, Volume 5*, (Columbia, Missouri: University of Missouri Press, 1999); Clifford F. Porter, 'Eric Voegelin on Nazi Political Extremism', *Journal of the History of Ideas*, 63, no. 1 (Jan., 2002), pp. 151–171; Ivan Solonevich, *Диктатура сволочи* [Bastard Dictatorship], (Russian Word, 1995).

in the Allied Commission from 1944 to 1947.[20] Unsurprisingly, many of those listed pursued not so much scientific as political objectives, from which the objectivity and credibility of their research could not but suffer.

As for objective historical studies, as Emilio Gentile noted, 'before the early 1960s even Italian historians showed little interest in studying Fascism. The books on the subject that appeared after 1945 were written either by Fascists or anti-Fascists and were a straightforward narrative. Any serious attempts to place Fascism in a historical context were not influential'.[21] It was only in the 1960s that interest in the study of Fascism emerged among Western historians and an approach that could be classified as intellectual history began to take shape. Studies by Italian, American, and British scholars offered new angles of research into the phenomenon: Fascism was assessed as one of the consequences of European political history and culture; its own political and philosophical content was examined, and Fascism was seen as an independent political phenomenon that deserved unbiased historical research.

For intellectual historical studies, the ideological aspects of Fascism, which are closely linked to the historical and spiritual context of the era, are key to understanding the whole phenomenon, as are the institutional characteristics, spiritual climate, and intellectual atmosphere that prevailed in the Fascist states. In Italy, such an understanding only emerged in the 1960s when the question of an in-depth study of

20 As noted in the preface to the collection of his works on Fascism, G. S. Filatov 'was a witness to the agony of Fascism and the struggle for a new, democratic Italy'. Jurij Andreevič Krasin, 'О научном наследии Г. С. Филатова' [On the Scientific Legacy of G. S. Filatov] in G. S. Filatov, *Фашизм, неофашизм и антифашистская борьба в Италии* [Fascism, Neo-Fascism and the Anti-Fascist Struggle in Italy], (Moscow: Nauka,1984), p. 4.

21 Emilio Gentile, 'Fascism in Italian Historiography: In Search of an Individual Historical Identity' in *Journal of Contemporary History*, 21, no. 2, Twentieth Anniversary Issue (Apr.,1986), p. 180.

Fascism was raised by historians Renzo de Felice[22] and Nino Valeri.[23] Roberto Vivarelli's *Postwar Italy and the Formation of Fascism* was published in 1967,[24] examining, among other things, the psychological

22 Renzo de Felice was one of the leading scholars of Fascism in Italy. In the post-war period he produced a body of work on Fascism in general and on Mussolini in particular. De Felice distinguished between 'Fascism as a movement' and 'Fascism as a regime'—in his view, while the former can be seen to have ideological foundations rooted in the Enlightenment, the latter is mostly a 'superstructure' to Mussolini's personal dictatorship. That said, de Felice was one of the first Italian scholars to insist that the ideological foundations of Fascism should be impartially examined from a scientific point of view, for which he was repeatedly criticised by the Left. See: Renzo de Felice, *Le interpretazioni del Fascismo* [Interpretations of Fascism], (Bari: Editori Laterza, 2012); de Felice, *Il Fascismo. Le interpretazioni dei contemporanei e degli storici* [Fascism. The Interpretations of Contemporaries and Historians], (Bari: Editori Laterza, 2008). Of all the works by Renzo de Felice, it is necessary to single out the biography of Mussolini in eight volumes, on which the historian worked for over thirty years: de Felice, *Mussolini il rivoluzionario. 1883–1920* [Mussolini the Revolutionary. 1883–1920], (Milan: Il Giornale—Biblioteca Storica, 2015); de Felice, *Mussolini il Fascista. La conquista del potere. 1921–1925* [Mussolini the Fascist. The Conquest of Power. 1921–1925], (Milan: Il Giornale—Biblioteca Storica, 2015); de Felice, *Mussolini il Fascista. L'organizzazione dello stato Fascista. 1925–1929* [Mussolini the Fascist. The Organisation of the Fascist State. 1925–1929], (Milan: Il Giornale—Biblioteca Storica, 2015); de Felice, *Mussolini il duce. Gli anni del consenso. 1929–1936* [Mussolini the Duce. The Years of Consensus. 1929–1936], (Milan: Il Giornale—Biblioteca Storica, 2015); de Felice, *Mussolini il duce. Lo Stato totalitario. 1936–1940* [Mussolini the Duce. The Totalitarian State. 1936–1940], (Milan: Il Giornale—Biblioteca Storica, 2015); de Felice, *Mussolini l'alleato. L'Italia in guerra. 1940–1943. Tomo primo. Dalla guerra "breve" alla guerra lunga* [Mussolini the Ally. Italy at War. 1940–1943. Volume One: From 'Short' to Long War], (Milan: Il Giornale—Biblioteca Storica, 2015); de Felice, *Mussolini l'alleato. L'Italia in guerra. 1940–1943. Tomo secondo. Crisi e agonia del regime* [Mussolini the Ally. Italy at War. 1940–1943. Volume Two: Crisis and Agony of the Regime], (Milan: Il Giornale—Biblioteca Storica, 2015); de Felice, *Mussolini l'alleato. La guerra civile. 1943–1945* [Mussolini the Ally. The Civil War. 1943–1945], (Milan: Il Giornale—Biblioteca Storica, 2015).

23 Nino Valeri, *Trent'anni di storia politica italiana, 1915–1945* [Thirty Years of Italian Political History, 1915–1945], (Turin: ERI, 1962).

24 Roberto Vivarelli, *Il dopoguerra in Italia e l'avvento del Fascismo* [Postwar Italy and the Formation of Fascism], (Naples: Istituto italiano per gli studi storici, 1967).

aspects of Italy after World War I. In Germany in the same decade, Ernst Nolte's book *Three Faces of Fascism* (1963)[25] was published, in which the author suggested the concept of considering Fascism as a radical form of resistance to Marxism, bourgeois values, and the spirit of modernity. Later on, similar studies were actively developed in the UK and the USA.

When analysing the body of contemporary intellectual historical research aimed at explaining Fascism, a number of key points of discussion can be identified: the origins and foundations of Fascist theories, the mythological basis of Fascism, Fascism as a political religion, and Fascism as a doctrine.

25 Ernst Nolte, *Three Faces of Fascism: Action Française, Italian Fascism, National Socialism,* (New York: Henry Holt & Company, 1966).

Among such works of contemporary scholars are those by Roger Eatwell,[26] Stanley G. Payne,[27] David D. Roberts,[28] Roger Griffin,[29] Emilio

26 Roger Eatwell, *Fascism: a History*, (New York: Penguin Books, 1997). Eatwell identifies the following origins of Fascism: German Romanticism, Hegel's philosophy, nineteenth-century nationalism, theories of race, and elitist theories.

27 Stanley G. Payne, *A History of Fascism 1914–1945*, (Madison, Wisconsin: University of Wisconsin Press, 1996). According to Payne, Fascism is a product of the 'ideas of 1789', derived from the secular aspects of the Enlightenment. An important theoretical contribution of Payne is the debunking of a number of ideological myths about Fascist regimes — in particular that they were supposedly all imperialist as well as racist. Both of these apply mainly to German National Socialism, which in this case is rather an exception to the rule. Fascist nationalism tended to be defensive in nature, a consequence of a specific instinct to protect national identity. Imperialism was certainly characteristic of Italian Fascism and German National Socialism, but other similar regimes did not have a pronounced ambition to conquer new lands.

28 David D. Roberts, *Syndicalist Tradition & Italian Fascism*, (Chapel Hill, North Carolina: University of North Carolina Press, 1979). Roberts's approach is interesting in that the author demonstrates the logic of the intellectual evolution of Italian Revolutionary Syndicalism, tracing the latter's obvious influence on Fascist doctrine.

29 Roger Griffin, *Fascism*, (Oxford: Oxford University Press, 2009). Griffin sees a common basis for Fascist theories not on an ideological, but a mythological plane. He builds a certain typology of characteristic features of Fascism. For him, Fascism has ten key features that have a doctrinal, philosophical and ideological character: anti-liberal Fascism, its anti-conservatism, reliance on charismatic power, anti-rationalism, socialist elements, totalitarianism, heterogeneity of social support for Fascism, racism, internationalism (anti-Communist universalism), and eclecticism (variety of social and philosophical approaches within the same regime).

Gentile,[30] A. James Gregor,[31] Marco Piraino and Stefano Fiorito.[32]

The intellectual historical studies conducted by Italian, American and British scholars over the last fifty years have resulted in a corpus of ethically neutral, non-ideologised texts that allow us to trace a certain internal logic in the intellectual evolution of Italian Fascist doctrine, identify the origins and foundations of Fascist theories, recognise the

30 Emilio Gentile, 'Fascism, Totalitarianism and Political Religion: Definitions and Critical Reflections on Criticism of an Interpretation', *Fascism, Totalitarianism and Political Religion* / Ed. by Roger Griffin, (London and New York: Routledge, 2005); Gentile, 'Fascism as Political Religion', *Journal of Contemporary History*, 25, no. 2/3 (May-June, 1990), pp. 229–251. According to Gentile, the key to explaining Fascism is the idea of the 'political religion', i.e. the type of religion that relegates an ideology, movement or political regime to the realm of the sacred by deification of a secular essence transformed into a myth.

31 A. James Gregor, *Mussolini's Intellectuals. Fascist Social and Political Thought*, (Princeton, New Jersey: Princeton University Press, 2005); A. James Gregor, *Totalitarianism and Political Religion. An Intellectual History*, (Redwood City, California: Stanford University Press, 2012). This author rejects the early interpretations of Fascism as an ideologically empty, irrational movement devoid of intellectual content, and opposes viewing Italian Fascism in conjunction with German National Socialism, because, in his opinion, significant ideological differences are obvious between the two revolutionary regimes. According to Gregor, the origins of the Fascist doctrine lie in the idealist philosophy of Giuseppe Mazzini, the Italian nationalism of Enrico Corradini, Giovanni Gentile's theory of the ethical state, and Alfredo Rocco's national political economy. James Gregor's theoretical approach rooted Fascist ideologies in European history and political culture, which was necessary to further develop a corpus of unbiased scholarly texts on the subject.

32 Marco Piraino and Stefano Fiorito, *Fascist Identity. Political Project and Doctrine of Fascism*, (Lexington, KY, 2013). According to Piraino and Fiorito, Fascism is a modernist totalitarian political movement that opposes both liberalism and Marxism-Leninism. In their understanding, Fascism does not fit into the classical ideological framework of the Left or Right, as it offers a strictly unitary model of state and nation. The ideological essence of its doctrine is based on the ethico-idealist evolution of socialist and nationalist thought; it is the opposite of liberalism and Marxism. The basis of the doctrine is the ethical totalitarian state, the source of spiritual and political imperialism. According to Piraino and Fiorito, Fascist imperialism is deeply rooted in European and Italian culture and philosophy.

mythological basis of Fascism, and identify its main ideas. The array of scholarly texts published in Italian and English over the last twenty-five years makes it possible to examine the ideological content of Fascism without any moral preconceptions, from a scientific point of view.[33]

It is now appropriate to return to the issue of Russian-language studies of Fascism, covering the post-Soviet period (1991–2016). The vast majority of the literature published on the subject in the Russian period is centred in one way or another around the personality of Benito Mussolini. First of all, the works of the historian L. S. Belousov[34] and the journalist M. M. Ilyinsky[35] must be acknowledged. The trans-

33 The abundance of references to English-language texts in this book, and the polemic mainly with American and British authors, probably require additional clarification. The fact is that for Italy itself the Fascist question remains a rather sensitive and ambiguous one. From my experience of numerous trips to Italy, especially from conversations with representatives of older generations who witnessed (even as children) the Fascist era, I can say that in the country there is no straightforward attitude towards this period of history — one can see a marked contrast with Germany and its unconditional 'guilt' surrounding Nazism and certain parallels with our country and its Bolshevik past. The state of national consciousness is undoubtedly reflected in the ethos of the academic community as well — of course, Fascism is studied in Italy and some scholars have undertaken outstanding research in volume and quality (for example, the works of Renzo de Felice, Emilio Gentile, Nino Valeri, and Roberto Vivarelli, to which we have referred above). At the same time, the Anglo-American sources are particularly useful because their authors are completely unbiased and can talk about Fascism as peacefully as they do about ancient Rome or the Inca Empire, without experiencing any moral quandaries. Therefore, when I set out to achieve objective results, I focused mainly on Americans and Britons.

34 L. S. Belousov, *Муссолини. Диктатура и демагогия* [Mussolini. Dictatorship and Demagogy], (Moscow: Mashinostroenie, 1993); Belousov, *Режим Муссолини и массы* [Mussolini's Regime and the Masses], (Moscow: Moscow State University Press, 2000); Belousov and A. I. Patrushev, *Любовь диктаторов. Муссолини, Гитлер, Франко* [The Love of Dictators. Mussolini, Hitler, Franco], (Moscow: AST Press Book, 2001).

35 M. M. Ilyinsky, *Жизнь и смерть Бенито Муссолини* [The Life and Death of Benito Mussolini], (Moscow: Veche, 2000).

lated biographies of the Duce[36] as well as some translations of original texts (mostly biographical in nature)[37] are also abundantly available in Russian. The Russian philosopher A. L. Zorin also translated into Russian the major works of Giovanni Gentile. The publication of *Selected Philosophical Works of Giovanni Gentile*[38] in seven volumes, each preceded by an article by the scholar from Krasnodar, can be seen as a significant step towards the discovery of actual idealism (which formed the philosophical basis of *The Doctrine of Fascism)* for the Russian-speaking reader. In addition, A. L. Zorin has written and published a number of scholarly works on the Italian neo-idealism of Gentile, Croce, and their students.[39] As for Russian-language doctoral

36 Christopher Hibbert, *Benito Mussolini: The Rise and Fall of Il Duce*, (London: Penguin, 1975); Jasper Ridley, *Mussolini: A Biography*, (Maryland: Cooper Square Press, 2000); Denis Mack Smith, *Mussolini*, (New York: Knopf, 1982).

37 Benito Mussolini, *Третий путь: без демократов и коммунистов* [The Third Way: Without Democrats and Communists], (Moscow: Algorithm, 2012); Romano Mussolini, *My Father, Il Duce*, (Carlsbad, California: Kales Press, 2006).

38 *Selected Philosophical Works of Giovanni Gentile*; translation from Italian, preface, commentary, and indication of names by A. L. Zorin, (Federal Agency on Culture and Cinematography, Federal State Educational Institution of Higher Professional Education, Krasnodar: Krasnodar State University of Culture and Arts Press, 2008–2012); Zorin, *Персонализм итальянских спиритуалистов XX в.* [Personalism of the Italian Spiritualists of the Twentieth Century], (Krasnodar: Krasnodar State University of Culture and Arts Press, 1998); Zorin, *Кросчеанцы в поисках субъекта истории и морали* [Croceans in Search of the Subject of History and Morality], (Krasnodar: Krasnodar State University of Culture and Arts Press, 1998); Zorin, *Философские искания левых джентилеанцев* [Philosophical Quests of the Left-Wing Gentileans], (Krasnodar: Krasnodar State University of Culture and Arts Press, 1999); Zorin, *Этика итальянских неоидеалистов. Проблема обоснования морали и метода* [Ethics of Italian Neo-Idealists. The Problem of the Justification of Morality and Method], (Krasnodar: Krasnodar State University of Culture and Arts Press, 1999); Zorin, *Философско-этические взгляды крочеанцев и джентилеанцев* [Philosophical and Ethical Views of the Croceans and the Gentileans], (Krasnodar: Krasnodar State University of Culture and Arts Press, 2001).

39 A. L. Zorin, *Philosophical and Ethical Views of the Croceans and the Gentileans.*

studies, we should mention the following dissertations: *The Actual Idealism of Giovanni Gentile* by A. Generalov,[40] *Moral Philosophy of Italian Neo-Idealism in the 20th Century: The Problem of Justifying Morality* by the abovementioned Zorin,[41] and *Fascism, the Working Class and Mass Consciousness in Italy, Late 1920s-1943* by historian L. Belousov.[42] In other dissertation studies on similar subjects (S. V. Kotov's *European Fascism: Social and Cultural Pseudo-Values of a Political Movement*[43] and his doctoral dissertation, *Neo-Fascism as a Political Phenomenon of Modernity: Philosophical and Political Origin and Conceptual Genesis*;[44] G. E. Davydova's doctoral dissertation, *Philosophical and Anthropological Foundations of European Fascism*;[45] and V. K. Sakhibgoryaev's dissertation *Fascism as a Phenomenon and Concept of Philosophy of Culture*[46]) neither actual idealism, nor the po-

40 A. I. Generalov, *Giovanni Gentile's 'Actual Idealism'*, Dissertation Candidate of Philosophy (Moscow, 1996).

41 A. L. Zorin, *Моральная философия итальянского неоидеализма XX в.: проблема обоснования морали* [Moral Philosophy of Twentieth-Century Italian Neo-Idealism: The Problem of Moral Justification], Doctoral dissertation in Philosophy, (St. Petersburg, 1999).

42 L. S. Belousov, *Фашистский режим, рабочий класс и массовое сознание в Италии, конец 1920-х — 1943 гг* [The Fascist Regime, the Working Class and Mass Consciousness in Italy, Late 1920s-1943], Doctoral candidate in History, (Moscow, 1999).

43 S. V. Kotov, *Европейский фашизм: социокультурные псевдоценности политического движения* [European Fascism: Social and Cultural Pseudo-Values of a Political Movement], Dissertation candidate in Philosophy, (Rostov-on-Don, 2005).

44 S. V. Kotov, *Неофашизм как политический феномен современности: философско-политические истоки и концептуальный генезис* [Neo-Fascism as a Political Phenomenon of Modernity: Philosophical and Political Origin and Conceptual Genesis], Doctoral Dissertation in Political Science, (Rostov-on-Don, 2011).

45 G. E. Davydova, *Философско-антропологические основания европейского фашизма* [Philosophical and Anthropological Foundations of European Fascism], Dissertation candidate in philosophy, (Rostov-on-Don, 2005).

46 V. K. Sakhibgoryaev, *Фашизм как явление и концепция философии культуры* [Fascism as a Phenomenon and Concept of Philosophy of Culture], Doctoral

litical philosophy of Italian Fascism are distinguished from the general group of 'Fascist' theories in which the key role is played, as a rule, by German National Socialism, which differs significantly from Italian Fascism both in its origins and its doctrinal content. In historiography, such an approach to Fascism is commonly referred to as 'expansive'. This study attempts to significantly 'narrow' the material under examination to Italian Fascism as an independent intellectual and political phenomenon.

Our Research Principles and Key Definitions

It is clear from the above that not a single attempt at a comprehensive historical and philosophical reconstruction of the political philosophy of Italian Fascism has been made in Russian. Soviet era thinkers created ideologically engaged texts, reproducing the arguments of Marxist ideologues, while in contemporary Russian scholarship and journalism, only the direction of research related to the personality of Benito Mussolini has developed considerably.

The above-mentioned studies by Western scholars can be characterised as having been carried out in accordance with the methods of 'intellectual history', which can be defined as the study of intellectuals, ideas, and intellectual structures over time. Intellectual history often uses a very detailed reconstruction of philosophical arguments and in this aspect is almost indistinguishable from the history of philosophy. Moreover, the discipline tends to view ideas as derived from history, understood in the broadest possible context, be it that of institutional change, social confrontation, or intellectual biography.[47]

At the same time, for our purposes, in order to meet the aims and objectives set out above, the research must be historical *and*

---

dissertation candidate in Philosophy, (Rostov-on-Don, 2008).

47 It should be noted, however, that intellectual history places more emphasis on the cultural, biographical, and social aspects of the formation of particular attitudes and traditions of thought than does the history of philosophy.

philosophical. Why is intellectual history insufficient to answer questions about the political philosophy of Italian Fascism?

First of all, we should note the fragmentary nature of the historical and philosophical excursions undertaken by intellectual historians. The line of reasoning in the vast majority of the published works does not go beyond the first decade of the twentieth century, covering, at best, the pre-war period (the exception are the texts of A. James Gregor and a few modern Italian authors who have begun to analyse the philosophical foundations of Fascist ideology, primarily based on the works of Giovanni Gentile). If we look carefully at the primary sources (*The Doctrine of Fascism* by Mussolini, *The Political Doctrine of Fascism* by Rocco, and numerous works by Gentile), we can find a much deeper intellectual and philosophical foundation, which was referred to by the Fascist ideologists themselves: the Renaissance philosophers, Risorgimento thinkers (primarily Mazzini, Gioberti, Rosmini, Spaventa), and German classical philosophy (mainly the works of Hegel). As a rule, insufficient attention is paid to the tradition of Revolutionary Syndicalism going back to Sorel and its Italian interpretation (only David D. Roberts puts an emphasis on this). This is the first reason why a historical-philosophical approach is called for, including a semantic reconstruction and description of Fascist arguments, as well as hermeneutic comprehension of the origin and evolution of this political tradition.

Secondly, the central figure in the intellectual history of Fascism and co-author of *The Doctrine of Fascism* is Giovanni Gentile, an academic philosopher. Gentile's arguments, an understanding of which is necessary to reveal the political ontology of Fascism, are intelligible only with a proper depth of historical and philosophical immersion in his intellectual heritage. Unfortunately, this research perspective is virtually absent from the modern intellectual history of Fascism. Without correlating Gentile's arguments and the positions of both nineteenth-century Italian thinkers (Rosmini, Gioberti, Mazzini) and the great philosophers of the past (Plato, Aristotle, Bruno, Berkeley,

Kant, and Hegel, to whom Gentile often refers in *The Theory of Mind as Pure Act*) it is impossible to reconstruct the political philosophy of Italian Fascism qualitatively.

Thirdly, a historical-philosophical study can provide a deeper basis for interpreting non-philosophical but highly relevant texts such as Alfredo Rocco's *The Political Doctrine of Fascism*. The author was a lawyer and not a philosopher. However, his text contains many references to Dante, Machiavelli, Vico, and Mazzini, which reveal how Fascist philosophising was rooted in the Italian intellectual tradition, a fact that undoubtedly deserves careful study from a historical-philosophical point of view.[48]

Taking into account the aspirations outlined above, this study answers questions that have long remained unanswered and broadens the understanding of the intellectual foundations of Italian Fascism.

The question of our own methodological dispositions, namely the methods of the history of philosophy, understood as a science of the spirit and comprehended hermeneutically, should be explored in more detail.

Wilhelm Dilthey wrote that 'the human eye is drawn not only to the immeasurable spaces of the celestial bodies, discovering in them the proportionate structure of the cosmos, but also to the depths of one's own heart'.[49] Emilio Betti, in turn, remarked that 'there is nothing closer to the human heart than understanding other people. And there is no more seductive audacity for the capacity to understand than the attempt to understand the erased human traces that suddenly appear before it and appeal to it. Wherever we discover meaningful

48 A word of caution: in the case of Fascism, it seems extremely difficult to draw a clear-cut distinction between purely philosophical content and ideological content. The solution I propose is to present the philosophical as the origin and root of the ideological, as exemplified by Gentile, whose philosophical ideas formed the basis of both his own political beliefs and the ideological model that he sought to convey to the public.

49 Wilhelm Dilthey, *Introduction to the Human Sciences*, (Detroit: Wayne State University Press, 1988).

forms through which another spirit speaks to our spirit, our ability to interpret is challenged to deduce the meaning conveyed in them'.[50]

The key methodological foundations of this work are the main hermeneutical principles, which, in our point of view, enable us to achieve the main goal of historical and philosophical research in the most authentic way. Let us present the key hermeneutical canons (as interpreted by Betti) and substantiate the relevance of their application to achieving the aim of the research.

The canon of hermeneutic autonomy of the object states that 'meaning-containing forms should be understood according to their own regularities, according to their specific laws of formation, on the basis of their intended context, in their necessity, coherence and contiguity: the scale applied to them must be immanent to their original purpose — the purpose which the created form was supposed to serve from the author's point of view'.[51] By applying this principle to our study, we aim to show the texts of the ideologues of Italian Fascism and their predecessors in the context of their respective eras and, by resorting to historical material, to highlight the values, political attitudes, and impulses that ideologues embedded in these texts and which they themselves saw as relevant.

The canon of totality and coherence of the hermeneutic consideration requires one to identify 'the relationship and coherence between separate constituent parts of speech, as well as any expression of thought in general, and also their common correlation with the whole, whose parts they are: correlation with each other and with the whole, which makes possible the mutual clarification of meanings and clarification of meaning-bearing forms through the relation of the whole to its constituent parts and vice versa'.[52] Applying the requirement of this canon in the course of the study, we examine the

50 Emilio Betti, *Hermeneutics as a General Methodology of Sciences of the Spirit*, (Oxfordshire: Routledge, 2021), p.10

51 Ibid., p. 29.

52 Ibid., p. 31.

often-contradictory viewpoints embedded in the package of a single doctrine, which, through correlation with the fundamental principles and intensions of doctrinal aspirations characteristic of Italian Fascism as a whole, allows for an analysis of the necessary details and particular principles proposed by individual ideologues in their relation to the whole.

The canon of the relevance of understanding asserts that 'the interpreter has to go through (in a reverse motion) the path of creativity in himself, to reconstruct it from within, from within to carry out a reverse translation of another's thought, fragment of the past, or remembered experience, into his own vital relevance, that is, to adapt them to his own spiritual horizon within his own experience (through a kind of relocation)'.[53] In reality, the aspiration to completely level one's own subjectivity in relation to the subject of historical-philosophical research often fails.[54] At the same time, we have attempted to be as objective as possible in our analysis of the subject of research. By internally reconstructing Fascist arguments and not feeling any emotional sympathy for the vast majority of them, we have focused on following the logic of Fascist ideologists and the meanings relevant to them, merging with their aspirations for the time of the research and becoming immersed in them. In our opinion, there is no other way, because, as Giambattista Vico rightly noted, 'this whole world of culture, of course, is created by human hands and spirit, so its principles and regularities can again be found in the ways of existence of the spirit of this very man, and that is where they should be sought'.[55]

The final, fourth hermeneutical canon, according to Betti, the canon of the semantic adequacy of understanding (or the canon of hermeneutical semantic correspondence) asserts the need for the

53 Ibid., p. 40.

54 Sometimes there is no such aspiration at all, as we see in the targeting of Soviet historians who raised the subject of Italian Fascism.

55 Cited from Betti, *Hermeneutics as a General Methodology of Sciences of the Spirit*, p. 124.

interpreter to synchronise with the inner promptings emanating from the object of study. 'If it is true that only spirit can speak to spirit, it is also true that only a spirit of equal level and congenial predisposition can access and adequately understand the speaking spirit',[56] explains Betti. It is difficult to judge whether this canon is conceptually feasible in our case. The author does, however, dare to hope that he has been able to grasp and authentically convey the political motivations that inspired the authors of the texts reviewed in this study.

Following the hermeneutic canons outlined above allows for a systematic and comprehensive reconstruction of the investigated subject matter from a historical and philosophical point of view, highlighting the key features of the Fascist phenomenon in its comparative historical juxtaposition with other contemporary political doctrines.

In addition to the above, it should be noted that where there is an accessible primary source in Italian and a translation into another language (including Russian), preference was given to the original work (wherever possible).[57]

It should be mentioned separately that the descriptive nature of this work is largely due to its methodological peculiarities. When trying to make a hermeneutic entry to the political philosophy of Fascism, it was kept in mind that the leader of Fascism, Benito Mussolini, was not a philosopher, despite the fact that he was a well-read man, and it was the academic philosopher Gentile who gave the direct philosophical content to the Fascist doctrine. Thus, the diversity of names, theories, and references to different layers of European intellectual heritage, which abound in this work, is necessary to achieve the aim of the study and reasonable from the point of view of the chosen methodology.

56 Ibid., p. 117.

57 Friedrich Schleiermacher pointed out that 'hermeneutic analysis can only have the original as its subject'. Friedrich Schleiermacher, *Hermeneutics*, (St. Petersburg: The European House, 2004), p. 231. However, for the purposes of this study, we were forced in some cases to resort to translations due to the inaccessibility of the original works.

Without reference to all the above-mentioned variety in its totality, an objective reconstruction of the political philosophy of Italian Fascism is not possible.

In addition to the purely methodological aspects listed above, it seems crucial to define some of the key concepts used in this work: 'political ontology', 'intellectual', 'Right' and 'Left'.

According to the hypothesis argued in this study, the political philosophy of Italian Fascism is based on a specific comprehensive philosophical worldview, grounded in the Neo-Hegelian actualist doctrine of Giovanni Gentile. In this worldview, the ethical, social, and political aspects of the Fascist doctrine are rooted in a fundamental conception of the structure of being, as well as its temporal, spatial, and epistemological aspects. This holistic theoretical construction, which includes fundamental ontological statements from which normative requirements for the socio-political order are derived, is proposed in the text of this work to be referred to as political ontology. Thus, the political ontology of Italian Fascism is represented as a set of beliefs held by the authors of the doctrine, containing a coherent and cohesive view of the essence of the world, society, the state, and the individual.

The political philosophy of Italian Fascism was created by intellectuals. The intellectual is a new type of thinker who emerged in the first half of the twentieth century. This figure 'combines the writer, the publicist, and the politician'.[58] Unlike the scientist, by definition incapable of crossing the boundaries of the impassioned ethics that is the condition of scientific activity, and the public politician, all of whose actions are inevitably directed towards one main goal (the seizure of power and the subsequent realisation of his own domination), the intellectual was usually not bound by any framework other than the one he had chosen for himself within the discourse in which he lived and

58 A. Mikhailovsky, 'Германия' [Germany] in *Мыслящая Россия. История и теория интеллигенции и интеллектуалов* [Thinking Russia. History and Theory of the Intelligentsia and Intellectuals], (Moscow: Eurasia Heritage, 2009), p. 117.

worked. In this sense, the independent intellectual can be described as the most consistent and principled advocate of any ideals or principles. The key character of this research, the academic philosopher Giovanni Gentile, possesses all the necessary traits of an 'intellectual', as do many other Fascist thinkers. However, it should be noted that the social role of the intellectual in politics is closely linked to the Dreyfus affair and the use of this term has clear temporal limits. For this reason, the term 'intellectual' is not used in this sense in relation to Rosmini, Gioberti, or Mazzini.

Since this work will repeatedly make some reference to political signification, it is useful to clarify exactly what the author understands by 'Left' and 'Right'.

'Leftist' is commonly understood as those ideologies and political movements whose representatives share the values of the French Revolution of 1789 — 'Liberty, Equality, and Fraternity' is the foundation of their ideology. The cultural and philosophical basis of any left-wing movement can be traced back either to emergent British liberalism (the political ontology of John Locke) or to the republican ideas of the French Enlightenment (the ideas of Helvétius, Rousseau, and Saint-Simon). In the nineteenth century, left-wing ideas found their most radical embodiment in the writings and political attitudes of Karl Marx. The Left is characterised by rationalism, egalitarianism, materialism, progressivism, and mechanicism.

'Right-wing' refers to those forces which did not embrace the ideals of the French Revolution or the moral attitudes of the Enlightenment. In the history of recent centuries, the first exponents of sentiments that would later be considered typically right-wing were the Storm and Stress movement in German culture (Hamann, Goethe, Schiller), who revolted against the rationalism of the 'Enlighteners'. In the nineteenth century, the Right was characterised mostly by conservatives (Joseph de Maistre, Edmund Burke), who were horrified by the consequences of the French Revolution. Right-wing thinkers can be considered both classical idealists (Fichte) and irrationalists (Schopenhauer, Nietzsche).

The Right is typified by elitism, a commitment to tradition, a focus on the ideal of an organic community (as opposed to mechanicism), and idealism (broadly speaking, this may be a subset of transcendentalist ontology as well as a commitment to a particular religion). Based on an emphasis on the need to preserve traditional continuity (and through it the 'eternal', as opposed to the 'temporal' and 'transient' of the progressives), the right-wing idea is often traced to the great sages of antiquity — Plato, Cicero, Marcus Aurelius. In the twentieth century, the right-wing worldview also found its own radicals in the form of representatives of various 'Fascist' movements.

It should be noted that in the post-1945 world, the classical right-wing worldview is expressed somewhat tacitly on the political spectrum and is largely marginalised, which is why, for example, consistent liberals like Friedrich Hayek and similar thinkers who oppose an egalitarian worldview are conventionally referred to as 'right-wingers'. Despite the fact that it seems incorrect to do so based on the classical system of political signification, which it is useful to take as a framework, there are references in this work to 'left-wing' and 'right-wing' liberalism, owing to the fact that these systems of political belief in the modern world are often justifiably opposed to one another. 'Left-wing liberalism' refers to a system of liberal political beliefs whose core value is justice and whose core aspiration is the typical left-wing propensity for egalitarian practices. By 'right-wing liberalism' we mean a political worldview whose core value is liberty and whose main aspiration is its practical achievement. In practice, as the particular case of Italian Fascism demonstrates, 'left-wing liberals' tended to find themselves in the camp of other left-wing forces — socialists and Communists — while 'right-wing liberals', by contrast, formed political alliances with monarchists and Fascists, which seems logical given that they saw Communism (and its radical egalitarianism) as the main threat to liberty.

CHAPTER ONE

THE ORIGINS OF ITALIAN FASCISM

§1. Risorgimento. The Emergence of the Italian National Identity

1.1. The Historical Significance of the Unification of Italy as a 'Point of Reference'

AT THE TURN of the nineteenth century, the Napoleonic Wars brought an end to the feudal state formations that had prevailed in the Italian Peninsula since the Middle Ages. Napoleon Bonaparte was proclaimed King of Italy in 1805. After his fall, the victorious powers redrew the map of Europe during the Congress of Vienna, which lasted ten months from September 1814 to June 1815. The aim of the Congress was to re-establish absolute monarchies that had been shattered by the French Revolution and Napoleon's armies. In Italy, the power of the monarchies under the considerable influence of the Austrian Habsburg dynasty was restored. The Congress of Vienna restored the Kingdom of Sardinia, the Kingdom of the Two Sicilies, the Kingdom of Lombardy-Venetia, the Papal Region, and the Duchies of Tuscany, Parma and Modena[1] on the Italian peninsula. It is from

1 Of these states, the most powerful was the Kingdom of Sardinia, which received Genoa as a result of the Congress of Vienna, retaining strategically important territories on the French border and a greater degree of independence from

the Congress of Vienna that historians generally begin the timeline of the Risorgimento, the period of Italian unification, statehood, and national consciousness that spanned 55 long years.

Italy came to the end of Napoleonic rule in a very poor state. As Austrian Chancellor Klemens von Metternich declared, it was 'only a geographical expression'.[2] The vast majority of Italians were uneducated, spoke local dialects (no more than 2.5 percent of the population spoke Dante's language), and were agrarian and clerical. National unity was perceived as a myth and a dream. [3] However, a number of factors made the dream come true. Firstly, the legacy of French domination introduced radical variations of Enlightenment ideas in Italy, which in turn brought about the rejection of feudal privileges and the unlimited power and authority of the Catholic Church, and paved the way for the replacement of religious education institutions with secular schools. The second factor was the rebirth of statehood on Italian territory. After the expulsion of the French, Italian monarchs returned to power. Although influenced from abroad, formally most of the states re-established on the peninsula were independent and sovereign, making it possible to strive for consolidation and unification. The third factor was the Industrial Revolution, which reached, albeit slowly, the northern regions of the future Italy, as well as the development of trade. As economic ties between the Italian states grew ever closer, the doctrine of free trade became more popular and the desire for a common currency, common units of measurement, and

---

Austria than all the others. See Lucy Riall, *Risorgimento. The History of Italy from Napoleon to Nation State,* (London: Palgrave Macmillan, 2009), p. 11.

2 Martin Clark, *The Italian Risorgimento*, (Edinburgh: Pearson Education Limited, 2009), p. 4.

3 Even this assertion could be described as overly bold. From the Renaissance to the Risorgimento, Italian elites had little ambition and operated in their territories in the shadow of the Catholic Church, under the influence of major external powers. A. W. Salomone, 'Statecraft and Ideology in the Risorgimento. Reflections on the Italian National Revolution', *Italica*, 38, no. 3 (Sep., 1961), pp. 163–194.

common regulators across the peninsula became more and more desirable. The construction of railways and the emergence of steamships were of particular importance.[4] Economic integration thus created the foundation for political integration. Finally, the fourth factor, which arguably proved the most important, was a value factor, a philosophical factor in the broad sense. The first half of the nineteenth century was an era of new philosophical, ideological, and political doctrines. In Italy, the Enlightenment was spreading and German classical idealism was gaining influence. Social and philosophical debate among Italian thinkers with different worldviews was becoming more and more active. It was Italian priests and philosophers who defined and justified the desire for the unification of the country, transforming it from a disembodied dream into a concrete plan of action. Their role in making the Risorgimento a reality cannot be overstated.

The Italian word *risorgimento* has several meanings: 'rebirth', 'renewal', 'resurrection from the dead'. The main political motives behind the Risorgimento were aspirations for 'independence, unity, and freedom'.[5] Independence from external domination by France and Austria. Unification of the many kingdoms and duchies into a single state. Freedom — both civil and spiritual. The Risorgimento was a secular, liberal, nationalist, and largely anti-clerical movement.

One of the most important driving forces behind the Risorgimento were the various circles and secret societies that fought against both French rule and Austrian influence in the Italian Peninsula. The most well-known of these was the Carbonari, a Masonic-type organisation whose ambition was to create a constitutional monarchy or republic in Italy. The means used by the Carbonari ranged from assassinating 'enemies of liberty' and creating the grounds for armed insurrections, to promoting liberal ideas through the publication of pamphlets,

4 Kent Roberts Greenfield, 'Economic Ideas and Facts in the Early Period of the Risorgimento (1815–1848)', *The American Historical Review*, 36, no. 1 (Oct., 1930), pp. 31–43.

5 Clark, *The Italian Risorgimento*, p. 3.

manifestos, and proclamations. In addition to the Carbonari, we know of other similar organisations — Young Italy, which we will describe in more detail below, and the Knights of Freedom, whose aim was to assassinate Charles Felix, King of Sardinia.

However, much of the credit for the successful unification of the country is usually attributed to individual heroes — personalities who made a particularly important contribution to the achievement of the Risorgimento. The 'fathers' of Italian unification were numerous — Giuseppe Garibaldi and Alessandro Gavazzi, Camillo Benso di Cavour and Victor Emmanuel II. Alongside the political and military leaders, thinkers such as Antonio Rosmini, Vincenzo Gioberti, Bertrando Spaventa and Giuseppe Mazzini are prominent and highly influential figures of the era. Their legacy influenced not only their contemporary affairs, but the whole of twentieth-century Italy. In particular, the ideas of Mazzini and the Italian idealists fuelled the historico-philosophical quest of Giovanni Gentile, which led not only to Gentile's political commitment, greatly contributing to the integration of Italian intellectuals into national and global political processes in the first half of the twentieth century, but also to the production of major philosophical works that defined the Fascist doctrine.

1.2. The Nineteenth-Century Italian Idealism of Antonio Rosmini, Vincenzo Gioberti, and Bertrando Spaventa

It is useful to start examining the main themes of Italian idealism in the nineteenth century with a brief overview of the group of authors who shaped the development of Italian philosophy up to the mid-twentieth century. They are Antoni Rosmini-Serbati, Vincenzo Gioberti and Bertrando Spaventa.

It must be said that Italian philosophy, until the emergence of Rosmini, Gioberti, and Spaventa, had contributed little to world thought since the Renaissance. While in England, Germany, and France the philosophical stars of the New Age and the Enlightenment were rising, the rationalists were arguing with the empiricists,

Romanticism battled Enlightenment ideas and German classical idealism, and Italian thought was on the periphery of European intellectual history. The genius Giambattista Vico, author of *The New Science* and father of modern philosophy of history, was largely ignored by his contemporaries. Only in the first half of the nineteenth century was Italian philosophy able to catch up with modern speculative European philosophy. Two thinkers played a particular role in this — Antonio Rosmini and Vincenzo Gioberti. The third, Bertrando Spaventa, made a significant effort to adapt German classical idealism to Italians, thus giving birth to the Italian neo-idealism of the twentieth century, of which Gentile and Croce were the leading representatives.

Antonio Rosmini

Blessed Antonio Rosmini (1797–1855), a Roman Catholic priest and philosopher, became famous not only as a thinker, but also as the founder of his own monastic order, the Rosminians. In the years following the Congress of Vienna, he took up the main ideas of German Romanticism and set Italian thought on a return to medieval Christian idealism, emphasising in particular its Platonic elements.[6] Rosmini was among the first Italians to give his philosophy a truly critical and speculative character. Although he was a Catholic thinker, Rosmini was writing in the nineteenth century and he rejected the widely accepted view of philosophy as 'the handmaid of theology', stressing that philosophy was a science of the ultimate foundations of being.[7] He defended freedom of thought, stressing that true faith must find its justification in rational reflection. As such, Rosmini urged philosophy to 'come to the aid' of theology.[8] The philosopher was also an advocate of an active education policy. Rosmini argued that 'purification' of the Catholic Church was only possible if the clergy's level of education was significantly increased. Although opposed to dogmatism, Rosmini was convinced that the Church should be the main vehicle for knowledge and that education should be Catholic. He opposed secular schools controlled by the state, seeing in them a threat to the true freedom of the individual.

---

6 Rosmini defined his idealist philosophy as 'ideological psychologism'. He insisted on the objectivity of the 'innate idea of being', which, having been given to us, allows us to know; in other words, on the objectivity of the ideal granted to our consciousness. This is the starting point of his philosophy. See Jules Chaix-Ruy, 'Philosophie et religion chez rosmini d'apres G. Rovea' [Philosophy and Religion in Rosmini after G. Rovea], *Les Études philosophiques, New World Series*, 10, no. 1 (January/March, 1955), pp. 114–116.

7 Rosmini's other definitions of philosophy are: 'the science of being', 'the science of ideal being'. Michele Federico Sciacca, 'Le problème de l'origine des idées et l'objectivité de la connaissance selon À. Rosmini' [The Problem of the Origin of Ideas and the Objectivity of Knowledge According to À. Rosmini], *Revue de métaphysique et de morale* [Journal of Metaphysics and Morals], 60, no. 3 (July-September 1955), p. 299.

8 How much theology, in the eyes of the Catholic Church, needed the 'aid' of philosophy beyond what had been developed by the scholastics is an open question. It is a fact that a few decades after Rosmini's death some of his writings fell under the disapproval of the Catholic Church. In particular, the philosopher was suspected of an implicit pantheism. Francis Winterton, 'The Papal Condemnation of Rosmini', *Mind*, 13, no. 52 (Oct., 1888), pp. 622–626.

Rosmini's political ideal was the creation of a confederation of Catholic states under the authority of the Pope.

Although Rosmini's main philosophical ambition was to prove the existence of God and develop his own doctrine of theodicy, much of the philosopher's legacy was linked to reflections aimed at reconciling new political trends (such as 'natural human rights') with the traditional political aspirations characteristic of Catholic thinkers.[9] Against radical variations of republican and Enlightenment thought, Rosmini argued that in politics, it was the preservation of the foundations of society that was fundamental, rather than the pursuit of infinite progress. The real aim of society, according to Rosmini, is the pursuit of virtue — if this condition is fulfilled, society will be governed justly.

Rosmini's political ideal was to create a confederation of Catholic states under the authority of the Pope. As a friend and advisor to Pope Pius IX, Rosmini was invited to become Prime Minister of the Papacy and played a significant role in ensuring that Rome was governed by the Holy See on the basis of constitutional principles. Rosmini is not

9 A contemporary of the thinker presents Rosmini's philosophy as 'a compromise between theocracy and liberalism, between religion and science'. Giacomo Barzelloti, 'Philosophy in Italy', *Mind*, 3, no. 12 (Oct., 1878), p. 508.

directly identifiable as a supporter of the Risorgimento, but was nevertheless one of the most influential figures of Italian intellectual life, inspiring more than one generation of idealist thinkers.[10]

Vincenzo Gioberti (1801–1852), a Catholic priest, philosopher, essayist, and politician, developed his own ontological concept. Although he was an opponent of Rosmini, he too based his thought on idealist principles.[11] Gioberti's political influence compared to that of Count Camillo Benso di Cavour, and his impact on nineteenth-century Italian thought was second only to that of Rosmini. The peak of Gioberti's political career was as Prime Minister of the Kingdom of Sardinia in 1848–1849. As a political thinker, it was his work *On the Moral and Civil Primacy of the Italian Race* (1843) that brought him fame.

---

10 A recent author claims that Rosmini was one of the originators of a new Italian idealist philosophical tradition based on 'encyclopaedic knowledge, which derived from principles different than those of Diderot's French encyclopaedists'. See Michel Adam, 'Actualité de Rosmini', *Revue philosophique de la France et de l'étranger*, 184, no. 2, (April-June 1994), pp. 195–202.

11 The main philosophical influences on Gioberti were Plato, St. Augustine, Leibniz, Kant, Bruno, Campanella, and his contemporary Alessandro Manzoni. See: J. F. Renauld, 'Quelques livres de philosophie italienne' [Some Titles of Italian Philosophy], *Revue de Métaphysique et de Morale*, 27, no. 4 (October 1920), pp. 517–536.

Vincenzo Gioberti, philosopher, journalist, and Prime Minister of the Kingdom of Sardinia (1848–1849)

In this work, Gioberti argued that Catholicism was the foundation of the Italian national character, and that true political independence of the Italian lands could only be achieved peacefully under the leadership of the Pope. When he wrote *On the Moral and Civil Primacy of the Italian Race,* Gioberti shared Rosmini's Guelphic vision of a confederation of Italian states under the direct authority of the Pope as a presidential figure. The philosopher set out to create a harmonious synthesis between a Christian universalism characteristic of Catholic philosophy and contemporary political liberalism, two systems of thought which his contemporaries saw as diametrically opposed at their core assumptions. Gioberti's thought evolved in the opposite direction to that of Mazzini, which will be discussed in detail shortly — while the latter hoped for a civil uprising, the former wanted organic reforms 'from above' that the Roman Curia could carry out. Gioberti was one of the first to try to define the essence of a common Italian identity — for him it was inextricably linked to Catholicism. It was precisely the religious factor, according to Gioberti, that was to play a decisive role in finding a national consensus upon which to unite the country. This explains his deference to religious revelation, without which, according to him, no knowledge could be conceivable. For the Italian philosopher, it was impossible to arrive at progress in any field without relying on the Catholic frame of reference. As a political ideologist, Gioberti relied on the assumption that in the mind of the ordinary Italian, revolution was always regarded as synonymous with terror, violence, and chaos, while the Church was perceived as the very opposite of this. Church and state have been so closely linked in the minds of Italians since Roman times that the separation of these two entities seemed unnatural to many. In the turbulent times of uprisings and revolutions, Neo-Guelphism seemed to be a doctrine that could bring about progressive change without losing the foundations of national identity (indeed, even reinforcing them). From this perspective, linking Catholic doctrine and the national identity may have yielded positive results. However, the fact that Gioberti did not go far beyond the Catholic tradition in the fundamental premises of his philosophical and political system also had obvious disadvantages in terms of the effectiveness of his political message on the target audience — educated citizens and the military aristocracy. As Bruce Haddock rightly points out, the greatest astonishment for his contemporaries must have been how an educated liberal could have pinned so much hope on the institution of the papacy, which had fallen on hard times under Pope Gregory XVI.[12]

12 See: Bruce Haddock, 'Political Union without Social Revolution: Vincenzo Gioberti's Primato', *The Historical Journal*, 41, no. 3 (Sep., 1998), pp. 705–723.

Vincenzo Gioberti was an advocate of 'reform from above'. Gioberti's Neo-Guelphism was expressed in his hopes for the Roman Curia as a force capable of uniting Italy into a single state.

Gioberti, like Rosmini, saw modern liberalism not as a threat to Christianity, but as a means by which the true church could obtain a definitive victory. In particular, he saw the liberal conception of the absolute freedom of the individual as a modern interpretation of the Christian postulate of the immortality of the soul. He tried to reconcile the foundations of Catholicism with reason.[13] As Giovanni Gentile later explained, in his philosophising Gioberti 'did not divide man into two parts, one of which could philosophise freely, while the other was to surrender to a higher power that would enslave it by the force of an inexplicable mystery'.[14]

13 Some commentators on Rosmini and Gioberti use the term 'Catholic liberalism' to define the political beliefs of these thinkers, contrasting them with 'social liberalism'. For example, see: Anthony Scarangello, 'Major Catholic-Liberal Educational Philosophers of the Italian Risorgimento', *History of Education Quarterly*, 4, no. 4 (Dec., 1964), p. 233.

14 Cited in Scarangello, 'Major Catholic-Liberal Philosophers', p. 237.

Gioberti later changed his mind — in one of his last works, *Del rinnovamento civile d'Italia* (1851; *On the Civil Renewal of Italy*), he expressed scepticism about the possible political leadership of the Catholic Church in the unification of Italy and spoke very negatively of the Jesuits, accusing them of corrupting the Church.[15] In the last years of his life, which Gioberti spent in Paris after resigning as prime minister and entering diplomatic service, the philosopher pinned his hopes on the Kingdom of Sardinia and, although he did not live to see the climax of the Risorgimento, these hopes were fulfilled by the Sardinian monarch Victor Emmanuel II who eventually united the country.

Bertrando Spaventa (1817–1883) was a major philosopher in Italy in the second half of the 19th century who developed Hegelian idealism. Originally from Bomba, Abruzzo, in Central Italy, Spaventa received his basic education at the diocesan seminary in Chieti. He then studied in Naples, where, having mastered German and English, he had the opportunity to read the original works of foreign philosophers. From 1858 to 1860, Spaventa chaired the philosophy departments at the Universities of Modena, Bologna, and Naples. He was determined to prove that although modern idealist philosophy had reached its peak in Germany, it originated in Italy. Spaventa compared Descartes with Campanella, Spinoza with Bruno, and Kant with Vico. According to him, Renaissance thinkers were the immediate precursors of German idealist philosophy. This line of enquiry by Spaventa had one goal — to free Italian philosophy from a sense of mediocrity in comparison to the German intellectual tradition. At the same time, Spaventa emphasised that the progress of Italian thought was significantly constrained by

15 In the end, the Papacy proved to be the most resolute of all the opponents of the Risorgimento. A unified Italian kingdom was formed in 1861 and Papal Rome joined it only in 1870, until then maintaining its independence from the rest of Italy thanks to the presence of Napoleon III's French troops in the city. Frank J. Coppa, "'Realpolitik" and Conviction in the Conflict between Piedmont and the Papacy during the "Risorgimento"', *The Catholic Historical Review*, 54, no. 4 (Jan., 1969), pp. 579–612.

religious dogmatism.[16] For this position, as well as for the 'pantheism' of his decidedly Hegelian ontology, Spaventa was severely criticised by adherents of orthodox Catholicism. [17]

Bertrando Spaventa, philosopher and member of parliament, was the greatest propagator of Hegel's thought in Italy in the second half of the nineteenth century.

Like Gioberti, Spaventa was no stranger to politics — for four terms (8th, 10th, 11th, and 12th) he was elected to the Italian parliament. During his parliamentary career he defended secular legislative practices and spoke out in favour of universal suffrage. As a philosopher, Spaventa had a profound influence on both Croce and Gentile, and largely shaped the focus of twentieth-century Italian neo-idealism.[18]

16 N. D. Alfonso, 'Bertrando Spaventa', *The Journal of Speculative Philosophy*, 17, no. 4 (October, 1883), p. 432.

17 Guido de Ruggiero and Constance M. Allen, 'Philosophy in Italy', *Journal of Philosophical Studies*, 3, no. 12 (Oct., 1928), p. 514.

18 It should be noted that Bertrando's brother Silvio Spaventa (1822–1893), also a member of the Italian parliament, was Benedetto Croce's second cousin and had a great influence on the young Croce. Silvio, like Bertrando, was a supporter of Hegel's political philosophy and a prominent figure in Italian liberalism.

Returning to Rosmini and Gioberti, it is worth noting that their political aspirations, characteristic of the Risorgimento era, were of a consensus nature. Hoping for the unification of the country without civil wars, revolutions, or much bloodshed, these Italian thinkers linked their hopes to the papacy and the Catholic Church. Their contribution to the formation of the contemporary Italian national consciousness was very important and these idealist philosophers were actively referenced during the Fascist era. Ultimately, however, it was the republican intellectual with a conflicted political ontology, Giuseppe Mazzini, who was to become the greatest ideologue and thinker of the Risorgimento. Of all the Italian intellectuals of the nineteenth century, it was he who had the greatest influence on the twentieth century, namely on the formation of the political doctrine of Italian Fascism.

1.3. Giuseppe Mazzini's Social Philosophy

Alongside Rosmini and Gioberti, Giuseppe Mazzini (1805–1872) is one of the most brilliant Italian thinkers of the nineteenth century. In his time, Mazzini was perceived as a European figure whose influence was on a par with that of John Stuart Mill, Karl Marx, and Alexis de Tocqueville.[19]

Philosopher, publicist, revolutionary — Mazzini wore many hats in his lifetime. He was born in 1805 in Genoa, a city which became part of the Kingdom of Sardinia in 1815 as a result of the Congress of Vienna. The political climate of Mazzini's youth was imbued with the spirit of Italian patriotism awakened in the years of French occupation. The future revolutionary was from the middle class (his father was a doctor), which allowed him to get a good education — he studied law, while also being actively interested in literature. From an early age Mazzini was drawn to idealist thought — he admired the works of Giambattista Vico, Herder, Fichte, Goethe, Schelling, and the Schlegel

19 For more on Mazzini, see: Dmitry Moiseev, 'Политическая мысль Джузеппе Мадзини' [Giuseppe Mazzini's Political Thought], *История философии* [History of Philosophy], 20. (Moscow: 2015), pp. 63–78.

brothers, as well as the Italian poets Dante Alighieri and Ugo Foscolo.[20] After graduating from the Faculty of Law of the University of Genoa in 1827, Mazzini became a journalist writing literary criticism. During this period he developed a passion for political philosophy, studying the work of the French thinkers Félicité de La Mennais and Henri de Saint-Simon. He joined the Carbonari, but soon broke with them — by then Mazzini was already convinced that lofty patriotic goals could not be achieved by the methods of a secret society which distanced itself from the masses. The path he chose, which he justifies in his political writings, was one of popular revolution that would lead to a democratic republican order. Sympathetic to revolutionary sentiments, Mazzini participated in word and deed in the many riots that shook Italy, for which he was imprisoned in 1831, and then went into exile — first in Paris, then in Geneva, and, finally, in London.

In 1831, while in France, Mazzini established the political organisation Giovine Italia (Young Italy), which could be considered the first modern Italian political party. Giovine Italia had its own newspaper, its own propaganda machine, and, crucially, the capacity to convey its message to its target audience (the Italian middle class) and coordinate national liberation activities in Italy. At the same time, Mazzini wrote the most famous of his early works, *The Manifesto of Young Italy*. The idealistic character of Mazzini's Manifesto is evident almost immediately: 'Great revolutions are the work of principles, not bayonets'.[21] Mazzini argues that in order to achieve concrete, tangible victory, one must first win the minds and hearts of people on the field of morality. For Mazzini, this is a long process: since the human intellect is not

---

20 Mazzini was especially influenced throughout his life by Dante, whom he viewed not only as a genius but also as a paragon of civic virtue, stressing that Dante's attitude towards Florence can be seen as a model of patriotism. Andrea Ciccarelli, 'Dante and Italian Culture from the Risorgimento to World War I', *Dante Studies, with the Annual Report of the Dante Society*, 119 (2001), p. 126.

21 Giuseppe Mazzini, 'Manifesto della Giovine Italia' [The Manifesto of Young Italy] in *Mazzini G. Scritti editi e inediti. Vol. 1.* [Mazzini G. Published and Unpublished Works. Volume 1], ed. G. Daelli, 1861. p. 123.

capable of immediately grasping the principles of freedom, it is necessary to gradually lead people to these ideas through constant educative efforts. This is work for many people, united by one higher purpose.

Mazzini proclaims three principles which must be followed to achieve the development and prosperity of Italy: unity, freedom, and independence. With this assertion he differentiates the Young Italy movement from those who are prepared to sacrifice the country's independence from external forces for the sake of uniting the Italian lands under the single will of a tyrant and from those who, fearing violence, are not prepared to pursue the complete unification of the Italian territories, content with expanding the borders of one of the many Italian states. Mazzini opposed any compromise dictated by fear. The only authority he recognised in his Manifesto is 'the will of the nation'.[22]

Giuseppe Mazzini, a revolutionary and the most influential thinker of the Risorgimento

Mazzini raises the question: by what means can a united, free, and independent Italy be created? He objects to those who, not believing in the very possibility that the people could rise up in defence of their

22 Mazzini, 'Manifesto della Giovine Italia', p. 125.

own rights and freedoms, nor in the rediscovery of a free popular consciousness, promote militant resistance using the same methods by which tyrants enslaved the nation. 'They do not understand that 26 million people who draw their strength from the pursuit of a good cause and have an indomitable will are invulnerable', Mazzini writes.[23] Are the propagandists of force themselves prepared to die for the liberation and unification of Italy? The author of the Manifesto doubts it. Those who call the people to the barricades, as a rule, stand aside themselves; or, otherwise, their appeals do not come to any concrete action, as the greatness of the task frightens even the potential organisers of the revolution. They have no faith in the people and await foreign help. The 'people of the future', who are destined to create a united Italian state, must learn from the mistakes of the past.[24]

Mazzini argues that the past should have taught Italians that freedom is never achieved by the bayonets of foreigners. For him, a true revolution is a clash of principles and convictions, a war of the masses. Only convinced idealists, living the ideals they promote, can inspire a revolution. 'Italy knows this, knows that the secret of strength is in faith, that the true virtue is sacrifice, and that the right way is to prove one's strength', he writes.[25] The ideas and aspirations of Young Italy should be organised into a unified system; Young Italy should become a new element of national life, one that will be able to create a unified Italian state in the nineteenth century. Mazzini assigns a special role in this process to literature, which should become a 'moral clergy'[26] giving form to true virtue'.[27]

23 Ibid., p. 126.

24 'They', the 'people of the past', with whom Mazzini polemicises in *The Manifesto of Young Italy*, are the Carbonari, a group of revolutionaries who set up a Masonic-type organisation with the aim of fighting for a constitutional transformation.

25 Ibid., p. 127.

26 Ibid., p. 128.

27 In his later work, *Philosophy of Music* (1836), Mazzini paid close attention to Italian opera in addition to literature. Mazzini's message was taken up by composers of his time — in particular by Giuseppe Verdi, in whose operas *Macbeth*

Reflecting on foreign policy, Mazzini is of the opinion that Italians should not become preoccupied with events in Europe, except in cases from which certain positive results can be drawn, or lessons learned about the struggle against the oppressors of mankind. Italians should reject both pity and assistance from other nations. For Mazzini, Europe had yet to learn what Italians were really like. In the end, Italy will have to show her foreign offenders all the crimes committed against her. Mazzini's Manifesto concludes, 'We will say to the nations: such are the souls you have bought and sold; such is the land you have condemned to isolation and eternal slavery'.[28]

The *Manifesto*, with all its revolutionary fervour and idealistic quest for a new, freer, and fairer world, was timed to coincide with the founding of the movement and a newspaper of the same name, which published a series of essays between 1831 and 1834 that detailed the political position of the early Mazzini. One of the most significant works of this kind is the article 'From the Staff of the "Young Italy" to their Compatriots' (1832), in which the Italian thinker elaborates his views on the optimal form of political power, defending the republican position against absolutist and constitutional monarchy and proclaiming the principles of universal suffrage, social justice, and renunciation of privileges.

For Mazzini, the key to success in any revolution is the concentration of as many people as possible on a single goal. A revolution cannot succeed if it does not have a symbol, a purpose, an image of the future. Mazzini proclaims the republic as such a symbol. The Italian people

and *Ernani* one finds motifs consistent with the ideological national rise of the Risorgimento. Alongside Verdi — who, incidentally, was in correspondence with Mazzini — the operas *The Italian Girl in Algiers*, *Moses in Egypt*, and *William Tell* stand out as works in which the cry of the Risorgimento can be heard — the struggle for freedom and national liberation against foreign invaders and oppressors. Philip Gossett, 'Becoming a Citizen: The Chorus in "Risorgimento" Opera', *Cambridge Opera Journal*, 2, no. 1 (Mar., 1990), pp. 41–64.

28 Ibid., p. 130.

have a positive historical memory of the republic.[29] They had to be convinced of the validity of republican principles and, by adhering to the pan-European trajectory of historical progress, make a historical leap through a single revolutionary uprising.

Thus, Mazzini proclaims the republic as the main goal. He polemises with those who portray constitutional monarchy as 'a form of transitional power' from absolutism to freedom. His argument is that by recognising the monarch it is necessary to transfer to him the power and right to reign, to decide on war, and to appoint the government. Furthermore, the principle of the inheritance of power, incompatible with the principles of equality and equal rights, remains in force. Mazzini argues that Young Italy should not rely on an alliance with any monarchs but should 'raise the banner of the Italian people',[30] call them to battle, abolish all privileges, and make the principle of equality a religious symbol. Only in this way can the monarchs and their aristocracy be defeated. 'We are men of progress; we look to the future and strive for independence, without regard for our age, condition or the place where we live',[31] asserts Mazzini.

---

29 In particular, Mazzini noted the experience of the Renaissance city-states. While the philosopher saw many advantages in the Italian experience of republicanism, the long history of multiple independent states in one territory, with their own traditions and, at a later stage of the Risorgimento, their own ideas about their place in the new unified Italy, was also fraught with great complications for the unification of the country. For more details, see: Steen Bo Frandsen and Adelaide Zocchi, 'Le città italiane fra tradizione municipalistica e gerarchia nazionale durante il Risorgimento' [Italian Cities Caught Between Municipalist Tradition and National Hierarchy During the Risorgimento], *Meridiana*, 33, Materiali'98 (November 1998), pp. 83–106.

30 Giuseppe Mazzini, 'I collaboratori della Giovine Italia ai loro concittadini' [The Collaborators of the Young Italy to Their Fellow Citizens] in *La giovine Italia. Serie di scritti intorno alla condizione politica, morale e letteraria della Italia, tendenti alla sua rigenerazione* [The Young Italy. Series of Writings on the Political, Moral and Literary Condition of Italy, Tending Towards Its Regeneration], (Marseille: Tipografia militare di Giulio Barile, 1832), p. 23.

31 Ibid., p. 38.

The method espoused by Mazzini is to discover genuine principles and then, by disseminating them, to apply them to all meaningful spheres: politics, economics, science, and more. The motto of the republican movement is formulated by Mazzini as follows: 'Freedom in all and for all. Equality in rights and duties, both social and political. The association of all peoples, of all free men, in a mission of progress embracing all mankind.'[32] This formulation can be considered Mazzini's guiding principle.

What is particularly interesting is the way in which Mazzini reveals his motto: 'The people form the basis of the social pyramid... It is what unites us all; it is the collective multitude that inspires us when we think and speak of revolution and the rebirth of Italy.'[33] By people, he means 'the total number of human beings who make up the nation.'[34] In the same place, he notes that a multitude of individuals is not a nation unless it is governed by the same law, by the same principles, and unless it is bound by the same fraternal ties. 'Nation is a word for unity: unity of principles, aims, and rights',[35] Mazzini concludes. According to him, it is that type of social relationship which leads a multitude of people into a homogeneous unity. Otherwise, what we have is not a nation but a crowd, a collection of barbarians, united temporarily by the task of conquest, pillage, and robbery. The nation, on the other hand, pursues the common goals of improving and developing all kinds of socially important activities for all the individuals who make it up. The way to build a nation is through the association of individuals. Mazzini deduces the antithesis of association: dissociation. The latter manifests itself when there is an internal conflict between different social classes

32 Ibid., p. 38.

33 Ibid., p. 42.

34 Ibid., p. 42.

35 Ibid., p. 42.

or old and new orders.[36] Dissociation, according to Mazzini, is one of the conditions under which revolution is possible.

Mazzini repeatedly returns to the question of privilege: 'When equal distribution of rights is not a universal law, then caste, privilege, domination, slavery, and dependence arise'.[37] Equality is essential to achieving social harmony, which is the condition for association. For Mazzini, all people are morally equal from birth. All are equally predisposed to progressive tendencies, if they are led by true principles. The only natural inequality in Mazzini's eyes was that of the intellect, and a nation could benefit from this inequality, if it were to use it well. All other inequalities are subject to law, and may be regulated by law.

Following this line of reasoning, he concludes: 'Equality, freedom, and association — only these three elements can create a genuine nation'.[38] He defines the nation as 'a multitude of citizens speaking the same language, united, under equal social and political rights, for the common purpose of the development and progressive improvement of all social activities and forces'.[39] The nation is the only legitimate authority; authority that does not emanate from the nation must be recognised as usurped.

According to Mazzini, the will of the nation, as expressed by the deputies elected to represent it, must be the law for all citizens. 'One nation, one national representation', he proclaims. This national representation must not be elected on the basis of any census (whether that of wealth, property, or any other), but on the basis of the will of all citizens. Every representative of the nation has to participate in the elections. If an individual avoids participating in elections, he has no right

---

36 Mazzini mentions examples of dissociation from the fall of the Roman Empire: praetors vs senators, plebeians vs patricians, Christians vs pagans, philosophers vs religious adherents. See: Mazzini, 'I collaboratori della Giovine Italia ai loro concittadini', p. 44.

37 Ibid., p. 44.

38 Ibid., p. 45.

39 Ibid., p. 45.

to call himself a citizen. Thus, according to Mazzini, it is incumbent on the representatives of the nation to improve and manage the social forces in order to create conditions wherein the common good can be pursued. All the public institutions that are created should develop the principles of social equality without compromising political equality. For Mazzini, the people's representatives have a duty to become the guardians of freedom, reconciling the desire for individual freedom of the individual citizen with the desire for the progress of society as a whole.

Between 1831 and 1834, Young Italy carried out clandestine activities, which Mazzini directed from France. In 1833 and 1834, the revolutionaries made several attempts to raise popular uprisings in Savoie and Piedmont, but were defeated. After wandering around France and Switzerland for several years, Mazzini settled in London in January 1837, where, rejuvenated, he re-immersed himself in revolutionary activities. He gradually gains an international reputation and his ideas are recognised among like-minded people from around the world. Young Italy transforms itself into Young Europe; organisations preaching Mazzini's principles are set up in Germany, Poland, Switzerland, and even Turkey. In 1843, the British Parliament is already discussing Mazzini: the discovery by the British authorities of his correspondence, which led to a Liberal rebellion in Bologna, is made public, and the Italian thinker becomes a hero of the English liberals. In 1848, Mazzini arrives in Milan, which has rebelled against Austrian rule. The Sardinian monarch, Charles Albert, soon launches a full-scale war of national liberation against the Austrian empire, in which he suffers a crushing defeat, after which Mazzini flees to Switzerland to join Giuseppe Garibaldi's forces.

In February 1849, Rome is declared a republic. Mazzini arrives in the city and is soon elected to the triumvirate, i.e. one of three rulers of the young state, along with Carlo Armellini and Aurelio Saffi. Although he tries to implement the reforms he has long envisioned, fate gives him only a few months to do so — in July the French army, summoned to the aid of Pope Pius IX, enters Rome and Mazzini is once again forced into hiding in Switzerland.

The Roman triumvirate was the peak of Mazzini's political career. After the unsuccessful uprisings in Mantua and Milan in 1852 and 1853, respectively, and the failure of a series of revolutionary demonstrations in Genoa in 1856, the thinker went from being one of the protagonists of the Risorgimento to a spectator of the coming events of his much-coveted unification of Italy. He flees once more to London,[40] where in 1860 he publishes his most famous work, *Doveri dell'uomo* (*On the Duties of Man*). This text, dedicated to the workers of Italy, is a quintessential example of his political, social, and ethical thought. Mazzini touches on 'the most sacred things of all — God, Humanity, our Country, the Family'.[41] He argues that, although for more than fifty years the European peoples have waged a struggle of national liberation against absolutist forms of government and hereditary aristocracy in the name of freedom and human rights, the first question that must be raised is that of duty. According to Mazzini the political movements

40 During another exile in London, shortly after the collapse of the Roman Republic, Mazzini created the 'Central European Democratic Committee' with the truly prophetic political task of creating a United States of Europe. For Mazzini, the populations, freed from the tyranny of the monarchs, would have a natural tendency towards international association, as an expression of their desire to live in peace and harmony and develop in a systematic manner. In addition to a political association, similar in principle to the modern European Union, Mazzini proposed the creation of a single European Court of Justice, which would be able to make legally sound decisions in the event of international disputes. It must be noted that it was not Mazzini who proposed the very idea of a United States of Europe, but another Italian democrat, Carlo Cattaneo, leader of the Milan Uprising of 1848, but it was Mazzini who took concrete political actions to achieve this aim. See: Giuseppe Mazzini, 'From a Revolutionary Alliance to the United States of Europe', ed. Stefano Recchia and Nadia Urbinati, in *A Cosmopolitanism of Nations. Giuseppe Mazzini's Writings on Democracy, Nation Building and International Relations*, (Princeton, New Jersey: Princeton University Press, 2009), pp. 132–135.

41 Guiseppe Mazzini, *I doveri dell'uomo* [An Essay on the Duties of Man], (Stabilimento tipografico Richiedei, 1872), p. 7.

of the nineteenth century, which had set out to liberate the nations, did not achieve any meaningful results in the form of improving the living conditions of the workers. He argues that there is no point in recognising someone's rights if people have no real opportunity to exercise these rights. What sense does free speech and equality in education make if people do not have the time or ability to derive any value from them? What opportunities does freedom of trade give to someone who has nothing to trade? These are fundamental questions, to which Mazzini gives a direct and clear answer: '...the theory of rights may be enough to motivate people to overcome some obstacles, but it cannot do anything when the task is to create long-term harmonious relations between people from which a nation can grow'.[42]

Following a theory of rights that affirms the happiness of the individual as the highest good results in a society of egoists gripped by the same motives as in the bygone era of monarchies. Thus, according to Mazzini, the primary task becomes education of peoples, education capable of breeding them with fortitude and readiness for self-sacrifice. In other words, a sense of duty. People, as children of one God, must follow one law for all. Their task should not be the selfish pursuit of their own good, but self-improvement in pursuit of virtue and the advancement of their fellow man. Mazzini stipulates that he is by no means calling on people to relinquish their rights, but that the rights themselves can only be the result of a fulfilled duty. The pursuit of material interests alone has disastrous consequences.

The first topic that Mazzini expounds on is divine law. 'God gave you life; thus God gave you the law. God is the only true lawmaker for humanity',[43] he writes. Divine law contains the basis of every morality and every duty. Without knowledge of divine laws, human beings cannot claim any rights. For Mazzini, the consciousness of the individual and the opinion of others are 'two wings that lift one up to God'.[44]

42 Ibid., p. 14.

43 Ibid., p. 19.

44 Ibid., p. 31.

Political movements that overemphasise the former lead society to anarchy. Movements that sacrifice the freedom of the individual for 'social rights' lead societies to petrification, depriving them of mobility and any possibility of further progress.[45] 'Our consciousness may assure us that there is law; however, it cannot teach us the duty that follows from this law',[46] Mazzini notes. It needs a torch to illuminate the darkness, and this torch is human reason.

People live and die, but their good deeds, and the knowledge they attain and pass on to posterity, remain in eternity. Man learns for as long as he lives, but the learning of humanity is infinite. For Mazzini, humanity is 'the living word of God'. From one age to another, humanity becomes more and more aware of itself, of its mission, as well as of the laws of God. 'As there is one God, so there is one law of God,'[47] writes Mazzini. 'But we discover it line by line, through the experience of previous generations, in accordance with the increasing movement towards the association of human races, peoples, and individuals,'[48] the author continues his thought. No one can claim to know God's law. However, man's first duty is to work together to elevate humanity to that level of education and that level of perfection which God and time have prepared for it. 'I believe in humanity, the only interpreter of God's law on earth',[49] Mazzini concludes.

The second topic that Mazzini explores is the individual's duty to humanity. He writes: 'You are human beings; this means that you are rational and social beings, capable of intellectual development through association'.[50] Possessing a unique nature, human beings must not

45 Here Mazzini notes prophetically that if Communism ever wins, giving the state a monopoly on all the means of production, it will lead to the creation of an 'immobile society' and the 'terrors of tyranny'.

46 Ibid., p. 33.

47 Ibid., p. 34.

48 Ibid., p. 34.

49 Ibid., p. 37.

50 Ibid., p. 37.

only serve the interests of their family and country, but must fulfil their duty to all mankind — to educate and improve themselves and those around them; to work not only for themselves but also for the progress of all mankind. Mazzini proclaims the truth of the Christian message that there is one God and that all men are his children. From the understanding of one God, according to him, follows an understanding of one humanity. The life of peoples in close cooperation with one another is how Mazzini defines the ideal to which humanity should aspire. 'The fraternity of the peoples of Europe, and then of the whole world',[51] is how the Italian thinker formulates this goal. When acting in the interest of one's family and country, one must ask oneself how one's actions benefit all of humanity.

The next subject is man's duty to his homeland. By creating nations and peoples, God gave man a way to increase his strength. For Mazzini, a country is 'an association of free and equal people, bound together by fraternal bonds, pursuing a common goal'.[52] A country is not a mass but an association of individuals. Equality of rights and freedom from privilege are the foundation of any country. In addition to God's law, a country must have 'secondary laws' governing its life, and all the citizens of that country must take part in drafting them. Here, he also notes that those countries that recognise freedom only within their own borders, while systematically violating it internationally, must pay a price for their egotism.

Mazzini then touches on the question of freedom. A man deprived of freedom cannot fulfil his duty, cannot live a truly moral life, because he is not free to choose good or evil. Freedom is sacred. From these postulates, Mazzini deduces that all men have the right to freedom, as well as the right to pursue it by any means. The republic is the only logical and legitimate form of government precisely because free citizens participate in its functioning. Freedom of movement, freedom

51 Ibid., p. 44.

52 Ibid., p. 51.

of religion, freedom of opinion and expression in public, freedom of association with others, freedom of work, and freedom of trade cannot be taken away from a person. All these are sacred for Mazzini. Freedom is, however, only a means and not an end. 'Freedom is not the negation of all authority; it is the negation of any authority that does not express the collective purpose of the Nation or that seeks to establish itself contrary to social consensus.'[53] According to Mazzini, freedom will be sacred as long as it is guided by the idea of duty, the belief in a universal perfection.

Finally, the author touches on economic issues. Mazzini speaks to the poor, the underprivileged members of the working class. The Italian thinker realises that it is pointless to address their debt to humanity, to talk to them about political rights and freedom of speech, as they are engaged in a bitter struggle for existence. With this in mind, he urges them to think of themselves as part of one big family, of one nation, where they, with fairer wages from work, will have more free time and more opportunities to develop themselves. Labour is the basis of every economy. Appealing to a sense of justice, Mazzini offers workers the idea of a national revolution capable of eliminating the tyranny of capital. He insists that the right to property is as sacred as freedom itself and criticises the utopian socialists. Mazzini notes that the distribution of property in his era was unfair, as a considerable amount of it was acquired through violence and oppression. 'We must not try to abolish property; we must only create the conditions in which many can acquire it',[54] Mazzini concludes in passing. He is convinced that once class distinctions are finally abolished in European societies, the conditions for greater social justice will be created. For Mazzini, economic justice is about everyone getting a wage equal to the value they produce through their work.

53 Ibid., p. 73.

54 Ibid., p. 93.

Looking at *On the Duties of Man* in the context of Mazzini's life and the evolution of his thought, against the background of his earlier works, it can be seen that his political, social ideal has not changed: a republican polity that guarantees maximum rights and freedoms, but which also imposes a moral and ethical duty on citizens to improve themselves and pursue national development. In the statements above, Mazzini reveals the significant influence German classical idealism had on his political ontology—both Hegel's philosophy of history (with regard to the self-knowledge of God through progress in the consciousness of freedom) and Kant's ethics (morality aspiring to the proper rather than the existent). Compared to his earlier works, the role of the religious factor (an appeal to divine laws, from which he derives his political ontology) is noticeably amplified. However, Mazzini is not to be denied consistency, as he declares the same fervent attachment to the republican ideal he had at the time of Young Italy. He adapts his political theory to the new challenges of the time—for instance, to the Communist threat, which by 1860 was already very clear. At the same time, in the fundamentals of his political thought, Mazzini remains a convinced liberal and nationalist who is committed to a free and independent united Italy.

Mazzini was lucky enough to see his dream come true in his lifetime—in 1861, King Victor Emmanuel II of Sardinia proclaimed a united Italian state, the Kingdom of Italy; in 1871, following the final defeat of Pope Pius IX and the capture of Rome, the unification of the Italian lands was successfully completed. However, Mazzini's relationship with the victorious monarchy did not work out; in 1867 the thinker even declined the mandate of deputy offered to him.[55] In 1872,

55 It must be noted that many of those who lived to see the climax of the Risorgimento were disappointed with the results. Unification was achieved economically and politically, but there was no spiritual and intellectual unity as envisioned by Mazzini and the Italian idealists. The idea that the Risorgimento promised much but did not deliver on all its promises was embedded in the emerging Italian national consciousness. During the twentieth century, the radical representatives of the Italian political field (including the Fascists) actively speculated on this

Mazzini died in Pisa. More than a hundred thousand people saw him off for his final journey.

Mazzini became one of the major heroes of the Risorgimento period in Italy; he is still revered as one of the fathers of the nation, on a par with Garibaldi and Victor Emmanuel II. His nationalism and fierce rejection of socialism led many radical thinkers of both the pre-Fascist period and the Fascist era itself to regard him as one of their primary teachers. For example, the Syndicalist Sergio Panunzio, in a 1917 article written for Mussolini's newspaper *Il Popolo d'Italia*, urged everyone to study Mazzini, 'the greatest Italian since Dante'.[56] At the same time, Panunzio noted that Mazzini's work must be 'purged of religious ballast',[57] leaving only 'the living elements — association, education, and the nation's mission'.[58] Another prominent Syndicalist, Angelo Oliviero Olivetti, urged: 'Forward, towards the Italian People, foretold by Mazzini!'[59] As David Roberts observes, 'for the Syndicalists, Mazzini was a symbol of the broken promise of the Risorgimento, because he aspired to a different kind of Italian unity, a popular community with close psychological ties and deep social commitments'.[60]

---

notion. Raymond Grew, 'How Success Spoiled the Risorgimento', *The Journal of Modern History*, 34, no. 3 (Sep., 1962), pp. 239–253. The Fascists were particularly critical of the institution of parliamentarism, which was brought into Italy by the Risorgimento and which, they believed, had no positive influence on national development. Henry Stuart Hughes, 'The Aftermath of the Risorgimento in Four Successive Interpretations', *The American Historical Review*, 61, no. 1 (Oct., 1955), pp. 70–76. While Marxists (e.g. Antonio Gramsci) described the Risorgimento as a 'passive revolution' (*rivoluzione passiva*), right-wing radicals more often used the term 'failed revolution' (*rivoluzione mancata*). A. W. Salomone, 'The Risorgimento between Ideology and History: The Political Myth of rivoluzione mancata', *The American Historical Review*, 68, no. 1 (Oct., 1962), pp. 38–56.

56 Roberts, *The Syndicalist Tradition and Italian Fascism*, p. 167.

57 Ibid., p. 167.

58 Ibid., p. 167.

59 Ibid., p. 167.

60 Ibid., pp. 167–168.

Giuseppe Mazzini's philosophy inspired both the Left and the Right. Mazzini did as much for the emergence of a united Italy as did Giuseppe Garibaldi or Victor Emmanuel II.

As for the 'Fascist era', Mazzini's influence is evident in several key protagonists of the time. For the philosopher Giovanni Gentile, Mazzini was a great idealist who clearly distinguished good from evil, a true warrior of the idea, with which he waged an irreconcilable struggle. He argued that Mazzini was a true prophet of Italian nationalism, and the religious foundations that permeated his political teaching only served to bolster his belief in a free and strong Italian nation.[61] Giuseppe Bottai, founder of *Critica Fascista* (Fascist Critic), also presented Mazzini as a proto-Fascist. In the context of Mazzini's consensus-based economic theory, he was written about as the forerunner of corporatism. Fascist leader Benito Mussolini also did not deny Mazzini any reverence — several volumes of Mazzini's works were always lying on his desk.

The influence of the Risorgimento thinkers on Fascism was both direct (such as the examples discussed above) and indirect. It was during the Risorgimento era that any projection of Italy as a sovereign

61 See: Roland Sarti, *Mazzini: A Life for the Religion of Politics,* (Westport, Connecticut: Greenwood Publishing Group, 1997), p. 227.

state or consideration of Italians as a single modern people, with all its attributes, first became possible. Without the intellectual and spiritual breakthroughs of Rosmini, Gioberti, Spaventa, and Mazzini, neither Italian nationalism in the late nineteenth century nor Fascism in the twentieth century would have been possible.

§2. The Left-Wing Roots of Fascism: Revolutionary and National Syndicalism

2.1. The Revolutionary Syndicalism of Georges Sorel

Another origin of Fascism, fundamentally different from the idealism of the Risorgimento era, can be found in France at the turn of the twentieth century. French philosophy, which gave the world the most radical variations of Enlightenment political philosophy, is at the same time 'responsible' for the contrary political tradition, which can be called modern political conservatism. Both directions of French political thought — the left, egalitarian, republican direction, which gained its momentum from Claude Adrien Helvétius, Jean-Jacques Rousseau, and Henri de Saint-Simon, had a significant influence on Marx and, through him, on the whole 'leftist' radicalism of the twentieth century; and the right, counter-revolutionary, conservative, reactionary, and elitist direction, inspired by the thought of Joseph de Maistre and Louis de Bonald — found their vivid followers in France, who in turn influenced the intellectual climate of the unified nation-state of Italy. The influence of left-wing radicalism on Fascism is evident when we turn to Mussolini's numerous statements (including in his *Doctrine of Fascism*) regarding the value of Sorel's philosophical insights, which influenced the representatives of Italian National Syndicalism who had joined the Fascist movement (including as prominent ideologues). We will consider the key ideas of the French thinker.

The philosopher Georges Eugène Sorel (1847–1922)[62], a theorist of Revolutionary Syndicalism, was a native of Cherbourg from a family of wine traders. He graduated from the École Polytechnique in Paris and pursued a career as a civil engineer. In 1891, at the age of 44, he was awarded the Legion of Honour for outstanding services to civic life. Soon after, in 1892, Sorel retired and settled in Boulogne, Paris, where he remained for the rest of his days. One year after his retirement from public service, Sorel reveals his commitment to Marxism and begins to publish in the French Marxist journals *L'Ère Nouvelle* and *Le Devenir Sociale*. He develops an anti-elitist left-wing radical theory of Revolutionary Syndicalism that justifies trade union violence, which he systematically presents in *Reflections on Violence*.[63] Sorel's theory influenced the formation of both left- and right-wing radicalism.[64] The thinker himself welcomed both the victories of the Bolsheviks and Mussolini's early successes.[65] However, in the last years of his life, he strongly condemned both the seizure of Fiume by D'Annunzio's supporters and Fascism, which proved to be a radical opponent of Bolshevism, in which the French philosopher had placed his hopes of realising his theories.

Sorel developed a theory of Revolutionary Syndicalism, deriving it from his own Marxist-inspired politico-economic studies and

62 See: Dmitry Moiseev, 'Революционный синдикализм Жоржа Сореля и его влияние на становление фашизма в Италии' [Revolutionary Syndicalism of Georges Sorel and Its Impact on the Formation of Fascism in Italy] in *Материалы Международного молодежного научного форума «Ломоносов-2015»* [Proceedings of the International Youth Scientific Forum 'Lomonosov-2015'], ed. A. I. Andreev, A. V. Andriyanov and E. A. Antipov, (Moscow: Max Press, 2015). [Electronic Resource]

63 The work was first published in 1906 in the French edition of *Le Mouvement socialiste*, then in book form in 1908.

64 This thesis is substantiated not only by what Mussolini said about Sorel as a teacher—which we will discuss shortly—but also by Sorel's collaboration with the French nationalists of Charles Maurras' Action française in 1909 and 1910.

65 It should be noted that until the outbreak of World War I, Mussolini was positioned as a left-wing politician, one of the leaders of the Italian Socialists.

observations of his contemporary political and economic situation. In *Introduction à l'économie modern* [*Introduction to the Study of Modern Economy*] (1903), the French philosopher made three methodological demands, significant in the context of his later studies. His first thesis was that 'for sociology it is essential, first and foremost, that it take an openly subjective stance from the outset, that it knows what it wants to do, and that it subordinate all its research to the solutions it preaches'.[66] Thus, Sorel declares that the ultimate ideological goal of research is more important than anything else; the results must be subordinate to it. In the case of socialism, this ultimate goal is the final victory of the proletariat in the class struggle.

Georges Sorel, the author of the Revolutionary Syndicalist doctrine

The second rule is formulated as follows: 'Reality must be seen in images which, one by one, encompass it as a whole and which are integrated into a system that corresponds to the goal that has been set.'[67] Asserting this thesis, Sorel insists we cannot 'sacrifice reality to the demands of formal investigation'.[68] The variety of human activity

66 Georges Sorel, *Introduction à l'economie moderne* [Introduction to the Study of Modern Economy], (Charleston, South Carolina: Nabu Press, 2013), p. 254.

67 Ibid., p. 257.

68 Ibid., p. 257.

cannot be exhausted, and that which seemed insignificant yesterday may turn out to be fundamentally important today.

Sorel defines the third rule as follows: 'Ideological constructions are necessary, but they are also the most frequent causes of our delusions; therefore, we must discard everything that is not the result of reflection on institutions, customs and empirical rules, which have acquired in practice rather definite forms.'[69] The essence of his reasoning is this: idealism of any kind is a fallacy and a lie; one must focus on observing the concrete aspects of the economic life of society. Sorel's own adherence to the above principles is evident in an analysis of his seminal work, *Reflections on Violence.*

In another politico-economic work by Sorel, *Social Sketches of Modern Economics: The Degeneration of Capitalism and the Degeneration of Socialism*,[70] the philosopher points out that 'strikes, which in the past were the ferment of revolutionary ideas, nowadays give rise to constant communication between the leaders of the workers' syndicates and the bourgeoisie, under the patronage of the government. At the same time, the ideas of economic fatalism, non-solidarity, and the class struggle are disappearing'.[71] Sorel declares that 'the science of the new socialists recognises only the society, albeit divided into two parts and often pursuing opposing interests, but united by deep solidarity'.[72] In the quoted work, he examines in detail the vari-

69 Ibid., p. 257.

70 *Insegnamenti sociali dell'economia moderna. Degenerazione capitalista e degenerazione socialista* was first published in Palermo, Italy, in 1907. In the preface to the first Russian edition, which appeared in the same year, Sorel notes that the French text of the work was completed in 1903, and the delay in publication was due to personal circumstances of the Italian translator of the text, Professor Racca. Thus, this text can also be attributed to the period of Sorel's work which predates *Reflections on Violence*.

71 Georges Sorel, *Социальные очерки современной экономики. Дегенерация капитализма и дегенерация социализма* [Social Essays on Modern Economics. The Degeneration of Capitalism and the Degeneration of Socialism], (Moscow: Krasand, 2011), p. 355.

72 Ibid., p. 355.

ous aspects of the crisis of the socialist movement, caused, in his view, by consensus-based sentiments both in the bourgeoisie and amongst 'leftist' leaders. He sees a radicalisation of the situation, including by violent means, as the way out of this crisis.

In *Reflections on Violence* (1906), Sorel polemicises with his contemporaries about the current state of political processes taking place in Europe. Reasoning in Marxist terms, he notes that the weakening bourgeoisie is gradually losing its class consciousness, trying to compromise with the proletariat, expressing a certain concern for it, and, in this way, relieving the class struggle. Sorel accuses parliamentary socialism of betraying the class interests of the proletariat, indeed of being reactionary, and insists on its destruction. He views violence on the part of the proletariat as a key element capable of turning the historical process once again to the path of progress outlined by Marx, which can lead to a drastic harshness in the attitude of the bourgeoisie toward the proletariat (and, accordingly, an awakening of the class consciousness of the bourgeoisie), which will inevitably lead to a new round of class struggle aggravation and proletarian revolution. According to Sorel, this requires disseminating the doctrine of hatred, which is capable of giving ideological meaning to proletarian uprisings.

Cover of the Spanish edition of Georges Sorel's *Reflections on Violence*

Sorel's intellectual ferocity is directed against 'conciliators', both inside and outside the socialist camp. He finds the attempts of the big bourgeoisie to present themselves as 'pious men', concerned for the fate of the workers, ridiculous and repugnant. At the same time, he denounces working-class leaders who forget the class interests of workers and negotiate with state representatives and industrialists: 'Many workers wonder if syndicate organisation is not becoming a kind of politics, a means of making a career.'[73] Meanwhile, all the parliamentary clamour 'serves only to cover up the government's true motives'.[74] Moreover, if the leaders of the syndicate provoke conflict, they achieve their goals much faster and more effectively. By intimidating municipal and industrial leaders with popular demonstrations, they force the weakening bourgeoisie to promptly surrender their positions. Thus, in the first

73 Georges Sorel, *Reflections on Violence*, (Cambridge: Cambridge University Press, 1999), p. 6.

74 Ibid., p. 12.

chapter of his work, Sorel concludes that 'the social policy of the bourgeoisie, which is founded on cowardice and is constantly compelled to yield to threats of violence, leads to the conclusion that the bourgeoisie is sooner or later condemned to death and that its disappearance is only a matter of time'.[75] From here, Sorel reaches the conclusion that proletarian violence is a vanguard component of socialist tactics.

Sorel points out that the concept of proletarian violence may appear to many Marxists as a regression, a throwback to barbarism. At the same time, noting numerous cases of parliamentary socialists betraying genuine (by Marx's standards) workers' interests, Sorel argues that 'revolutionary syndicalism does not need to be led by so-called parliamentary socialists'.[76] According to Sorel, the parliamentary Left is a 'dictatorship of incompetence'; instead of 'explaining to the proletariat all the greatness of its revolutionary role',[77] they lead workers towards the of loss of revolutionary energy and make a full-fledged uprising impossible. He argues that Europeans are 'dumbed down by humanism';[78] they need to recover their old energy. According to Sorel, there is no other mechanism than proletarian violence.

Of critical importance is a passage in chapter three ('Prejudice against Violence'), in which Sorel examines eighteenth-century legal consciousness and its impact on the events of the French Revolution. According to the French thinker, during the old regime, justice seemed designed to exalt royal power, and its true purpose was upholding the state, not the law. He notes that the legal profession gave the revolution many important and influential figures, the most famous of whom was Robespierre. Indeed, the jurist revolutionaries adopted the principle of state terror from the old regime. Eighteenth-century revolutionary legislation enshrined this principle. Sorel goes on to explain that '[i]t used to be that the State was always seen as good and wise, and

75 Ibid., p. 14.

76 Ibid., p. 21.

77 Ibid., p. 24.

78 Ibid., p. 27.

therefore any opposition to it was a grave offence'.[79] Interestingly, this thesis is also directed against the revolutionary state. Sorel states: 'Maybe, we are no better and no more compassionate than the people of '93; I am even ready to admit that the country is morally inferior now, but we are not under the power of the State, of that Moloch to which our fathers sacrificed so much'.[80] Borrowing the concept of the exceptional value of the state from the monarchists, Sorel explains the cruelty of the members of the Convention. Syndicalism needed to liberate itself from the old prejudices. In this case, 'social conflicts will have the character of a pure struggle, quite analogous to the struggle between two hostile armies'.[81] According to Sorel, 'the syndicalists do not set out to reform the state like the leading minds of the eighteenth century, they want to destroy it altogether, because they want to implement Marx's idea: the social revolution must not seek to replace one ruling minority with another'.[82]

Sorel then turns to the question of the general proletarian strike. For the French philosopher, the strike is analogous to a military campaign which must lead to a final victory — a 'great final upheaval'.[83] The drive for a general strike is proclaimed as key for Revolutionary Syndicalists. At the same time 'the movement of the revolutionary masses must be presented in such a way that it produces an inspiring impression on the indignant souls of the proletarians'.[84] Sorel writes that 'the general strike is precisely that mythological concept in which all socialism resides; a set of images capable of arousing precisely those feelings that correspond to the various manifestations of the socialist struggle against modern society'.[85] Thus, the idea of a general strike is

79 Ibid., p. 44.

80 Ibid., p. 45.

81 Ibid., p. 49.

82 Ibid., p. 50.

83 Ibid., p. 52.

84 Ibid., p. 54.

85 Ibid., p. 58.

translated into a myth in a positive sense, a breathing image of a future worth fighting for. Sorel argues that 'the general strike excludes the ideological consequences of any social policy; its supporters consider even the most democratic reforms bourgeois, for them nothing can weaken the class struggle underlying social organisation'.[86] According to Sorel, even intellectuals 'thinking on behalf of the proletariat' are not necessary for real socialism — one 'pure and clear idea' is enough, and this idea is, of course, the general strike. He rebukes the 'worshippers of an empty and false science' as followers of popular illusions without any practical sense.[87] In Sorel's view, 'small science' only creates sophisms, unable to produce either an accurate prediction of future events or an intelligible prediction of their consequences.

In addition to the general proletarian strike, Sorel introduces the concept of a general *political* strike, 'which combines the economic causes of the upheaval with many other phenomena of a completely different order'.[88] The French philosopher views this concept negatively — according to Sorel, it is a weapon in the hands of demagogues. First of all, 'the general political strike does not presuppose a class struggle between the proletariat and the bourgeoisie'.[89] Socialist politicians often act as skillful intermediaries between the proletariat and the bourgeoisie, solving the problems of the latter. Moreover, the preoccupation with beautiful speeches is a sign of a degenerate class, not an energetic and future-oriented one. Sorel also believes that the 'supreme educational value'[90] of socialism can only be found in the unconditional upheaval carried out by the Syndicalists. In his opinion, any bourgeois politicking could do irreparable harm to the movement. For Sorel, the Syndicalist movement must be protected from these 'charlatans'. Representatives of this camp tend to justify wars waged

86 Ibid., p. 63.

87 He is particularly referring to Auguste Comte and the positivists.

88 Ibid., p. 80.

89 Ibid., p. 80.

90 Ibid., p. 83.

by states for material gain. By strengthening the state, they weaken the working class, which turns out to be no more than 'cannon fodder' to win armed conflicts. The general political strike, according to Sorel, is a prologue to the demagogic dictatorship of politicians, to the usurpation of power by a select group of leaders who essentially betray the interests of those who follow them. The victory of this type of protest could lead to a social revolution that will result in unprecedented slavery.

After examining the essential differences between the two types of strike, Sorel moves on to justify the ethical value of violence. Drawing on examples from the history of the formation of Christianity, illustrating his idea with various examples from American, Corsican, and Norwegian life, Sorel proves the idea that 'civilisation is by no means threatened by the consequences of developing violence, since the idea of the general strike allows the notion of the class struggle to be maintained through such events that would seem insignificant to bourgeois historians'.[91] Thus, he resorts to a direct apology of violence: if sacrifices and extreme measures are necessary in order for socialism to fulfil its historical role, then the harshest tactics possible must be resorted to.

Sorel finishes his work by talking about morality. In his view, it is necessary to start creating 'the morality of future manufacturers', different from the bourgeois morality, which he sees as pathetic and vulgar. The philosopher proclaims: 'Syndicalism sets out to create a truly proletarian ideology, and whatever the bourgeois scholars may say, the historical experience to which Renan refers indicates to us that this is very possible, and that from here the salvation of the world may come.'[92] According to Sorel, Syndicalists must be devoid of pride, of 'desires to become princes', of aspirations for material gain. Thus Sorel extols self-denial in the name of 'the higher moral ideal of socialism'

91 Ibid., p. 103.

92 Ibid., p. 141.

as the main virtue of the Syndicalist. Moreover, the process of forming such a revolutionary morality should not be one of creating a new religion, as described by intellectuals, but should have the features of an 'emerging virtue'[93] — that is, it should be a natural product of the Syndicalist's commitment to the ideal of socialism. Drawing on examples from Nietzsche, contemporary American experience, and the attitude of Napoleon's revolutionary armies, the French philosopher examines the values of heroic morality created by 'gentlemen' — fearless and energetic enthusiasm, violent by necessity. According to him, 'the same spirit can be observed in the workers' groups stirred up by the general strike'.[94] For Sorel, 'the general strike, like the wars of liberation, is the most brilliant expression of the individualist spirit in the rising masses'.[95] The selfless morality of the Revolutionary Syndicalist also allows him to work effectively in the workshop without a 'master', as he is committed to endless progress, both quantitatively and qualitatively.

93 Ibid., p. 142.

94 Ibid., p. 155.

95 Ibid., p. 156.

Cover of the Spanish edition of Georges Sorel's presentation of the main points of Revolutionary Syndicalism, 1934

As a result of his *Reflections on Violence*, Sorel comes to the conclusion that 'socialism owes to violence the high moral values by which it brings salvation to the modern world'.[96] Thanks to Sorel, the idea of a general proletarian strike becomes part of Syndicalist mythology, receiving from the French philosopher a moral and ethical justification as a necessary violence for historical progress and the achievement of a radical break in the class struggle between the proletariat and the bourgeoisie. The thinker substantiates a thesis about the high instrumental value of proletarian myth by comparing it to the ideas that inspired previous generations — be they the motives of the fearless Homeric heroes, the figures of the French Revolution, or the soldiers of Napoleon's army. For him, myth is the force by which history is made.[97] Sorel vehemently denounces parliamentary socialism for indulging the interests of the conservative bourgeoisie, arguing that the

96 Ibid., p. 163.

97 For more detail, see: Paul Kahn, 'Mythe et Réalité Sociale chez Sorel' [Myth and Social Reality in Sorel], *Cahiers Internationaux de Sociologie*, 11 (1951), pp. 131–154.

future belongs to syndicates bound by the 'manufacturer morality'. It is the syndicates that are the mechanism of future solidarity; they 'create powerful and lasting ties among the working class'.[98]

Sorel's radical Syndicalism had a significant impact on the trade union movement in Italy[99] which, in turn, played a role in the political victory of Fascism. Moreover, through the writings of thinkers such as Sergio Panunzio and Angelo Oliviero Olivetti, certain aspects of Revolutionary Syndicalism were incorporated into Fascist doctrine. In the 1890s, against the background of the Syndicalist crisis in France, the situation in Italy seemed more optimistic to Sorel, so he actively pursued cooperation with Italian authors and Syndicalist activists (Alceste de Ambris, Michele Bianchi, Filippo Corridoni), among whom he was considered a true patriarch. After Sorel's renunciation of Syndicalism[100] and his turn to right-wing movements (between 1909 and 1910 he actively collaborated with the French right-wing radical

98 Michael Curtis, *Three Against the Third Republic: Sorel, Barrès and Maurras.* (New Brunswick, New Jersey: Transaction Publishers, 2010), p. 258.

99 Here it should be noted that during his life Sorel had an active correspondence with many Italian thinkers, including Benedetto Croce and Vilfredo Pareto. Sorel did not conceal that he was influenced by Italian thinkers — in the works identified above he actively refers to the arguments and examples of Giambattista Vico, who, as Hutton shows, had a great influence on him — Sorel had a special interest in the concept of cyclical development proposed by Vico. Patrick H. Hutton, 'Vico's Theory of History and the French Revolutionary Tradition', *Journal of the History of Ideas*, 37, no. 2 (Apr.–Jun., 1976), pp. 241–256. Sorel's significant influence on the French 'Left' is evident in the letters written to Sorel by the leading Italian Marxist, Antonio Labriola (1843–1904), which were translated into Russian and published in the pre-revolutionary period. This correspondence has recently been republished. See: Antonio Labriola, *Исторический материализм и философия: Письма к Жоржу Сорелю* [Historical materialism and philosophy: Letters to Georges Sorel], (Moscow: LKI Publishing, 2011).

100 In December 1910, a letter from Sorel was read out at a Syndicalist congress in Bologna in which he renounced his former beliefs. See Jack J. Roth, 'The Roots of Italian Fascism: Sorel and Sorelismo', *The Journal of Modern History*, 39, no. 1 (Mar., 1967), p. 35.

leader Charles Maurras[101]) the French philosopher did not lose his popularity in Italy — as he himself admitted, he was correctly understood by Enrico Corradini, who claimed that Syndicalism and nationalism had much in common. Some Italian thinkers and Syndicalist figures have modified Sorel's ideas, but invariably found inspiration in him. For example, Filippo Corridoni, one of the active figures of the Italian Syndicalist Union, replaced Sorel's notion of a general proletarian strike with that of a 'revolutionary war for freedom'; the Syndicalists loyal to him, much like Sorel, drew inspiration from the ideals of the Risorgimento, chanting 'Viva Italia!' at demonstrations of like-minded 'leftists'.

Sorel closely followed the post-war rise of the young Fascist movement, evidenced in particular by his correspondence with Croce.[102] He noted that combining social and national myths into a single concept was an original invention of Mussolini's. Sorel believed that after the Fascists came to power, the new regime would seek to transform social life inside the country and expand Italy into an empire abroad. Sorel was not destined to see his suppositions confirmed — he died in August 1922, at the age of 74, a few months before the March on Rome.[103] In the Fascist era, especially after Mussolini publicly claimed Sorel as his

101 As Zeev Sternhell writes, referring to *The Birth of Tragedy from the Spirit of Music*, 'Sorel and Maurras complemented each other, like Apollo and Dionysus. Apollo and Dionysus had a common enemy, Socrates, the destroyer of tragedy, the precursor of Voltaire, the "archetype of the intellectual". The alliance of Maurrasian "Apollonianism" and Sorelian "Dionysianism" meant the end of Socrates and Descartes, the defeat of the eighteenth century'. Zeev Sternhell, *The Birth of Fascist Ideology. From Cultural Rebellion to Political Revolution*, (Princeton, New Jersey: Princeton University Press, 1995), p. 123.

102 Ibid., p. 40.

103 An obituary dedicated to Sorel by the Revue de Métaphysique et de Morale notes that 'the embittered old man sought, with the help of both right-wing and left-wing radicals, even the most desperate ways to do away with a debased civilisation'. Georges Sorel (1847–1922), Supplement to the *Revue de Métaphysique et de Morale*, 29, no. 4 (October-December 1922), p. 2.

teacher[104] and Panunzio and Oliviero Olivetti gained high positions in the party and academia, Italian interest in the French philosopher continued unabated. At the same time, Sorel was also actively criticised in Fascist circles — in particular, for his famous approving remarks regarding Lenin and Bolshevism.[105] Nevertheless, Sorel's theories on the ethical value of violence and the power of myth had a significant impact on the intellectual platform of Fascism and contributed to the success of the emerging radical movement.

As for the direct influence that Sorel had on Mussolini, it is necessary first of all to quote Sorel's own statement about the future leader of the Italian Fascists, made in 1912: 'Our Mussolini is no ordinary socialist. Believe me: one day you will see him at the head of the sacred battalions, saluting the Italian flag with his sword. He is a fifteenth century Italian, a "condottiere". It is not yet certain, but he alone possesses enough energy and ability to revive the power of the nation'.[106] Sorel and Mussolini were united in their hatred of the parliamentary state, the collapse of which they both passionately desired. Sorel repeatedly noted that there are as many types of socialism as there are nations on earth — indeed, the French philosopher took national characteristics into account, which is why he was not at all disturbed by the nationalist element in Italian Syndicalism and, accordingly, in the work and political experiments of the young Mussolini.[107] The Sorelian methodol-

104 In 1927, giving an interview to the Spanish newspaper *ABC Madrid*, when asked which of the three thinkers listed had influenced him most: Nietzsche, Jaurès, or Sorel, Mussolini replied 'Sorel'. He also stated that Sorel was his teacher in 1932, in an interview with the French journalist Émile Servan-Schreiber. James H. Meisel, 'A Premature Fascist? Sorel and Mussolini', *The Western Political Quarterly*, 3, no. 1 (Mar., 1950), p. 14.

105 See: James H. Meisel, 'Georges Sorel's Last Myth', *The Journal of Politics*, 12, no. 1 (Feb., 1950), p. 54.

106 Jean Variot, 'Quelques souvenirs: Le Père Sorel' [Some Memories: The Reverend Sorel] in *L'Eclair*, (Paris, Septembre 11, 1922). Cited from: Meisel, A Premature Fascist? Sorel and Mussolini, p. 14.

107 Sorel was comfortable with the fact that Fascism was both social and national. What mattered most to him was that it was revolutionary and against the old

ogy — according to which myth had considerably more political value than scientifically sound rational judgement — became an important component of the realpolitik implemented by Mussolini during the ventennio years.[108]

2.2. Peculiarities of Italian Syndicalism. National Syndicalism. Sergio Panunzio and Angelo Oliviero Olivetti

Italy's trade union movement was born in the late 1880s. The first Italian Workers' Chamber was set up in Milan in 1889, and by 1893 there were 14 such centres linked together in a national network. In 1890 the first mass demonstrations of workers took place in most major cities. The labour movement was gaining strength against a backdrop of an unprecedented socio-economic crisis between 1873 and 1895.

Despite the growing popularity of proletarian self-organisation ideology, Italian Syndicalism, understood as a political force and a particular intellectual tradition, was not the result of an entrenched labour movement, but crystallised against the background of the Italian Socialist Party's crisis. At the 1902 national congress of the Socialists there was a serious split in the party — its leadership decided on parliamentary support for the current government and sanctioned tactical alliances with 'progressive bourgeois parties'. The choice in favour of so-called 'reformism' was not unanimous; a group of activists led by Arturo Labriola and Enrico Ferri, not ready for political concessions,

parliamentary order. Jack J. Roth, 'Revolution and Morale in Modern French Thought: Sorel and the Sorelians', *French Historical Studies*, 3, no. 2 (Autumn, 1963), p. 215.

108 This was largely due to the fact that Mussolini completely shared Sorel's view that in the twentieth century it was irrationalism that was the best ideological weapon for offense, whereas rationalism was best for defence. In the eighteenth century the situation was just the opposite. Accordingly, the significance of tasks to be accomplished through mythological, figurative language increased, as did the effectiveness of their implementation. S. p. Rouanet, 'Irrationalism and Myth in Georges Sorel', *The Review of Politics*, 26, no. 1 (Jan., 1964), pp. 45–69.

broke away from the party.[109] In December 1902, Labriola founded his own weekly newspaper, *Avanguardia Socialista*, publishing, among others, the first Italian Syndicalists. Labriola and Ferri were successful in their struggle against the reformists—in 1904 they gained full control of the Socialist Party.

At the same time, Syndicalist sentiment within the party grew. By the next annual Socialist Congress in Bologna, in April 1904, the Syndicalists were an organised group within the party.[110] In September 1904, the first major national workers' strike in Italy took place. It ended in defeat for the Syndicalists and discredited their methods among the Italian Left, but at the same time such mass activity gave hope to supporters of a radical route. In January 1905, Enrico Leone and Paolo Mantica founded the journal *Il Divenire Sociale*, which became a forum for theoretical debate on Syndicalism. At the same time, the first congress of the Labour Resistance Organisations was held in Genoa, where the Syndicalists not only participated but proved themselves to be the strongest and most organised group.

In the meantime, the Socialist Party as a political whole continued to pursue the strategic course adopted in 1902 for collaboration with the government. The strategy of Giovanni Giolitti, a liberal and one of the country's leading politicians, who served as prime minister five times between 1892 and 1921, aimed to integrate the working class and left-wing intellectuals into an established political system. Giolitti believed that socialists would be more effective than other political

109 As Sternhell points out, the major point of divergence between the socialists and the new group of Syndicalists was this: the reformist socialists saw the unions only as associations formed along professional lines; the Syndicalists were convinced that this understanding was not enough and that the unions must become an instrument of the working-class struggle. Sternhell, *The Birth of Fascist Ideology. From Cultural Rebellion to Political Revolution*, p. 143.

110 In this context the regional aspect should be noted: radical Syndicalist sentiment was particularly strong in the southern, agrarian regions of the country ('alliance of the worker and the peasant'), while the more consensual reformist sentiment was stronger in the industrial north of Italy.

movements in reaching the disadvantaged and discontented, so that workers' living and working conditions could be improved and the most successful members of the 'systemic Left' could gain prominence in society without threatening the stability of the system as a whole. Overall, his plan succeeded, albeit temporarily — between 1900 and 1913, the socialists could well be seen as 'one of the interest groups within the system'.[111] This situation provoked the righteous fury of the Syndicalists, who argued that workers could establish their own values and social institutions and lead society into a new future in which there was no place for 'outmoded' liberal institutions. What were the characteristic beliefs of the Italian Syndicalists of the pre-war period in relation to their French and Spanish sympathisers? What did the Italian Syndicalists take from Sorel and Marx, and what did they reject from these 'left-wing' intellectual giants?

Unlike Spain and France, where the Syndicalist movement grew organically out of trade unions, in Italy the leading Syndicalists were intellectuals.[112] They had no understanding of the real situation on the factory floor. Their concepts were based on an abstract and unrealistic view of workers' needs or their real potential. The theorists of Italian Syndicalism were convinced that the proletariat was a new class of 'producers of the future', born in the process of industrialisation and equipped with a creative force capable of qualitatively changing society. Meanwhile, political practice revealed only unorganised, violent groups of aggressive workers.

Italian Syndicalism focused on the idea of developing new 'workers' values'. The main goal was to fundamentally change society and dismantle unjust bourgeois social institutions. Thus, the values of

---

111 Roberts, *Syndicalist Tradition and Italian Fascism*, p. 51.

112 By comparison, in Spain Syndicalism was particularly strong in Catalonia, the country's leading industrial region, which had the strongest trade union movement in 1908–1910, some of its leaders being middle-class intellectuals. In France, Sorel was reflecting on the real workings of trade unionism and proposing realistic tactics. By 1906 the French Syndicalists had held a national congress in Amiens as an independent political force.

solidarity and self-sacrifice for the sake of a high idea acquired special importance. The Syndicalists sought the psychological transformation of the proletariat, to establish a genuine brotherhood of workers, individual responsibility, and mutual support. The original target of the attack was bourgeois capitalist society, which, in a Marxist spirit, they proposed to destroy at once through revolution. The proletariat, according to the Syndicalists, must intervene in the course of the historical process and achieve its goal as quickly as possible. Here we see the first divergence between the Syndicalists and the orthodox Marxists, for whom the proletariat is not the highest social class, developing its own consciousness and psychological maturity, but an objective participant in the historical process, occupying a certain place in the economic process.

The image of the future that the Italian Syndicalists described lacked conceptual clarity. The new social order was supposed to be the result of a network of syndicates operating together, but a more detailed vision was not presented. According to the Syndicalists, society must somehow evolve to a point where it needs no governance, no bureaucracy, and no parliamentarianism, no *Realpolitik*. This political system could be defined as a 'direct democracy of producers', who have no need for intermediaries such as deputies and professional representatives. Such a society is thus highly decentralised. The influence of the anarchist tradition, with its radical anti-state and individualism, is evident in these aspects of the Syndicalist concept. The Syndicalists, however, denied this and insisted that it was their vision which was genuinely socialist. They saw the union as an organic middle ground between two opposing and equally destructive maxims—the cold, cynical individualism of bourgeois society and the dominating force of the state machine. The workers, bound together by the bonds of comradeship and united in syndicates, must overcome the purely individual worldview to create a society of the future based on solidarity. The Syndicalists also disagreed with anarchist methodology of struggle: according to anarchism, revolution was the result of armed uprisings of the masses; this vision is denied by the Syndicalists, who advocate, in the spirit of Sorel, a general strike, which takes time to prepare. The Syndicalists call for patience; the anarchists demand immediate violence.

Another important difference between Italian Syndicalism and its French counterpart is that Italian Syndicalists were not involved in the intellectual struggle against positivist and rationalist culture. Sorel's rejection of positivism was immense; his Italian colleagues did not share this view. Sergio Panunzio criticised Filippo Marinetti for his irrationalism and advocacy of cruelty as early as 1910, long before the outbreak of the First World War and the associated boom in futuristic militarism. Angelo Oliviero Olivetti, for his part, attacked the poet Giovanni Papini for 'reviving mysticism'.

While recognising the undoubted influence Georges Sorel had on the Italian Syndicalists, attention must also be drawn to a number of apparent contradictions between the French teacher and his Italian disciples. In particular, in 1918, Panunzio pointed out that the Italians were able to develop a clearer and more rational vision of the future for the syndicates than Sorel. The controversy dates back to 1905, three years before the publication of *Reflections on Violence.* With the publication of this famous work, the disagreement of the Italian Syndicalists with a number of Sorel's tenets became even more pronounced. In particular, the Italians did not share Sorel's conviction in the value of myth.[113] The workers' conversion to new values through a special mythology was denied on the grounds that the future seemed to be a natural evolution, whose foundation was the genuine assimilation by the proletariat of the values of comradeship and solidarity, a kind of 'maturation' of the working class, which did not need Sorelian 'superstructures'.

113 Paradoxically, it is this aspect of Sorelian Revolutionary Syndicalism that Mussolini — with whom many Syndicalist intellectuals would join — would later emphasise in particular.

The Italian Syndicalists also diverged from Sorel on an important premise of political ontology, namely the causes of the crisis of bourgeois society. For Sorel, bourgeois decadence was largely due to the excessive rationalisation of society, to its mechanisation. The worker, possessing a more primitive consciousness than the bourgeois, could be incited to revolutionary action through a myth that nurtured a revolutionary spirit. The Italians, for their part, disagreed with this premise — for them the evolution of workers' consciousness was linked precisely to a purposeful, rational system of thought.[114] The Marxist vision of progress eclipsed the more archaic anarchist mindset for them precisely because it represented a more rationalised, scientific approach to social issues. Workers, according to the Italian Syndicalists, do not need mythology. They completely overturn the Sorelian schema: it is not the myth that must educate the revolutionary spirit in the worker, but the worker's experience and his new morality that will be the source of his will for a new order, for social change. Labriola makes this quite clear: 'Myths, fairy tales, and revelations are the exact opposite of socialism, which teaches individuals how to reshape life "for themselves", how to construct their lives clearly'.[115]

Another aspect of Sorel's teaching that sparked controversy in Italy was the very doctrine of violence itself. The Italian Syndicalists pointed out that, of course, the turning point in the conflict between the old world and the new could be bloody and violent, and the proletariat would win if it proved stronger. But there is no creative potential in violence as such — the Italians were convinced of this, just as they were convinced that strikes do not have to be violent. For them, the most

114 This Syndicalist belief would later be characteristic of Fascist doctrine in general — despite Mussolini's personal preferences, the key ideologues of Fascism (the idealist Giovanni Gentile, the nationalist Alfredo Rocco, and the Syndicalist Sergio Panunzio who joined them) were opposed to any kind of irrationalism. See: David D. Roberts, 'How Not to Think about Fascism and Ideology, Intellectual Antecedents and Historical Meaning', *Journal of Contemporary History*, 35, no. 2 (Apr., 2000), pp. 185–211.

115 Roberts, *Syndicalist Tradition and Italian Fascism*, p. 78.

important thing was the psychological plane, on which the evolution of working-class consciousness was to take place.

Another particularity of the Italian Syndicalists' concept was elitism, which brought them closer to right-wing theorists (in particular the Pareto school of sociology). The Syndicalists agreed with Pareto that revolutionary change occurs when an active minority takes responsibility and brings new values to an inert majority. However, the Syndicalists were not defenders of a hierarchical order; their elitism was a tactical weapon of socialism, necessary to change the quality of society. The organisation of the trade union movement in Italy in the first decade of the twentieth century left much to be desired, so the Syndicalists saw themselves as class-conscious leaders who knew the interests of the proletariat better than the proletariat itself.

Having examined the key features of Italian Syndicalism from 1902 to 1913, it is now necessary to trace the line of Syndicalist thought that led many of them to support Fascism. A young journalist, Benito Mussolini, emerged on the socialist political scene during the Italo-Turkish War (1911–1912), where he organised protests against the Italian takeover of Libya and, after spending five months in prison, became editor-in-chief of the national socialist newspaper *Avanti!* Sergio Panunzio and Angelo Oliviero Olivetti knew Mussolini from the time the latter spent in Switzerland between 1902 and 1904 (they had notably attended the congress of the Union of Italian Socialists held in Zurich in March 1904). The future leader of Fascism embraced Sorel's teachings with great enthusiasm and often referred to himself as a Syndicalist.[116] In 1913 Arturo Labriola, convinced that Italy was not ready for Syndicalism and confident in the prospects of a movement led by Corridoni and De Ambris, was elected MP for Naples and began systematic work, culminating in his appointment as Minister of Labour in the cabinet of Giovanni Giolitti in 1920. However, on 28 July,

116 This did not prevent him, however, from stating in December 1910 that Syndicalism was a divisive, incoherent, and empty movement.

1914, World War I broke out. Italian society became divided between supporters and opponents of the country's entry into the war.

Leading Syndicalists favoured Italy's entry into the war on the side of the Entente. On 18 August, 1914, Alceste De Ambris made a statement in Milan in favour of participation in the war. His main argument was that a military victory by the Central Powers would cause irreparable damage to bourgeois society, which, in turn, was a prerequisite for the development and establishment of a Syndicalist society. The proletariat thus had to support Italy as a nation by fighting against the 'remnants of the Middle Ages'. De Ambris was supported by both organisers (Corridoni, Masotti) and intellectuals (Panunzio, Oliviero Olivetti).[117] The Socialists' pacifist position was considered reactionary.[118] The mood of the Syndicalists also influenced Mussolini, who in mid-October 1914 spoke for the first time in favour of going to war. In November 1914, he founded the newspaper *Il Popolo d'Italia*, in which Panunzio and De Ambris were frequently published. During this period the Syndicalists begin a gradual shift away from orthodox left-wing internationalism towards right-wing nationalism. While their arguments during this period still had a class character and class logic, something new (as Oliviero Olivetti said in 1915, 'something that transcends politics and partyism'[119]) was brought out in them during the war. Also in 1915, De Ambris came to the conclusion that the prevailing national solidarity should weaken liberal social institutions

117 For more detail, see: Glauco Licata, 'Il sindacalismo rivoluzionario italiano nel 1914' [Italian Revolutionary Trade Unionism in 1914], *Aevum*, 41, no. 3/4 (May-August 1967), pp. 304–326.

118 Such an opinion was expressed in particular by Oliviero Olivetti. See: Michel Ostenc, 'La guerre et le mythe de la "résurrection" chez les intellectuels italiens: Réforme morale et révolution nationale (1902–1915)' [War and the Myth of 'Resurrection' among Italian Intellectuals: Moral Reform and National Revolution (1902–1915)], *Guerres mondiales et conflits contemporains* [World Wars and Contemporary Conflicts], no. 227, Dossier: Artists and Intellectuals in War (July 2007), pp. 23–41.

119 Cited from Roberts, *Syndicalist Tradition and Italian Fascism*, p. 115.

and revolutionary forces should unite under the values outlined by Mazzini. Another Syndicalist, Ottavio Dinale, noted that the Italian people were finally outgrowing the established political system and taking the future into their own hands. Wartime Syndicalism represented an intermediate stage — the preparation for a new intellectual and spiritual synthesis, which was formulated in 1917.

The year 1917 was marked by a number of momentous events. The Italian army suffered a crushing defeat at Caporetto, the Bolshevik revolution was burning in Russia, and a civil war was breaking out. The events of the First World War changed not only the political, but also the intellectual climate in Europe. Italian Syndicalists felt that pre-war times would never return; it was necessary to come to grips with a changed reality. The Syndicalist Agostino Lanzillo, in *La Disfatta del Socialismo* (*The Defeat of Socialism*), published in 1917, declared that pre-war socialism was no longer possible. His message was echoed by Panunzio, who rejected the utopianism and economic reductionism of orthodox socialism. Both scholars remarked that the key factor in post-war Italian life would be the experience of war. A new elite was born in the trenches, gaining unique experiences of comradeship, solidarity, discipline, and the pursuit of a collective goal. In 1919, De Ambris recognised that the war had produced a new revolutionary force. He noted that an alliance of war veterans and workers could bring about the non-Bolshevik revolution that Italy needed.

1919–1920 is remembered in Italian history as the *Biennio Rosso*, the 'two red years'. This was a period of heightened social conflict, economic crisis, and a large number of protests and strikes. In Turin and Milan workers seized factories, in the south peasants went on strike. The left-wing radicals of the Unione Sindacale Italiana (Italian Workers' Union) mobilised at least 800,000 people under their banner.[120] Syndicalist intellectuals seriously feared that the Anarcho-Syndicalists

120 For more detail on the 'two red years', see: Charles L. Bertrand, 'The Biennio Rosso: Anarchists and Revolutionary Syndicalists in Italy, 1919–1920', *Réflexions Historiques*, 9, no. 3 (Fall 1982), pp. 383–402.

would provoke the Italian workers into a Bolshevik revolution. Their fierce rejection of Russian-style Bolshevism was yet another factor in the Syndicalists' alignment with the right-wing segment of the political field.

Giuseppe Mazzini became the new hero of the Syndicalists — the work of this father of the Risorgimento seemed particularly relevant to Panunzio and Oliviero Olivetti during this period. Panunzio claimed that Mazzini was 'the greatest Italian since Dante',[121] while Olivetti called Italians 'into the future predicted by Mazzini'.[122] The relevance of Mazzini may be explained by the fact that he was equally opposed to both mechanical liberalism and Marxism, proposing an idealist political ontology, a theory of association, advocating the value of education and self-development, and proposing a lofty mission of building the nation. By synthesising the theories of Mazzini and the living content that remained in Syndicalism from the period between 1902 and 1913, the Syndicalist intellectuals were able to captivate the young war veterans, who later formed the core of the Fascist movement (such as Dino Grandi and Italo Balbo), with their revolutionary struggle. The key thesis of the new Syndicalism was formulated by Ottavio Dinale: 'Besides reforming the bureaucracy, a new ethic must be created: parasitism must be suppressed and replaced by productivity and labour; individual group interests must be replaced by common interests; we must renew everything that is the essence of the Italian'.[123] The established spirit of change had to be kept alive by all means; the new historical context demanded compromise. An economic-political revolution of the 'pre-war' type was no longer required — a genuine revolution of the spirit had already taken place. Alceste De Ambris who became a close associate of the poet Gabriele D'Annunzio in his adventure in Fiume and co-author of the constitution of the city-state (*The Charter*

121 Roberts, *Syndicalist Tradition and Italian Fascism*, p. 167.

122 Ibid., p. 167.

123 Ibid., p. 175.

of Carnaro), also mirrored this bizarre synthesis — national and militant, hierarchical and free, corporate and poetic.

Sergio Panunzio, theorist of National Syndicalism

By the end of 1920, the neo-Syndicalist concept had captured the minds of many of Mussolini's associates in the fast-growing Fasci di Combattimento movement.[124] The most influential Syndicalists at the time saw the Fascists as just another political party, not worthy of special treatment, but between 1921 and 1923 many of them changed their minds.[125] In July 1921, Panunzio argued that Fascism could play a key role in the long-term development of socialism. His position was supported by Enrico Leone. Angelo Oliviero Olivetti only

124 According to Dante Germino, the two main intellectual sources for the doctrine of Fascism were precisely nationalism and Syndicalism. Dante Germino, 'Italian Fascism in the History of Political Thought', *Midwest Journal of Political Science*, 8, no. 2 (May, 1964), pp. 109–126.

125 See chapter 'Origini e sviluppi storici del sindicalismo Fascista' [Origins and historical development of Fascist Syndicalism] in A. James Gregor, *Sergio Panunzio — Il sindicalismo ed il fondamento razionale del Fascismo* [Sergio Panunzio — Syndicalism and the Rational Basis of Fascism], (Edizione Lulu.com, 2014), pp. 213–250.

inclined towards this view in 1924.[126] In March 1922, Panunzio made the following resounding statement: henceforth he was convinced that Fascism should organise the masses as the basis for a neo-Syndicalist state. However, some prominent Syndicalists opposed an alliance with Fascism — in particular Alceste de Ambris, convinced that Fascism would not live up to expectations, fled to France in 1923, where he lived until his death (he passed away on 9 December 1934).

Panunzio continued his commitment to Fascism — in December 1923 he wrote: 'We must be the first to give Europe a real living example of a nation state based on syndicates, which is the essential task and necessary element of the Fascist spirit'.[127] Olivetti, who joined the Fascists in 1924, continued to advocate the need for a neo-Syndicalist revolution. However, both Syndicalists soon took part in developing the corporate principles that would later form the basis of the Fascist economy and system of representation. Eventually they both found their rightful place in the new Fascist state. Panunzio occupied various public offices from 1924 (deputy, deputy minister of communications, member of the National Council of Corporations) and continued his academic career (in 1925 he headed the University of Perugia, in 1927 he became head of the Department of State Doctrine at the political science faculty of the University of Rome). Olivetti was included in the Commission of Eighteen, which drafted constitutional reforms in 1925, and was a member of the National Council of Corporations.

126 Many scholars of Fascism have noted the divergent aspirations of the thinkers who contributed to the doctrine. As Geoffrey Schnapp argues, 'the Fascist doctrine was built on a flexible combination of the ideas of characters such as Georges Sorel, Sergio Panunzio, Paolo Orano, Enrico Corradini, Angelo Olivetti and Robert Michels. It attempted to fuse the organic nationalism of the nineteenth century with a Marxism purged of materialism'. Geoffrey Schnapp, 'Fascinating Fascism', *Journal of Contemporary History*, 31, no. 2, Special Issue: The Aesthetics of Fascism (Apr., 1996), p. 237.

127 Roberts, *Syndicalist Tradition and Italian Fascism*, p. 233.

§3. Right-Wing Roots of Fascism: Elitism, Nationalism, Secular Corporatism, Futurism

3.1. The Elitism of Gaetano Mosca, Robert Michels and Vilfredo Pareto

Despite the influence of Syndicalism, evidenced by many studies and clearly demonstrated above, Fascism is still an example of a right-wing rather than a left-wing movement, with a characteristic right-wing tendency towards idealism, elitism, hierarchy, statism, and a denial of progress. The creators of the sociological theory of elites, Gaetano Mosca, Robert Michels, and Vilfredo Pareto of the so-called 'Italian school of elitism', did Fascism a great service. The elitists argued for natural inequalities and the impracticability of democratic principles, and they were very persuasive in doing so.

Gaetano Mosca (1858–1941), graduating in 1881 from university in his native Palermo, moved to Rome and from 1887 worked in the Italian Chamber of Deputies, continuing his academic activity in three cities — Palermo, Rome and Turin. In 1909 he was elected a member of parliament, a position he held until 1919, the year in which he was appointed senator for life. Mosca renounced his life-long senatorship in 1926. As an opponent of Mussolini's dictatorial ambitions, he decided to retire from politics. Thereafter, Mosca devoted himself exclusively to scientific work.

Gaetano Mosca—founder of modern elitist sociology

The Italian philosopher's main scholarly achievements are associated with theories of elites, namely his works *Sulla teorica dei governi e sul governo parlamentare (Theory of Governments and Parliamentary Government*—1883) and *Elementi di scienza politica* (*The Ruling Class*—1895). Mosca argued from historical experience[128] that an elite, a 'ruling class', is unavoidable in any system of government. Mosca's thought is directed both against the doctrines of the 'organic state' and against theories of social Darwinism, racism, and Marxism purported by his contemporaries. He rejects the notions of social progress popular in his day, holding pessimistic views of human nature and human tendencies, which, being weak, emotional, and irrational, need others to govern them. The elite must take responsibility for the majority that is being governed, must adapt to changing internal and external political conditions, and must maintain social consensus. Mosca's sympathies in the field of economic policy are on the side of the laissez-faire doctrine; he acts as a strong opponent of socialism and an advocate of minimal state intervention in economic relations.

128 The political sciences, according to Mosca, are 'the mature fruit of the historical sciences'. Norberto Bobbio, 'Gaetano Mosca e la scienza politica' [Gaetano Mosca and Political Science], *Giornale degli Economisti e Annali di Economia, Nuova Serie* [Journal of Economists and Annals of Economics, New Series], 18, No. 9/10 (Sept.- Oct. 1959), p. 472.

Democratic mechanisms are always a risk factor for the elite—they contribute to the erosion of responsibility and have a negative impact on the moral qualities of the 'ruling class'. In this context democracy is, according to Mosca, a threat to social stability. Nevertheless, he declares himself as an opponent of hereditary aristocracy—in the post-war edition of *The Ruling* Class, Mosca argued that a reasonable republican system of representation is needed in modern conditions.[129] In addition to excessive democracy, a significant danger to social consensus is the extremely cumbersome bureaucracy, which, becoming gigantic and unwieldy, turns into a 'thick layer' between the elite and the people, making their mutual understanding much more difficult. The governing and the governed should share the same feelings and aspirations. The former must be imbued with a sense of moral and social responsibility. It is worth noting that Mosca himself was quite sceptical about the aforementioned 'demands' on the elite, questioning whether they were even feasible in the modern world. As such, one can argue that Mosca's elitism is not normative, but positive. In other words, he, who spent most of his active life in parliamentary work, was not in favour of authoritarian models of power, but insisted that a 'ruling class' was itself an inevitability, whether the state was liberal, Fascist, or Communist.

Mosca's doubts about democracy have greatly outlived both himself and the political context in which they were written, becoming the basis for modern elitist sociology.[130] Mosca became a classic during his

129 See: Thomas I. Cook, 'Gaetano Mosca's "The Ruling Class"', *Political Science Quarterly*, 54, no. 3 (Sep., 1939), p. 445.

130 In contemporary Western humanities, Mosca is often compared with Marx, usually with the comparison being in his favour. The political history of the twentieth century testifies to the truth of Mosca's 'eternal class realism' over Marx's utopian aspirations of a 'classless society', particularly citing the experience of Communist dictatorships, which had an even more strict and uncompromising hierarchy than any 'bourgeois' dictatorship. See Eugenio Ripepe, 'Après Karl Marx est-ce le temps de Gaetano Mosca?' [After Karl Marx is it Gaetano Mosca's Time?], *Revue européenne des sciences sociales* [European Social Science Journal], 21, no. 65 (1983), pp. 135–141; Heinrich Best, 'Marx or Mosca? An

lifetime, as one of the first to show that the dominance of an organised minority over an unorganised majority is inevitable because each individual belonging to a majority finds himself alone against the totality of an organised minority group which claims right to rule. Mosca's analysis reveals the political power of organisation while emphasising that being in a minority is preferable for exercising a claim to power.[131] In this respect, the persuasiveness of Mosca's theoretical constructions played into the hands of radicals eager for power. However, Mosca himself could hardly be called a defender or even a supporter of Fascism — he was an opponent of Mussolini and made no secret of it.[132]

The elitist sociologist Robert Michels

Inquiry into the Foundations of Ideocratic Regimes', *Historical Social Research / Historische Sozialforschung*, 37, no. 1 (139), Elite Foundations of Social Theory and Politics (2012), pp. 73–89; John Higley and Jan Pakulski, 'Elite Theory versus Marxism: The Twentieth Century's Verdict', *Historical Social Research / Historische Sozialforschung*, 37, no. 1 (139), Elite Foundations of Social Theory and Politics (2012), pp. 320–332.

131 See: John E. Tashjean, 'Mosca Revisited: Exegesis of an Elitist Argument', *Revue européenne des sciences sociales* [European Social Science Journal], 10, no. 27 (1972), pp. 123–126.

132 In 1925, a year before he left the Senate, Mosca signed the *Manifesto of the Anti-Fascist Intellectuals* written by Benedetto Croce.

Robert Michels (1876–1936) had a very different view of Fascism. A German by birth, he was a pupil of Max Weber, Werner Sombart, and Achille Loria.[133] Born into a wealthy Cologne family, Michels studied in England, Paris, Munich, Turin, Leipzig, and Halle. He began his academic and political career in Germany—at the University of Marburg and the German Social Democratic Party. In 1907, Michels was promoted to assistant professor at the University of Turin, and in 1911 he moved to Basel, where, as in Turin, he taught political economy.[134] Ten years later, Michels finally moved to Italy, adopting Italian nationality and continuing his academic career at the universities of Messina and Perugia (at the University of Perugia, Michels was made professor of economics and the history of doctrines in 1928), residing permanently in Rome. In 1924, Michels joined the Italian Fascist Party, supporting Mussolini.

Michels is best known for a work entitled *Political Parties: A Sociological Study of the Oligarchic Tendencies of Modern Democracy*, first published in 1911. In this work, Michels, drawing on Mosca's elitist theory, argues that in any political party, regardless of its political affiliations, real power belongs to a small group of people (the party leadership), while the ordinary members are in the position of a governed majority. Partly sharing Mosca's anti-democratic view that the majority is physically incapable of governing itself, Michels examines

133 The relationship between Michels and Max Weber was particularly productive. The two became very close between 1906, when Michels began to publish in Weber's *Archiv für Sozialwissenschaft und Sozialpolitik*, and 1915, when the relationship was severed by a disagreement between Michels and Weber over attitudes towards the First World War. During these nine years Weber read and commented extensively on Michels, not missing any of his significant works. Lawrence A. Scaff, 'Max Weber and Robert Michels', *American Journal of Sociology*, 86, no. 6 (May, 1981), pp. 1269–1286.

134 According to Achille Loria's recollections of Michels, the latter 'never called himself a technical economist'. Michels was not concerned with economics in the Marginalist sense, but rather with 'political economy' in its traditional (eighteenth and nineteenth century) sense. Achille Loria, 'Obituary: Robert Michels (1876–1936)', *The Economic Journal*, 46, no. 182 (Jun., 1936), pp. 372–373.

a particular phenomenon of modern society—the political party.[135] According to Michels, any political party is a mechanism for achieving power. It is a mistake to identify it with the absolute totality of its members or, to put it in Marxist terms, with the 'class' it supposedly represents.

A key concept in Michels' social philosophy is the 'iron law of oligarchy', according to which any democratic organisation is governed by a certain elite (this elite is whom he calls the 'oligarchy'). Otherwise, in the modern world, in which organisations are extremely complex, it is impossible to run an organisation. Thus, according to Michels, the pursuit of 'direct democracy' is nothing more than a myth and real power in any organisational structure belongs to a minority that is either democratically elected or has come to power by other means. Moreover, 'there is not much difference, if we talk about practical results, between an individual dictatorship and the dictatorship of a group of oligarchs'.[136] Once in power, one group or another, regardless of its beliefs, will do everything possible to maintain and consolidate that power, even at the expense of its supporters. Supporters of even the most democratic parties are not immune to the possibility that a different agenda may emerge among the party's elite in the course of a political struggle, overriding the party programme. The victory of the Socialists in elections does not mean the victory of socialism.

---

135 John May provides some apt definitions of Michels' political leanings, calling him a 'pessimistic romantic revolutionary' and 'pessimistic scientific paternalist'. This view of Michels reflects both the Syndicalist-socialist outlook of the German sociologist's early life, in which he himself was a candidate for the Reichstag elections (in 1903 for the German Social Democratic Party), and his deep scepticism about contemporary political participation mechanisms. John D. May, 'Democracy, Organization, Michels', *The American Political Science Review*, 59, no. 2 (Jun., 1965), pp. 417–429. Other scholars directly derive Michels's ideas from Syndicalism and the 'left-wing' beliefs of Rousseau and Proudhon. For example, see: Philip J. Cook, 'Robert Michels's Political Parties in Perspective', *The Journal of Politics*, 33, no. 3 (Aug., 1971), pp. 773–796.

136 Robert Michels, *Political Parties: A Sociological Study of the Oligarchical Tendencies of Modern Democracy*, (Ontario: Batoche Books, 2001), p. 229.

This social fact is what Michels calls a 'tragic inevitability'[137] — the majority is destined to be led by a minority forever. No social revolution can mark a change in this balance between majority and minority, mass and elite — according to Michels, the entire historical experience of human civilisation is a testament to this.

Michels' conclusion is that 'leadership is a necessary phenomenon in any form of social life',[138] and it is not the task of the social sciences to speculate on any moral coloring of this empirical fact. However, according to Michels, 'there is great scientific value in demonstrating that any leadership system is incompatible with the most important tenets of democracy'.[139] The leadership phenomenon is directly linked to the 'iron law of oligarchy' — the political leader goes through certain psychological changes on his way to power, according to which the further he advances on the road to success, the more he distances himself from the masses, cherishes his achievements, and seeks to strengthen his position. This conclusion, according to Michels, can be extrapolated to any modern organisation as a whole, so he makes a relevant digression concerning 'the psychology of the organisation as such', after which he arrives at the following statement: 'The organisation generates the domination of elected over electors, of proxies over trustees, of delegates over delegatees. He who says "organisation" really says "oligarchy"'.[140]

Michels' theoretical model contains strong arguments against any utopia that pins its hopes on the 'moral high ground' of the new elite which a particular ideology or revolutionary milieu could potentially produce. At the same time, Michels himself was not a complete pessimist — he believed that Mussolini, as a charismatic leader, with the support of Italian workers, and free from the bureaucratic shackles of any large organisation, could achieve real positive change for the

137 Ibid., p. 233.

138 Ibid., p. 240.

139 Ibid., p. 240.

140 Ibid., p. 241.

masses, especially the unprotected masses. Michels' hopes were only partially fulfilled — the Fascist party grew rapidly, and the elitist's arguments about the 'psychology of the organisation' became as applicable to it as they were to any other organisation, yet Michels continued to work alongside the party.[141]

The third major representative of the 'Italian elitists' is Vilfredo Federico Damaso Pareto (1848–1923). The son of the fugitive Genoese marquis Raffaele Pareto, a nationalist and supporter of Mazzini, Vilfredo was born in Paris and lived the first ten years of his life abroad. In 1858 the Pareto family was able to return to Italy. Vilfredo received a brilliant education and at the age of 21 received a doctorate in engineering from the Polytechnic University of Turin. By this time, Pareto was already a staunch supporter of liberalism. He recalled that in his youth he was ready to forgive democracy all its faults, believing that 'freedom is a universal panacea'.[142] Pareto joined the Adam Smith Society of Florence and began a career in business. Having achieved success, he even stood as a candidate for parliamentary elections, but did not receive a seat. At the same time he continued his involvement in science. Interested in the positivism of Comte and the Marginalism of Walras, Pareto delved into economic sciences. In 1882 Pareto's father dies. The thinker himself resigns in order to achieve the title of professor of economics. Unfortunately, neither he, nor his ally Maffeo Pantaleoni, were able to confirm his position in Italy at that time. In 1893, Pareto, now forty-five, left for Switzerland for the University of Lausanne, disillusioned with both Italian science and Italian politics.[143] In Lausanne, Pareto reconsiders many of his views. He departs from

141 Some scholars have even classified Michels as a 'regime ideologue' — this does seem excessive, however. Larry Carney, 'Sociology in the Throes of Fascism: Parsonian Meliorism and Myths of Triumphalism', *International Journal of Politics, Culture, and Society*, 7, no. 3 (Spring, 1994), p. 478.

142 Vincent J. Tarascio, 'Pareto: A View of the Present through the Past', *Journal of Political Economy*, 84, no. 1 (Feb., 1976), p. 110.

143 In particular, Pareto came to realise that 'the word "democracy" means both everything and nothing'. Ibid., p. 112.

liberal dogma and henceforth considers it unscientific. It is 'the scientific' that became his new guiding star — Pareto strives for the highest possible degree of abstraction in his writings and reasoning. He reconsidered all the idols of his early life — Adam Smith, Jean-Baptiste Say, and Claude-Frédéric Bastiat. The Dreyfus Affair, which Pareto watched closely, finally convinced him of the imperfection of democracy — in his opinion, despite all the repugnance of the charge against Dreyfus, its defenders were using the same dirty Sophistic techniques as the opponents. The illusions of progress and the 'perfection of mankind' espoused by the young Pareto were abandoned by the mature thinker — in an era of declining values and the triumph of 'interests' over principles, the Italian sociologist experienced the collapse of his deepest liberal convictions.

Young engineer and economist Vilfredo Pareto

In 1906, Pareto left Lausanne University. In the last years of his life, he focused on sociology, in which 'questions of ethical neutrality were even more important than in economics.'[144] Pareto set himself the positivist task of building a sociology whose principles would be

144 Tarascio, p. 115.

indistinguishable from those of physics, chemistry, and the natural sciences. His task was to free himself from 'sectarian passions, national and party prejudices, utopian exaggerations, ideals, etc.'[145] In his struggle for a 'pure sociology', he initially failed to find any allies, positioning his approach in opposition to both socialism and liberalism.[146]

Vilfredo Pareto's elitist sociology gave the Fascist movement many convincing anti-democratic arguments.

145 Cited from: E. V. Osipova, *Социология Вильфредо Парето: политический аспект* [The Sociology of Vilfredo Pareto: A Political Aspect], (St Petersburg: Aletheia, 2004), p. 11.

146 Pareto was subsequently fiercely criticised from both camps. His two-volume *Les Systèmes Socialistes* (1902–1903), devoted to an analysis of the history of socialist thought, appalled Lenin with its detailed criticism of leftist ideas, while his later sociological works were described by Raymond Aron as 'colossal aberrations' for their 'ideological character'. Tarascio, 'Pareto: A View of the Present through the Past', p. 116. Raymond Aron's attitude towards Pareto, however, was very complex — at different stages of his work he has, from time to time, used Pareto's theoretical sociological apparatus. See Stuart L. Campbell, 'The Four Paretos of Raymond Aron', *Journal of the History of Ideas*, 47, no. 2 (Apr.–Jun., 1986), pp. 287–298.

As a sociologist, Pareto adheres to three basic principles that characterise his views on the nature of society. First, according to Pareto, people tend to act illogically but assume that others perceive their actions as logical. Pareto identifies six classes of so-called 'residues' (passions, instincts), which are social facts, but at the same time threaten social equilibrium. Because of their irrational tendencies, people commit many social acts that are fraught with change. Secondly, in thinking about society, it is necessary to distinguish between the scientific validity and social utility of a particular doctrine. Even the most absurd doctrines can be socially useful. Thirdly, the distinction between the individual and the social must be taken into account, especially with regard to the practical aspects of doctrinal construction. As a rule, when proposing certain social changes, the proposer himself acts blindly — based on his own beliefs, aspirations or knowledge, which is far from exhaustive. He understands the ultimate goal, where society should go, but he cannot be sure that it will want to go there, nor that it will reach the goal set by the reformer. Understanding these risks, Pareto proposes to follow personal interests, as short-term and achievable as possible.

In his major sociological works *Trattato di sociologia generale* (*Treatise on General Sociology* — 1916) and *Compendio di sociologia generale* (*Compendium on General Sociology* — 1920), Pareto introduces his own concept of ideology, analyzing it in detail from a psychological and sociological perspective. He provides his own classification of the verbal tactics by which ideologists take control over the consciousness of the masses. The first class is assertions-axioms (sayings from sacred books; the transmission of ideas already established in society); the second, incompetent judgements with reference to authority; the third, appeals to people's various feelings. The aim of Pareto's analysis of ideologies is to present them as false, pseudoscientific, illogical worldview systems. However, faithful to his second methodological principle (about the potential social utility of the absurd), he did not deny ideologies a mobilising power and a certain social role.

Finally, a key concept in Pareto's sociology is that of the 'elite'. He defines it as 'a class of people with the highest score in their field of activity'.[147] Pareto divides the entire population into two layers: the non-elite and the elite, which, in turn, are divided into the ruling and the non-ruling. Society is a pyramid, with the elite at the top. Society is a pyramid, with the elite at the top. An individual can rise from the non-elite level to the elite level by virtue of his innate psychological qualities, exceptional talents, and achievements, or, on the contrary, descend from the elite to the masses. Thus, there is a 'circulation of elites'. The elite manipulates the masses, playing on the feelings and beliefs of the latter, making the non-elite serve the interests of the elite. Humanism, according to Pareto, is a suicidal ideology of the elite; democracy is an empty and meaningless notion. With the passage of time, the elite loses its power and, in cases of complete degradation, is replaced by another elite in a process of revolution, whose task it is to restore the lost social equilibrium.[148] It is not only the wretchedness and powerlessness of the ruling elite that is the prerequisite for revolution, but also the existence of a strong interest group capable of carrying out a coup. In this context, Pareto justifies violence that serves the purpose of restoring balance, order, and stability. In this sense, the Italian sociologist, as a historical pessimist, expresses support for forces ready to 'rule with an iron fist', to suppress dissent, and to persecute

147 Vilfredo Pareto, 'Treatise on General Sociology. Thesis 2031' in Osipova, *The Sociology of Vilfredo Pareto*, p. 132.

148 'Social equilibrium' is an important concept of Pareto's sociology, taken from Leon Walras' economic theory of general equilibrium and reinterpreted. Society, according to Pareto, is a complex system consisting of many elements. An imbalance in the system resulting from the irrational aspirations of individuals, or from the weakness or incompetence of the ruling elite, leads to social cataclysms resulting in the replacement of one elite by another. See Giovanni Busino, 'La science sociale de Vilfredo Pareto' [The Social Science of Vilfredo Pareto], *Revue européenne des sciences sociales*, 46, no. 140, La sociologie en quête d'une théorie générale (2008), pp. 107–132.

their political opponents. In other words, he shows himself to be an advocate of authoritarian methods of governance.[149]

The young Fascist movement, of which Pareto caught only the early years (the thinker died in 1923, ten months after the March on Rome), could be seen through the lens of Pareto's elitism precisely as a strong, young elite, rushing to replace the definitively rotten Italian liberalism which had lost any creative potential and desire for power. Fascists saw Pareto's sociology as a guide for action and relayed much of his reasoning.[150] Pareto's anti-democratic arguments — presenting democratic mechanisms as instruments of 'golden calf' power, an oligarchy seeking only to maximise its own profit and hiding behind false arguments about the public good and popular representation — were actively used in Fascist propaganda.[151] Mussolini put Pareto's theoretical recommendations into practice after he came to power; the Duce discredited and practically wiped Italian liberals off the political scene, promoted private enterprise, lowered property taxes, and increased the authority of religious education (Pareto considered religion an important element of manipulation). Personally, Pareto was treated with great deference by the Fascists — he was introduced into the Senate,[152]

149 However, as Joseph Femia rightly points out, we should not forget that this is the same Pareto, according to which the welfare of a community is identical to the sum of the welfare of each of its members. In other words, despite Pareto's approach to governance, one should not look for signs of Holism à la Marx in the writings of the Italian sociologist; Pareto does not have any metaphysics of the state, which would later be characteristic of Fascist philosophy. See Joseph V. Femia, *Pareto and Political Theory*, (Oxfordshire: Routledge, 2006), p. 65.

150 A striking example is Mario Palmieri's ideological work *The Philosophy of Fascism* (1936), published by the Dante Alighieri Society and praised by Mussolini himself, which presents society as a pyramid with a rigid hierarchy, and those in power, who find themselves at the top, are there because of their exceptional innate abilities. See James W. Vander Zanden, 'Pareto and Fascism Reconsidered', *The American Journal of Economics and Sociology*, 19, no. 4 (Jul., 1960), pp. 403–404.

151 For more details on this, see chapter 3 of this work.

152 Pareto resisted this with all his might — he was ill, he practically never left Switzerland, and he did not want to work in parliament. He was only willing

published articles in Mussolini's Fascist magazine *Gerarchia,* and was even supposed to represent Italy at the Geneva Conference, but declined, citing ill health. In a letter to his friend Pantaleoni on August 11, 1922, he wrote: 'When I wrote the Treatise, no one could have foreseen Fascism; and yet I demonstrated this historical law—when the state refuses to protect its citizens, private forces appear and seize power. Was I wrong?'[153] Despite Pareto's obvious influence on the Fascists, it is difficult to regard him as one of the sincere supporters of the fledgling movement and the emerging doctrine.[154] He was, first and foremost, always a scholar, and did not seek to engage in politics in any way.

Elitist ideas were highly appealing to Italian right-wing radicals who had no opportunity to operate within the early twentieth-century parliamentary system, which was rigid and resistant to any social mobility. They constituted a strong set of arguments against the theory of democracy as such.[155] Calls for a change of Italy's ruling liberal elite were growing louder, and the elitist intellectual apparatus provided both the theoretical analysis of the issue and the practical solution. Unsurprisingly, these calls were picked up first by Italian nationalists[156] and then by Fascists.

---

to accept an honorary post that did not involve permanent employment—ultimately, he was willing because he did not dispute the contribution he made to his homeland as a scientist. Joseph Lopreato and Robert C. Ness, 'Vilfredo Pareto: Sociologist or Ideologist?', *The Sociological Quarterly*, 7, no. 1 (Winter, 1966), p. 35.

153 Cited from Ibid., p. 34.

154 Renato Cirillo provides a rather convincing argument in support of this thesis. See: Renato Cirillo, 'Was Vilfredo Pareto Really a "Precursor" of Fascism?', *The American Journal of Economics and Sociology*, 42, no. 2 (Apr., 1983), pp. 235–245.

155 According to some scholars, elitism provided 'a convenient propaganda method to criticise all intellectual positions defending democracy and socialism'. Raymond Barkley, 'The Theory of the Elite and the Mythology of Power', *Science & Society*, 19, no. 2 (Spring, 1955), p. 106.

156 Especially Enrico Corradini, described below—he and Michels started working together as early as 1910 on the nationalist magazine *La Lupa* (The Wolf Woman). Zeev Sternhell, 'The "Anti-Materialist" Revision of Marxism as an

3.2. Enrico Corradini's Pre-War Italian Nationalism

As mentioned above, a certain nationalism was already characteristic of the thinkers of the Italian Risorgimento. Gioberti's nationalism had a Catholic character, while Mazzini's had a republican one. A new type of nationalism emerged in Italy at the turn of the century, one which was rigid and pragmatic. Italy, by the beginning of the twentieth century, had changed little in relation to the era briefly discussed in the first paragraph of this chapter. Although Italy was a unified state and had a Parliament, this did not have much of an impact on the general way of life for Italians. Italy remained predominantly agrarian, was largely invisible on the world stage (its first attempt to colonise Ethiopia in 1896 was a failure), and was overall a marginal country on the European map in military, cultural, and industrial terms. However, it seemed obvious to many Italian intellectuals that a country with such a cultural and historical heritage should occupy a prominent place on the political map of a new Europe — a Europe of Nations.

A combination of social, cultural, and political factors led to the emergence of a new Italian nationalism, of which Enrico Corradini (1865–1931)[157] was the most prominent representative. The future leader of the Italian nationalists was born on 20 July, 1865, in the town of Samminiatello di Montelupo near Florence. He started to write when he was a student, but nationalist overtones only emerged in his

Aspect of the Rise of Fascist Ideology', *Journal of Contemporary History*, 22, no. 3 (Jul., 1987), p. 388.

157 See: Dmitry Moiseev, 'Ключевые особенности итальянского национализма конца XIX — начала XX вв. на примере литературных и философских работ Энрико Коррадини и его влияние на формирование доктрины фашизма' [Key features of Italian nationalism in the late nineteenth and early twentieth centuries as exemplified by Enrico Corradini's literary and philosophical works and his influence on the formation of Fascist doctrine] in *Материалы Международного молодежного научного форума «Ломоносов-2016»*, [Proceedings of the Lomonosov-2016 International Youth Scientific Forum], ed. I. A. Aleshkovsky, A. V. Andriyanov and E. A. Antipov, (Moscow: Max Press, 2016). [Electronic resource]

writings towards the beginning of the twentieth century. In 1903, he started the newspaper *Il Regno* (*The Kingdom*), thought this could hardly be considered a success, as it was shut down in 1906 due to a conceptual disagreement between its various authors. According to its founders, its main objective was to promote 'the moral restoration of a new nation infected with all the vices of decadence: anarchism and antinomianism, narcissism and sycophancy'.[158] Nationalists were opposed to both socialism, which threatened to crush the young Italian nation through class struggle, and the ruling class, which governed the country in a highly inefficient manner.

Enrico Corradini (centre, dark overcoat) was an Italian nationalist leader at the turn of the twentieth century.

According to Corradini, all healthy, natural human communities are built on the principle that actors within a group maintain relations of 'friendship' and 'mutual assistance', while any actors outside said group are perceived a priori as 'hostile'. Failure to respect this principle leads

158 A. James Gregor, *Mussolini's Intellectuals*, p. 25.

to the extinction of the group. The loss of intragroup solidarity is the main reason for the collapse of a community and its takeover by another community. One of the most important principles of Corradini's nationalist theory can be defined as 'a sense of community', which is the result of many generations belonging to the same group, on a territory chosen by the group, along with a commonality of linguistic, cultural, political, and economic ties. A nation is a group united not only by a 'sense of community', but also by the awareness of a common mission for all its members, a common global purpose, both economic and spiritual. A nation possesses a will that demands sacrifice and submission. According to Corradini, nations are the only subjects of international relations, and he interpreted all international politics as a struggle for survival in a spirit close to social Darwinism.[159] Since a nation ravaged from within by social conflict cannot survive in international competition, a strong 'sense of community' becomes key to its longevity. A healthy nation, in turn, always seeks expansion — or, in other words, to make its state an empire.[160]

Like the Italian Syndicalists, the moral and philosophical stratum of a political doctrine was extremely important to Corradini, not from an idealist point of view but from a functional one. Beliefs are a vital mechanism in mobilising a nation. What Sorel wrote about 'myths' was largely shared by Corradini.[161] For nationalists, this term did not have any negative connotations — on the contrary, myths seemed to them a

159 Roldan Sarti, 'Fascist Modernization in Italy: Traditional or Revolutionary', *The American Historical Review*, 75, no. 4 (Apr., 1970), p. 1034.

160 'There is only one way to be a nationalist,' Corradini wrote, 'imperialistically'. Cited in: Gene Bernardini, 'The Origins and Development of Racial Anti-Semitism in Fascist Italy', *The Journal of Modern History*, 49, no. 3 (Sep., 1977), p. 450.

161 In addition to Sorel, we can also note the influence of the French nationalists Charles Maurras and Maurice Barrès on Corradini. The militarist, anti-parliamentary, nationalist aspirations of French Action and the League of Patriots found a certain resonance in Italy among nationalists, although it is extremely difficult to speak of any widespread influence on Fascism. See: Enzo Santarelli, 'Le socialisme national en Italie: Précédents et origines' [National Socialism in

vivid and convincing image of a desired future for which people would be prepared to die, sacrificing themselves, seeing in it something more valuable than their own lives. In addition to their shared understanding of the effectiveness of mythology, nationalists and Syndicalists were united by similar ideals, their disdain for parliamentary institutions, and their rejection of orthodox Marxist methodology. At the same time, they successfully modified some Marxist concepts — for example, they saw the notorious 'class struggle' in traditional Marxism as destructive of social bonds within the national group, but a class struggle in terms of international politics, interpreted as a struggle of 'proletarian' nations against 'plutocratic' nations, was perceived as an important element of the global worldview. 'Proletarian' nations were those that were late in their industrial development (e.g. Italians), while 'plutocrats' referred to the world's industrial leaders.[162] Corradini was one of the first Italian intellectuals to propose a corporate vision of the economy in which the productive forces, while having economic freedom, are politically organised by the state.[163]

Italy: Precedents and Origins], *Le Mouvement social* [The Social Movement], no. 50 (Jan.–Mar., 1965), pp. 41–70.

162 This theory was adopted completely by the Fascists — in December 1919, Mussolini, from the pages of *Il Popolo d'Italia*, argued that 'proletarian Italy must fight against the Western plutocracies'. Quoted in Clarence H. Yarrow, 'The Forging of Fascist Doctrine', *Journal of the History of Ideas*, 3, no. 2 (Apr., 1942), p. 165.

163 It is worth noting that Corradini gave literary expression to his ideas in a number of popular works, the best known of which are the novellas *La patria lontana* (*A Distant Fatherland*, 1910) and *La guerra lontana* (*A Distant War*, 1911). In the latter, Corradini recounts the unsuccessful Italian military campaign in Abyssinia. The war in the story appears 'distant' because the Italians failed to grasp its political and symbolic meaning. The protagonist, Ercole Gola, is at first a misguided man, as are many others, but later becomes a fervent patriot and supporter of expansion. The antagonist of Corradini's novellas is Count Anselmo Lambio, a typical representative of the liberal aristocracy, for whom only cultural expansion is conceivable. The line of opposition between the militarist nationalist ideal and the liberal pacifist ideal continues in *A Distant Fatherland*. This short story had been published earlier, but in its meaning it

Another important issue that Italian nationalists analysed closely was the problem of emigration. Hundreds of thousands of Italians were leaving the country in search of work, few were returning home.[164] For the ruling liberal elite in the latter half of the nineteenth century, this was not a problem; on the contrary, they regarded mass migration as a positive factor characteristic of the liberal era, a time of opening borders and markets. For them it was a natural consequence of social progress. For nationalists, by contrast, such a large outflow of human capital was a disaster. They rightly believed that mass labour migration was seriously damaging both the image of the country, making it look like a provider of cheap labour in the eyes of other nations, and the national dignity of Italians remaining in the country. The nationalist environment was greatly agitated by the 'de-Italianisation' of emigrant compatriots, who easily adapted and integrated into the national communities that welcomed them abroad.

continues the storyline of *A Distant War*. The key theme of *A Distant Fatherland* is the problem of emigration. The protagonists, Ercole Gola and his pupil Piero Buondelmonti, travel to Argentina and Brazil respectively. They come to realise that patriotism is not just a sentiment, but a fact of economic nature. Genuine patriotism is nationalism, which, according to Corradini, can only be imperial in nature. Enrico Corradini, *La guerra lontana* [A Distant War], (Milan: Editori Fratelli Treves, 1911); Corradini, *La Patria lontana* [A Distant Homeland], (Milan: Editori Fratelli Treves, 1911). For more on Corradini's literary work, see: Tullio Pagano, 'From Diaspora to Empire: Enrico Corradini's Nationalist Novels', *MLN*, 119, no. 1, Italian Issue (Jan., 2004), pp. 67–83.

164 R. S. Cunsolo, 'Italian Emigration and Its Effect on the Rise of Nationalism', *Italian Americana*, 12, no. 1 (Fall/Winter 1993), p.63.

Enrico Corradini—writer, essayist, thinker

Rebuilding the nation is a complex process that needs to be managed by a qualified minority, a 'revolutionary elite'. Referring to elitist theoretical concepts, nationalists insisted on the need for a 'new aristocracy' capable of responding adequately to the external challenges facing the country. In particular, they believed it was necessary to expand the industrial base as quickly as possible, which would give Italy sufficient strength for expansionary, imperial foreign policy.[165]

Born from the observations and aspirations of individual intellectuals, consolidated in the pages of newspapers and small conferences, the burgeoning Italian nationalism became a strong political movement in the first two decades of the twentieth century, a real training

165 If the question of expansion is raised, it was certainly desirable for the nationalists, but with a number of caveats. In particular, in order to expand the borders, a country must have sufficient domestic (industrial) capacity. The nationalists, despite their idealistic, typically right-wing aspirations, were therefore as rational as possible — for example, in 1905, Corradini argued in the pages of *Kingdom* against an Italian takeover of Libya, claiming that the country was not yet ready for it. He did, however, insist that Libya had to be invaded in the future. Ronald S. Cunsolo, 'Libya, Italian Nationalism, and the Revolt against Giolitti', *The Journal of Modern History*, 37, no. 2 (Jun., 1965), p. 186.

ground for the Fascist party.[166] In lengthy written and oral discussions, the nationalists worked out questions of social psychology and its impact on political behaviour in considerable detail — all that remained for the Fascists was to benefit from their work.[167] In December 1910, the first congress of Italian nationalists, held in Florence's Palazzo Vecchio, established a powerful nationalist organisation — the Association of Italian Nationalists (Associazione nationalista italiano, ANI).[168] The main agenda of the Association was to accelerate Italy's industrial growth, which would result in the country's emancipation from the influence of larger imperial powers — both economically and culturally. In the post-war years, the Corradini-led ANI became part of the Italian Fascist Party. Corradini himself was inducted into the Senate in 1923 by King Victor Emmanuel III of Italy, and in 1925 joined the Grand Fascist Council, of which he was a member until 1929.[169] Corradini died in Rome in 1931 at the age of seventy-six.

---

166 For example, one of the greatest ideologues of the Fascist regime, Alfredo Rocco, who will be discussed in the third chapter of this work, came to Fascism through nationalism.

167 The Italian nationalists undoubtedly anticipated Fascism in many ways, but it is a mistake to equate the two. In particular, Dante Germino, a renowned scholar of Fascism, rightly points out that 'the Nationalists' thought was considerably less dynamic and revolutionary in spirit', 'their doctrine was shrouded in an aura of morbid pessimism reminiscent of De Mestre' and, most importantly, 'the Nationalists failed to anticipate the most radical innovation of Fascism — a single totalitarian party'. Germino, 'Italian Fascism in the History of Political Thought', p. 114.

168 Richard Drake defines the Association as 'the first secular, anti-liberal, anti-socialist political party of the right in Italy'. Richard Drake, 'The Theory and Practice of Italian Nationalism, 1900–1906', *The Journal of Modern History*, 53, no. 2 (Jun., 1981), p.214.

169 It should be noted that during these years Corradini had little enthusiasm for Fascist state-building. In his personal notes from this period, he remarks that there is much more talk of Fascism than of Italy: 'Less Fascism and more Italy, less party and more nation, less revolution and more constitution'. Cited in Emilio Gentile, 'The Problem of the Party in Italian Fascism', *Journal of Contemporary History*, 19, no. 2 (Apr., 1984), p. 262.

3.3. Gabriele D'Annunzio's Secular Corporatism.[170] The Charter of Carnaro

Carl Schmitt, explaining the etymology of the word 'dictator' in his work *Dictatorship: From the Origin of the Modern Concept of Sovereignty to Proletarian Class Struggle*, finds this word related to the German 'Dichter'—'poet'.[171] In the history of Italian Fascism, two poets, Gabriele D'Annunzio and Filippo Tommaso Marinetti, claimed to be the dictator of Italy in the early stages of this right-wing movement.

The poet and author Gabriele D'Annunzio (1863–1938) became interested in politics at the end of the nineteenth century—in 1897 he was elected a member of parliament. In the 1890s, D'Annunzio abandoned decadence and moved to a position of pseudo-Nietzschean nationalism.[172] During the First World War he acquired the halo of a

170 It is appropriate to speak of secular corporatism when speaking of the Charter of Carnaro because religious corporatism, as an antidote to Marxism, was integrated into the social doctrine of the Catholic Church as early as 1891 (Pope Leo XIII's *Rerum Novarum* encyclical), which led to the establishment of the first Catholic trade unions.

171 See Natalia Skradol, 'Carnival of Exception: Gabriele D'Annunzio's "Dialogues with the Crowd"', *Rhetorica: A Journal of the History of Rhetoric*, 30, no. 1 (Winter 2012), p. 74.

172 Roger Griffin coined the term 'pseudo-Nationalism' to define the ethos of D'Annunzio's work in the 1890s. See: Roger Griffin, 'Gabriele D'Annunzio and Alceste de Ambris. The Regency of Fiume as the Harbinger of the New Italy' in *Fascism*, p.35. Other respected authors, such as Mary Ann Frése Witt and Michael Stanislawski, have also used this term to describe D'Annunzio's work. This term describes D'Annunzio's poetry from the late 1890s onwards, which displays motifs of glorification of the 'Italian race' and of the 'coming Italian superman', which is particularly evident in the cycle 'In Praise of Sky, Sea, Earth, and Heroes' (written from 1903 to 1912). The characterisation of such motifs as 'pseudo-Nietzschean' is quite popular, because if one takes Nietzsche's texts literally (which one should not, of course), one can also draw from them a celebration of war and violence ('You must love peace as a means to new wars' from Zarathustra; 'O my brothers, am I cruel? What goes down, I say, needs to be pushed! All that from today falls and falls apart: who would want to hold it up? But I—I want to push it still! And whom you will not teach to fly, you will teach—to fall faster!'), and calls to achieve the goal at any cost—and other

national hero, joining the army as a volunteer and becoming a military pilot at the age of fifty-two.

Gabriele D'Annunzio—poet, writer, politician

According to many scholars of Fascism, it was D'Annunzio, not Mussolini, who first showed the practical revolutionary potential of populist nationalism, fuelled by the world war and the post-war crisis. The most striking confirmation of this hypothesis is the short but colourful history of the Free State of Fiume. In October 1918, in Fiume (today's Croatian city of Rijeka), situated on the Adriatic Sea, and at the time predominantly populated by Italians (80%), the Italian Irredentists revolted, proclaiming it an independent republic aspiring to become part of Italy. The 1919 Paris Peace Conference recognised Fiume as a Free State.

aspects that will find practical development in various radical political regimes of the twentieth century. Why 'pseudo'? Because this reading is obviously grossly oversimplified. D'Annunzio, as a creative man, poet, and patriot, was certainly significantly influenced by Nietzsche, but the ideas he conveyed were primarily aesthetic rather than philosophical.

Although Italy was part of the victorious coalition, the outcome of the First World War did not satisfy D'Annunzio[173] — the Treaty of Versailles gave his country virtually nothing. Moreover, having tasted war, the poet longed for a continuation of such emotionally vibrant drama, in which he had begun to play a leading role.[174] He continued to search for his own political platform. Eventually D'Annunzio decided to rely on the *arditi* — the young front-line soldiers, veterans of the First World War, who formed their own volunteer regiments.[175]

During discussions at Versailles concerning the fate of Fiume, the Americans proposed that the city be handed over to the Kingdom of Serbs, Croats and Slovenes. In April 1919, D'Annunzio, at the time a celebrated war hero,[176] was asked to head the republican government of the rebellious city. On 11 September D'Annunzio, accompanied by a column of arditi, sets off on the 'March on Fiume'. On 12 September a group of veterans of the First World War, led by D'Annunzio, seizes power in the city without firing a single shot. The poet is appointed military commander and governor of Fiume. In his first address to the town, D'Annunzio exclaims: 'Italians of Fiume! In this unkind and

173 The poet refers to the war victory secured by the Treaty of Versailles as a 'mutilated victory' (*vittoria mutilata*). Thomas E. Peterson, 'Schismogenesis and National Character: The D'Annunzio-Mussolini Correspondence', *Italica*, 81, no. 1 (Spring, 2004), p. 44.

174 Having become an aviator at the age of fifty-two, in 1918 the poet carried out an unprecedented risky combat flight on Vienna, dropping bombs on the capital of the enemy state. D'Annunzio ended the war with the rank of lieutenant colonel and the status of an emblematic political figure.

175 This phenomenon was as prevalent in Italy as it was in Germany, with its famous Freikorps — anti-Communist volunteers. Filippo Tommaso Marinetti, addressing D'Annunzio's supporters, wrote: 'You became arditi out of love of violence and beautiful heroic deeds. A slap in the face to cowards, bastards and traitors in times of peace... You are the masters of the new Italy!' Quoted in Christopher Duggan, *Fascist Voices. An Intimate History of Mussolini's Italy*, (Oxford: Oxford University Press, 2013), p. 41.

176 As Roger Eatwell aptly points out, 'D'Annunzio saw himself not only as a synthesis of the "left" and the "right", but as a synthesis of the poet and the "man of action", of Dante and Caesar'. Eatwell, *Fascism: a History*, p. 48.

mad world, our city is today a unique island of freedom. This beautiful island, floats on the ocean and shines with undimmed light, while all the continents of the earth are submerged in the darkness of mercantilism and competition. We are a handful of enlightened people, mystical creators called to sow the seeds of a new power in the world that will sprout with bold determination and fierce illumination.'[177]

The political situation was such that in September 1919 D'Annunzio found himself not an associate but a direct rival to Mussolini in the struggle for radical sympathies and, for the time being, the poet was winning this struggle. Raising the flag with the eternal symbol of the Ouroboros and the boastful motto 'Quis contra nos?' (Lat. –Who is against us?), D'Annunzio immersed himself in bizarre state-building, decreeing the immediate goal to create a 'republic of beauty'. The dictator poet solves economic problems in a very straightforward way — he sets up a pirate fleet, plundering foreign ships in the Adriatic and supplying the city with everything it needs. As for the formation of the legal framework and political ideology, D'Annunzio approaches the matter like a true aesthete — he writes a constitution in verse. This document was never approved — at the last moment the poet listened to his colleagues, who convinced him that such matters should be approached in a less extravagant manner. Eventually D'Annunzio co-authored with the Syndicalist Alceste De Ambris the prose constitution of Fiume, the Charter of Carnaro (*Carta del Carnaro*).[178]

---

177 Cited from I. Kormiltsev, 'Три жизни Габриэле Д'Аннунцио' [The Three Lives of Gabriele D'Annunzio], *Иностранная литература* [Foreign Literature], no. 11, 1999.

178 For more detail, see: Dmitry Moiseev, 'Поэты и фашизм. Влияние Д'Аннунцио и Маринетти на становление и развитие итальянского фашизма' [Poets and Fascism. The Influence of D'Annunzio and Marinetti on the Formation and Development of Italian Fascism], *Философия. Язык. Культура* [Philosophy. Language. Culture.], no. 5. (St Petersburg, 2014), pp. 399–411.

Commendation sheet for Legionnaire Renato Cannella's commemorative medal, signed by Gabriele D'Annunzio, Commandant of the Italian Regency of Carnaro

The Charter of Carnaro was proclaimed as the main document of the Regency on 27 August, 1920. The co-authors were not entirely of one mind — De Ambris primarily tried to reflect the ideas of social equality, while D'Annunzio, for his part, concentrated on guaranteeing the conditions for human spiritual development and the 'beautiful life'. Structurally, the Charter consists of 65 articles divided into 20 chapters: 'Foundations', 'Citizens', 'Corporations', 'Communes', 'Legislation', 'The Executive', 'Judiciary Power', 'The Commandant', 'National Defence', 'Public Education', 'Constitutional Reform', 'Right to Initiative', 'Power of Appeal', 'Right to Petition', 'Reduplication of Offices', 'Recall', 'Responsibility', 'Renumeration', 'The Aediles', and 'Music'. In the preface to the Charter, the authors state that 'Fiume is a stronghold of Italian culture, the most distant land, bearing the stamp of Dante'.[179] They assert that both the history of Fiume, which goes back to Carnaro in Dante's time, and its science and culture confirm the fact that the sacred borders of Italy pass through Fiume. Fiume, endowed with will, heroism, and courage, built its own destiny in two years and is ready to defend its freedom in the name of a new Italy, as a liberated frontier land that is so 'by the will of God and Rome'.[180]

The first chapter of the Charter, Foundations, states that the sovereign people of Fiume declare their city '*corpus separatum*', that is, an 'independent city' with a special legal status. The outskirts of Fiume (the suburbs and nearby islands in the Adriatic), according to the Charter, constitute the province of Carnaro, which is a 'state elected by the people'.[181] As for the tradition of autonomy, the Charter refers to 'four centuries of our glorious period of communes'.[182] All citizens of Fiume are guaranteed equal rights without distinction as to race, sex, language, class, or religion. They are also guaranteed equality before the law and the right to practise any occupation, skill, or trade. However, a provision is prescribed that gives priority to the 'right of the producer' (*diritti dei produttori*),[183] while another assertion focuses on the desire for as little centralisation of power as possible, which would allow the commune to develop more vigorously and live in abundance.

The Foundations chapter also claims that citizenship of Fiume should be regarded by foreigners as a title of honour, 'as it was in the old

179 Gabriele D'Annunzio, La Carta del Carnaro. Della perpetua volontà popolare. Dei fondamenti, III. // D'Annunzio G. La Carta del Carnaro e altri scritti su Fiume. Roma, Castelvecchi, 2009.

180 Ibid., Della perpetua volontà popolare [Of the perpetual will of the people].

181 Ibid., Dei fondamenti [Of Fundamentals], III.

182 D'Annunzio, *La Carta del Carnaro,* Dei fondamenti, III.

183 Ibid., Dei fondamenti, IV.

days of Roman law' (*come era un tempo il vivere con legge romana*).[184] The Constitution also guarantees the citizens of Fiume fundamental freedoms: freedom of thought and speech, freedom of religion, freedom of assembly, and freedom of association. Citizens of both sexes are guaranteed schooling, physical exercise outdoors, paid work (with a set minimum wage), assistance in case of illness or inability to work, and pensions. A presumption of innocence is also established.

The right to property is not recognised as an absolute personal right, but as a 'useful and responsible social function' (*la piú utile delle funzioni sociali*).[185] The ninth article of the Charter states that property cannot be unconditionally owned by a citizen; an inactive and lazy owner can lose his property. It is proclaimed that the only legitimate right to own the means of production or exchange is labour (*unico titolo legittimo di dominio su qualsiasi mezzo di produzione e di scambio è il lavoro*).[186] The harbour, railway station, and railway tracks are recognised as state property. The institution of the National Bank of Carnaro is also introduced, with responsibility for issuing national currency and conducting credit operations. The thirteenth article of the Charter prescribes three fundamental elements whose joint powers control the management and development of the city: citizens, corporations, and communes. The fourteenth article is essentially a slogan. It prescribes 'three creeds' that take precedence over all other beliefs that exist within the borders of Fiume and the province of Carnaro: 'life is beautiful, it is right that a man born free should lead a dignified and profound life; a true man is the one who day by day awakens in his fellow citizens a devotion to humanity; Work, however simple and modest, when well done, adds beauty to the world' (*la vita è bella, e degna che severamente e magnificamente la viva l'uomo rifatto intiero dalla libertà; A man intiero is colui che sa ogni giorno inventare la propria virtù per ogni giorno offrire ai suoi fratelli un nuovo dono; il*

184 Ibid., Dei fondamenti, V.

185 Ibid., Dei fondamenti, IX.

186 Ibid., Dei fondamenti, IX.

lavoro anche il piú umile, anche il piú oscuro, se sia bene esguito, tende alla bellezza e orna il mondo).[187]

The second chapter of the Charter, 'Citizens', states that the inhabitants of Fiume acquire all civil and political rights when they reach the age of twenty. Without distinction based on gender, they receive the right to vote and to be elected. A number of offenders can be deprived of their political rights as a result of a formal sentence: those convicted by law, those who have not fulfilled their military obligations to defend the province, those who have not fulfilled their tax obligations, and the 'hopeless parasites of the community' (*parassiti incorreggibili a carico della comunità*)[188] who are unfit for work due to age or illness.

The third chapter, 'Corporations', states that, depending on the activity in which a citizen of Fiume is engaged, he is obliged to be a member of one of the ten corporations whose main focus is set by the commune, but which in turn are free to develop their activities as they see fit. The Charter approves the establishment of the following corporations. The first consists of wage earners in industrial, agricultural and commercial enterprises, craftsmen, and owners of small plots of land, working their own land with little or no recourse to the labour of others; the second includes all managerial and technical personnel in private enterprises, except business owners; the third includes all employees engaged in commercial activities, again with the exception of owners. The members of the fourth are those who create jobs in the fields of industry, agriculture, and commerce, who are not only business owners but, 'according to the spirit of the new statutes — shrewd conductors and assiduous growers of the company'.[189] The fifth corporation is made up of all city officials at any level. The sixth is made up of all those involved in the intellectual and artistic spheres, to which the authors of the Charter include professors and teachers, schoolchildren and students, sculptors and artists, decorators, architects,

187 Ibid., Dei fondamenti, XIV.

188 Ibid., Dei cittadini [Of Citizens], XVI.

189 Ibid., Delle Corporazioni [Of Corporations], XIX.

and musicians. The seventh is composed of persons belonging to the liberal professions whose members have not been assigned to one of the first six corporations. The eighth is made up of elected administrators of the various manufacturing societies. The ninth is composed of all those who work at sea. Finally, the tenth corporation is reserved for 'the mysterious forces of the people in torment and in ascendance' (*forze misteriose del popolo in travaglio e in ascendimento*).[190] As the authors of the Charter write, 'it is a voluntary sacrifice to the genius of the unknown, to the man of the future, to the coveted idealisation of daily work, to the liberation of the human spirit beyond the suffocating and bloody sweat of the present day' (*una figura votiva consacrata al genio ignoto, all'apparizione dell'uomo novissimo, alle trasfigurazioni ideali delle opere e dei giorni, alla compiuta liberazione dello spirito sopra l'ansito penoso e il sudore di sangue*).[191]

According to the Charter, all corporations are legal entities recognised by the state. They are guaranteed the authority and the right to issue their own decrees and regulations, form their own budgets out of deductions from the salaries of their members, fight to raise their status, choose their own symbols, establish their own rules, and hold ceremonies.

The fourth chapter of the Charter guarantees extensive rights to the communes, the local authorities. According to Articles 22–26 of the Charter, the communes, subordinate to the provincial central executive, are entitled to adopt their own municipal laws based on 'special customs and rules, both inherited and derived from their new identity' (*dalla consuetudine propria, dalla propria indole, dall'energia trasmessa e dalla nuova coscienza*).[192] The communes can enter into various treaties with each other, appoint judges, recruit police, and impose taxes. The provincial executive retains the right to act as peacemaker and negotiator in the event of conflict between the communes.

190 Ibid., Delle Corporazioni, XIX.

191 Ibid., Delle Corporazioni, XIX.

192 Ibid., Dei Comuni [Of Municipalities], XXIII.

Chapter five of the Charter, 'Legislature', establishes two elected legislative bodies, the Council of the Best (*Consiglio degli Ottimi*) and the Council of Corporations (*Consiglio dei Provvisori*). Any citizen of Fiume over the age of twenty-one may be elected to the Council of the Best. Elections to the Council of the Best are held every ten years on the basis of universal suffrage. The Council meets only once a year and is responsible for criminal and civil law, national defence, provincial-communal relations, and the arts. Members of the various corporations form the Council of Corporations, a legislative and representative body composed of sixty people, elected for two-year terms. The Council meets twice a year, in May and November. It is responsible for the regulation of labour law, commercial matters, transport, public works, tariffs, customs, industry, banking, and crafts. Once a year, in early December, the two Councils are required to meet in a joint session called the Great National Council — Arengo del Carnaro (*grande Consiglio nazionale sotto il titolo di Arengo del Carnaro*).[193] The Grand National Council is responsible for foreign policy, finance, higher education, changing the constitution, and the expansion of freedoms.

The sixth chapter describes the organisation of the executive, which consists of seven ministers: Economic Affairs, Education, Labour, Justice, Defence, and Finance, as well as the Minister of Foreign Affairs, who also serves as Prime Minister. Ministers are elected for a one-year term. They are eligible for re-election for a second term. Then, according to the Charter, there is a one-year term during which a minister cannot hold office. After one year, the former minister may be re-elected to the post.

193 Ibid., Del potere legislative [Of Legislative Power], XXXIV.

Gabriele D'Annunzio—Commandant of the Italian Regency of Carnaro

The seventh chapter of the Charter establishes that judicial power is vested in Justices of the Peace, Labour Judges, Supreme Court Judges, Criminal Court Judges and Administrative Court Judges. Justices of the peace[194] make decisions in civil and commercial disputes where the amount disputed does not exceed five thousand lire and the potential term of imprisonment of the offender does not exceed one year. Labour judges (*Giudici del Lavoro*) resolve disputes between employees and employers. The Criminal Court decides on all cases where the criminal sentence can be more than three years as well as on political cases. The judges of the Supreme Court decide on disputes in all matters outside the competence of justices of the peace, labour judges, and judges of the Criminal Court.

Chapter eight outlines the rights and duties of the Provincial Commandant, an office held by Gabriele D'Annunzio at the time of the constitution's writing. Article 43 of the Charter establishes that 'at a time when the Regency is in great danger, and its security depends on the will and devotion of one man, capable of uniting and leading all the popular forces in a single victorious impulse, the National Council,

194 Literally 'good men' (*buoni uomini*). Ibid., Del potere giudiziario [Of the Judiciary], XXXVIII.

during a sacred secret assembly in Arengo, may, by a vote of the word, elect the Commandant and transfer to him all supreme power, with no right of appeal' (*quando la Reggenza venga in pericolo estremo e veda la sua salute nel- la devota volontà d'un solo, che sappia raccogliere eccitare e condurre tutte le forze del popolo alla lotta e alla vittoria, il Consiglio nazionale solennemente adunato nell'Arengo può nominare a viva voce per voto il Comandante e a lui rimettere la potestà suprema senza appellazione*).[195] The Council determines the term of office of the Commandant; in doing so, the Council 'must not forget that in the Roman Republic the duration of the dictatorship was six months' (*non dimenticando che nella Repubblica romana la dittatura durava sei mesi*).[196] During the period of the Commandant's rule, he has the full extent of political, military, executive, and legislative power. The decision to remove the powers of the Commandant is taken by the National Council.

The ninth chapter, National Defence, declares all Fiume citizens of both sexes between the ages of seventeen and fifty-five to be subject to military conscription. Article 48 of the Charter spells out that the children of citizens killed in action shall be taken into the care of the state and their families shall receive all necessary support. Article 49 states that the province does not maintain a regular army in times of peace, but 'the whole nation remains armed' (*tutta la nazione resta armata*).[197]

The tenth chapter, 'Public Education', begins with the following words: 'For every race of noble origin the best weapon is culture' (*Per ogni gente di nobile origine la coltura è la piú luminosa delle armi lunghe*).[198] For the 'Adriatic race', as the Charter asserts, its culture is an invincible force, and for the people of liberated Fiume, it is a tool more effective than any other. Dante's language is proclaimed 'the

195 Ibid., Del Comandante [Of the Commander], XLIII.

196 Ibid., Del Comandante, XLIII.

197 Ibid., Della difesa nazionale [Of National Defence], XLIX.

198 Ibid., Dell'istruzione pubblica [Of Public Education], L.

priceless treasure of the people' (*il piú prezioso tesoro dei popoli*).[199] The education and culture of the people is proclaimed as the pinnacle of the constitution. Article 51 of the Charter prescribes the creation of a free University, as well as a School of Painting, a School of Decorative Arts, and a School of Music. The Council of the Best is entrusted with the oversight of secondary schools, the Council of Corporations with the vocational schools, and the National Council with higher education. The primary focus of all educational systems must be the Italian language.

Benito Mussolini and Gabriele D'Annunzio, 1925

Chapters 11 to 18 (Articles 55 to 62 of the Charter of Carnaro) prescribe the right of voters to address those whom they have elected, the right to appeal against court decisions, the right to legislative initiative, the rule that no citizen may simultaneously hold more than once office, the right to recall, salary issues for public figures, and the responsibility of public office holders.

199 Ibid., Dell'istruzione pubblica, L.

Of particular interest is Chapter 19 of the Charter, 'The Aediles'. It proclaims the creation of a provincial School of Aediles– 'wisely chosen men of taste, skill and modern education' (*eletto con discernimento fra gli uomini di gusto puro, di squisita perizia, di educazione novissima*).[200] Such a name for a social institution, recorded in the constitution, should refer us to the ancient Roman magistrates, but the authors of the charter stipulate that the new Aediles of Carnaro are a restoration of a fourteenth century tradition, in which such people were in charge of decorating the city. The Aediles are to be responsible for ensuring that no ugly buildings are built in Fiume, that city festivals and celebrations take place in an atmosphere of joy and wonder, to motivate citizens to decorate their homes, and to revive people's attention and love for beautiful things.

Finally, Chapter 20 of the Charter, 'Music', declares that 'in the Italian Regency of Carnaro, music is a social and religious institution' (*nella Reggenza italiana del Carnaro la Musica è una istituzione religiosa e sociale*).[201] Article 64 of the constitution states that 'a noble people is not one who created God in his own likeness, but one who created a song to honour him' (*un grande popolo non è soltanto quello che crea il suo Dio a sua somiglianza ma quello che anche crea il suo inno per il suo Dio*).[202] Music is heralded as the harbinger of the soul's rebirth; in between the sounds of music one hears the 'silence of the tenth corporation' (*il silenzio della decima Corporazione*).[203] The final, 65th article of the Carnaro Charter stipulates that in every commune of the regency there must be a choir and an orchestra maintained by the state. All musical performances must be absolutely free—'in the language of the Church, a gift from God' (*come dai padri della Chiesa è detto delle grazie di Dio*).[204]

200Ibid., Della edilità [Of the Aediles], LXIII.

201 Ibid., Della musica [Of Music], LXIV.

202 Ibid., Della musica, LXIV.

203 Ibid., Della musica, LXIV.

204Ibid., Della musica, LXV.

In terms of political history, there are a number of notable features in the Charter of Carnaro. Apart from a number of important exceptions, the document prescribes the establishment of a free democratic state, republican in nature, guaranteeing all fundamental rights and freedoms, delegating extensive powers to the municipalities, and governed collegially by regularly elected representative bodies. At the same time, the eighth chapter of the Charter, 'The Commandant', prescribes the de facto possibility of a dictatorship not limited by any legal framework, which did in fact take place — D'Annunzio, during the short period of Fiume's independence, felt himself to be a fully-fledged leader.

Another characteristic feature is the corporate principle of social organisation enshrined in the constitution — in other words, a citizen's occupation strictly determined his belonging to this or that working class, and his interests in the representative body were defended according to the class principle — an innovation that had a significant influence on the principles of the Fascist state in Italy.

The constitution also has clear meritocratic motifs — the main legislative body is called the 'Council of the Best', the Commandant is proclaimed 'the man able to unite and lead all the popular forces in a single victorious movement'. The Charter pays particular attention to education and culture, which follows from the piety for music and the Italian language. Lyrical passages alternate with strict legal formulations, references to the past are followed by a futuristic aesthetic, the self-administration of the communities around the time of the Medici rubs shoulders with the dictatorship of the Commandant.

The work of D'Annunzio and De Ambris did not go unnoticed in mainstream Italy — it was enthusiastically endorsed by Mussolini in *Il Popolo d'Italia*. By that time, however, the Regency of Carnaro had only two more months to live in freedom — on November 12, 1920, Italy signed the Treaty of Rapallo, which gave Fiume to the newly formed Kingdom of Serbs, Croats, and Slovenes. At the end of December of that year, D'Annunzio resigned and gradually withdrew from the political scene — the role of radical leader, *his* role, was taken by a young Mussolini, who had learned many lessons from the Fiume experiment.

3.4. Filippo Tommaso Marinetti's Futurism. The Fascist Manifesto

The poet Filippo Tommaso Marinetti (1876–1944), founder of the Futurist movement, also contributed to the formation of the Fascist doctrine. Marinetti's life and aspirations differ in many respects from those of Gabriele D'Annunzio, but at one point in history their aspirations were largely congruent — a rejection of Italy's position after the First World War and a desire for a radical renewal of society and the state. Born in 1876 in Alexandria, Egypt, Marinetti studied at the Jesuit College of St Francis Xavier. He then continued his education in Paris and Padua, earning a degree in jurisprudence. At the beginning of the twentieth century, Marinetti started to publish symbolist poetry. Gradually he came to a total rejection of both pessimism and romanticism, rebelling against the order of the world in which he found himself. On 20 February, 1909, the Parisian journal *Le Figaro* published Marinetti's *Futurist Manifesto*, which marked the beginning of the poet's public activity. Marinetti entered the public space, speaking in the press and holding various events aimed at popularising the ideas of Futurism. Eventually an entire school was formed to actively promote futurist ideas: 'Marinetti's indefatigable inventiveness, the exuberance of his ideas, his amazing *joie de vivre*, his attention to people of different countries and cultures was the reason why he was called the "Caffeine of Europe". Futurist paintings were exhibited in Berlin, Brussels, Paris, London, the USA, South America, Russia, Japan, and Northern Europe. The stagnation of intellectualism has been broken'.[205]

205 M. G. Wynne, 'Marinetti and Futurism', *The Yale University Library Gazette*, 57, no. 3/4 (April 1983), p. 108.

Filippo Tommaso Marinetti—Founder of Futurism

The original *Futurist Manifesto* consisted of eleven points, of which, in the context of this survey, the following are particularly significant. In paragraph 1 Marinetti states: 'We want to sing the love of danger, energy, and recklessness' (*Noi vogliamo cantare l'amor del pericolo, l'abitudine all'energia e alla temerità*).[206] In paragraph 7, the poet continues: 'Beauty exists only in struggle. There is no masterpiece that is not aggressive in nature. Poetry must be a fierce attack on the forces of the unknown; it must bend them before man' (*Non v'è' più bellezza, se non nella lotta. Nessuna opera che non abbia un carattere aggressivo puo essere un capolavoro. La poesia deve essere concepita come un violento assalto contro le forze ignote, per ridurle a prostrarsi davanti all'uomo*).[207] Paragraph 9 of the Manifesto expresses a militaristic idea: 'We want to glorify war — the only medicine of the world — militarism, patriotism, the destructive actions of anarchists, whose beautiful ideas kill and despise the feminine' (*Noi vogliamo glorificare la guerra — sola igiene del mondo — il militarismo, il patriottismo, il gesto distruttore dei libertari,*

206 Filippo Tommaso Marinetti, *Manifesto del futurism* [The Futurist Manifesto], (Pubblicato dal "Figaro" di Parigi il 20 febbraio, 1909).

207 Marinetti, *Manifesto del futurismo.*

le belle idee per cui si muore e il disprezzo della donna).[208] He continues: 'In Italy we proclaim this manifesto of destructive and outrageous violence, by which we today affirm the idea of Futurism, because we want to free Italy from this gangrene of various professors, archaeologists, tourist guides, and antique dealers' (*dall'Italia, che noi lanciamo pel mondo questo nostro manifesto di violenza travolgente e incendiaria, col quale fondiamo oggi il "Futurismo", perchè vogliamo liberare questo paese dalla sua fetida cancrena di professori, d'archeologhi, di ciceroni e d'antiquari*).[209] Marinetti concludes his Manifesto with an appeal to the reader: 'Look at us! We are not suffocated, our hearts are not worn out. Because they are fuelled by fire, hatred and speed! Does that surprise you? Because you don't even remember what it means to be alive. Standing on top of the world, we defy the stars!' (*Guardateci! Non siamo ancora spossati! I nostri cuori non sentono alcuna stanchezza, poichè sono nutriti di fuoco, di odio e di velocità...! Ve ne stupite...? E logico, poichè voi non vi ricordate nemmeno di aver vissuto! Ritti sulla cima del mondo, noi scagliamo una volta ancora, la nostra sfida alle stelle*).[210]

208Ibid.

209Ibid.

210 Ibid.

Marinetti posing with the original edition of the Futurist Manifesto (1909)

As Anne Bowler notes, 'Marinetti addresses the amorphous urban masses who await a call to action coming from a national leader'.[211] The *Futurist Manifesto* reveals a profound ontology of conflict—the old world versus the new, the impending; the past versus the future; the traditional versus the revolutionary. The war that Marinetti glorifies in 1909 is a protest against the established world order, against reverence for the past, for tradition, for foundations. At the same time, against this backdrop of calls for destruction, stands an Italy which is celebrated, which must awaken, which must establish a new aesthetic

211 Anne Bowler, 'Politics as Art: Italian Futurism and Fascism', *Theory and Society*, 20, no. 6 (Dec., 1991), p. 768.

and political world order. Thus, what follows from the Manifesto are national and political goals, the achievement of which could reverse crises in Italian culture as well as in Italian politics. For Marinetti, the victory of authentic Italian art, i.e. Futurist art, means the triumph of the entire Italian nation. The fusion of the aesthetic with the national is a key component of Italian Futurism — to Marinetti, the rejection of the homeland is tantamount to suicide.

In 1919 Marinetti founded the Futurist Political Party. The Futurists would soon join the young Fascist movement.

The neutrality of Italy, declared in August 1914, was a personal tragedy for the poet. The Futurists begin active militarist propaganda, seeing the world war as a unique chance to assert their own values. In April 1915 Marinetti was even arrested by the Italian authorities who were frightened by his militant agitation. However, in May 1915, Italy declared war on Austria, and the Futurists began assembling volunteer corps. It should be noted that the visual propaganda techniques used by the Futurists were soon adopted by Mussolini and his associates — examples include propaganda performances organised by Marinetti, mass gatherings, and processions. For the Futurists, art and politics merged into one, and the effect of this fusion impressed contemporaries.

In 1919, soon after the end of the war, which had left the victorious Italy with virtually nothing, Marinetti founded the Futurist Political Party, closely cooperating with Mussolini's radicals, the Fasci di Combattimento. It was during this period that Marinetti wrote *Il manifesto dei Fasci italiani di Combattimento* (*The Fascist Manifesto*) together with the aforementioned Syndicalist Alceste De Ambris. It would not be long before the Futurist Party merged with the Fascist movement.

The Fascist Manifesto was published in *Il Popolo d'Italia*, a newspaper founded by Mussolini and the mouthpiece of the Italian Fascist movement. It is composed of four sections, each of which sets out a specific challenge to the movement regarding one of the spheres of national life. The short work begins with the following lines: 'Italians! This is the programme of a truly Italian movement. It is revolutionary because it opposes dogmatism and demagogy, resolutely innovative and against prejudice' (*Italiani! Ecco il programma di un movimento sanamente italiano. Rivoluzionario perché antidogmatico e antidemagogico; fortemente innovatore perché antipregiudizievole*).[212]

The first section of the manifesto dealt with the political sphere. The authors declared the following requirements: 'Universal suffrage, exercised according to the regional principle, with proportional representation, the right to vote for women and the possibility for women to be elected; all citizens over the age of eighteen have the right to vote; all citizens over twenty-five years of age have the right to be elected; the Senate shall be abolished; the National Assembly shall be convened for a term of three years; the first task of the National Assembly should be to write the Constitution of the State; a National Council composed of specialists in the fields of labour, industry, transport, public health, communication, and so on should be formed; candidates should be selected from professional or craft collectives with legislative powers;

212 Filippo Tommaso Marinetti and Alceste De Ambris, 'Il manifesto dei fasci italiani di combattimento' [The Manifesto of the Italian Combat Fascists], *Il Popolo d'Italia* [The People of Italy], June 6, 1919.

candidates should be elected to the General Commission with ministerial powers.'[213]

The second section of the manifesto spells out the social demands of the Fascists: an eight-hour working day; the introduction of a minimum wage; the participation of labour representatives in industrial commissions; showing the same trust for decent trade unions as is shown for industrial leaders and civil servants; the rapid and complete systematisation of the railway and transport industries; the introduction of pensions for the disabled; the reduction of the retirement age from 65 to 55.[214]

The third section outlines the Fascist movement's demands for reform of the military sphere, consisting in the creation of a national militia with a short training period and exclusively defensive powers, the nationalisation of all military industry, and a national policy aimed at the peaceful promotion of Italian culture throughout the world.[215]

Finally, the fourth section deals with proposals to reform the financial sphere. It argues for a high progressive capital tax, confiscation of all the property belonging to religious associations, abolition of dioceses, and an audit of all military contracts and the withholding of 85% of their profits.[216]

Thus, in its early days the Fascist movement made a number of social and democratic demands, many of which (for example, universal suffrage, an eight-hour working day and a lower retirement age) are perceived as quite natural in the twenty-first century, but in 1919 sounded very radical. The strong anti-clerical injunctions of the Fascist programme are particularly harsh for Catholic Italy in the early twentieth century.

By 1920 Marinetti, one of the authors of the manifesto, was perceived as a Fascist politician in the Italian public consciousness as a

213 Marinetti and De Ambris, 'Il manifesto dei fasci italiani di combattimento'.

214 Ibid.

215 Ibid.

216 Ibid.

result of his joint activities with Mussolini. Nevertheless, it was in this year that Marinetti and Mussolini began to have significant differences. During the National Fascist Congress in Milan in 1920, an enraged and disillusioned Marinetti would leave the room with the words 'a bunch of passéists!'[217] and would soon leave politics too.

Ultimately, Futurism failed completely as an independent political project. When viewed as such, it had two principal aspirations: the political and the aesthetic. In terms of politics, Mussolini's policy largely aligned with what Marinetti proposed back in 1909 (a strong state, militarism, imperialism, nationalism, and a cult of health and violence). In terms of aesthetics, however, the ideas of Futurism proved too radical and, unable to survive its brush with reality, had no choice but to compromise with the cultural policy of the Fascist period.

§4. The Shaping of Benito Mussolini's Political Worldview

In discussing the origins of Fascism, it is impossible to ignore the key figure of Italy's Fascist movement—Benito Mussolini (1883–1945). The aim of this section is to outline the main strands of intellectual influence that shaped Mussolini's political position, on the basis of which Fascism became possible as a mainstream political movement, as well as to examine the key principles of the ideological platform with which the future Duce campaigned from 1918 to 1922, and which later, with the help of Giovanni Gentile and his actualist philosophy, were expressed in doctrinal terms.

217 This is the most unflattering definition Marinetti could utter to his interlocutor. In other words, 'reactionaries living in the past'. See Bowler, 'Politics as Art: Italian Futurism and Fascism', p. 787.

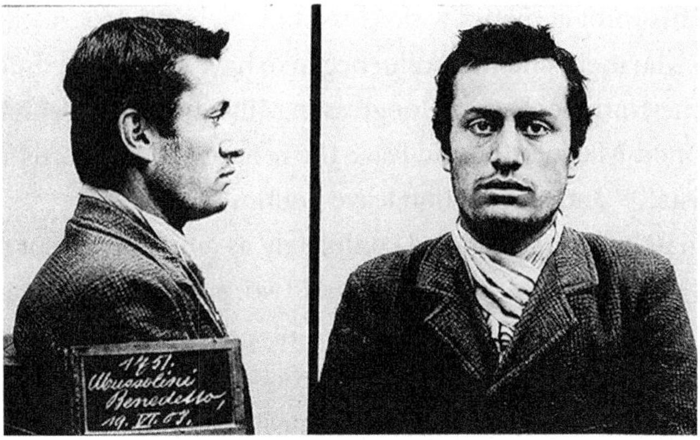

The young socialist Benito Mussolini. Photo from the Swiss police archives, 1903.

Benito Amilcare Andrea Mussolini was born on 29 July, 1883, in the village of Predappio, in the province of Emilia-Romagna in northern Italy. The future leader's childhood and youth were tied to these lands, which, as he notes in his autobiography, 'were well known in the thirteenth century because they were the birthplace of the famous families of the Renaissance'.[218] In describing the history of his family, Mussolini writes that 'the Mussolini family occupied a prominent position among the citizens of Bologna in the thirteenth century. In 1270, Giovanni Mussolini was the leader of this warlike, aggressive commune'.[219] The Duce continues: 'The destinies of Bologna and the internal struggles of its parties and factions, following the eternal conflicts and changes in all struggles for power, caused, at last, the exile of the Mussolinis

218 Benito Mussolini, *My Autobiography,* (New York: Scribner, 1928); Mussolini, *The Third Way: Without Democrats and Communists*, p. 15. The first publication of *My Autobiography* in the USA in 1928 was written by Mussolini with the help of a whole team of co-authors — his brother Arnaldo, his mistress Margherita Sarfatti, journalist Luigi Barzini Jr., and the American Ambassador to Italy Richard Child who wrote the foreword and published it in his home country. The first Italian edition of Mussolini's autobiography did not appear until 1971.

219 Ibid., p. 2.

to Argelato. From there they scattered into neighbouring provinces'.[220] Turning to a more recent era, he notes: 'Later, in the nineteenth century, the family tie became more clearly defined; my own grandfather was a lieutenant of the National Guard'.[221] Mussolini makes no secret that one of the first important influences on him was that of his father, Alessandro Mussolini, a blacksmith who was both passionate about the aspirations of the Risorgimento and the ideals of socialism. His father's idols were the Risorgimento heroes Giuseppe Mazzini and Giuseppe Garibaldi, the anarchists Carlo Cafiero and Mikhail Bakunin, and the socialist Carlo Pisacane.

According to the recollections of contemporaries who knew Mussolini personally, he was not an educated man. The socialist Angelica Balabanoff writes of the young Mussolini: 'He knows little of history, economics, and socialist theory... His mind is completely untrained'.[222] Balabanoff notes that 'Mussolini's radicalism and anticlericalism were only echoes from his early environment and a reflection of his own rebellious egoism, rather than the result of understanding and conviction'.[223] The historian Ernst Nolte argues that 'Mussolini was a lifelong condottiere, possessing faith or seeking faith. His whole history consists of the interplay between these two elements'.[224] Mussolini's lack of systematic education did not prevent him from becoming a journalist and a politician; he even turned this to his advantage in some respects by synthesising positions that are difficult to unify into a single concept from a historical-philosophical point of view; by changing 'banners' and political 'wings'; and by not adhering to any single and consistent theoretical ideal. Mussolini's thought is

220 Ibid., p. 2.

221 Ibid., p. 3.

222 Angelica Balabanoff, *Моя жизнь — борьба. Мемуары русской социалистки 1897–1938* [My Life — the Struggle. Memoirs of a Russian Socialist 1897–1938], (Moscow: ZAO 'Tsentrpoligraf', 2007), p. 52.

223 Ibid., p. 52.

224 Nolte, *Three Faces of Fascism*, p. 168.

eclectic; it combines many different beliefs and attitudes that evolved over his lifetime. Let us examine the most significant sources that fed the worldview of the leader of Italian Fascism.

In 1902 Mussolini (then a schoolteacher in Gualtieri in Reggio Emilia) escaped to Switzerland to avoid the army draft. He worked as a bricklayer in Geneva, Bern, and Freiburg. During his Swiss period, which lasted until 1904, Mussolini joined the socialist movement and was also actively engaged in self-education.[225] It was during this time that the foundations of Mussolini's worldview were formed.

The influence of the German philosopher Friedrich Nietzsche (1844–1900) on Mussolini can be traced back to 1909. The future Fascist leader spent 1909–1910 in Trent, at the time part of the Austro-Hungarian Empire, where he worked as editor of *L'Avvenire del Lavoratore* (*The Future of the Worker*). Mussolini's pieces from this period include quotations from Nietzsche, references to the German philosopher's teachings on the reassessment of all values and the will to power. Some Nietzschean overtones can also be detected in Mussolini's later speeches: calls to 'live dangerously', to overcome adversity, and to abhor weakness. Mussolini evidently studied the doctrine of the Superman, as expounded by Nietzsche in *Thus Spoke Zarathustra* with great care — he repeatedly declared that he was trying 'to make his life a masterpiece'.[226] Mussolini's life story is indeed reminiscent of an adventure novel, full of ups, downs and intrigue — from

225 Interestingly, having found himself in Lausanne in 1904, Mussolini attended a course of lectures on social philosophy by Vilfredo Pareto.

226 Cited from: L. W. Stewart, 'The Mentors of Mussolini', *The American Political Science Review*, 22, no. 4 (Nov., 1928), p. 850. In one of his speeches in 1926, Mussolini says: 'Politics is an art, of that there is no doubt. It is certainly not science, not empiricism. It is therefore an art. Also because there is a lot of intuition in politics. The political, like artistic creation, is a slow creation and a sudden revelation. In a moment the artist works with inspiration and the politician with determination. Both work with the material as well as with the spiritual... To provide people with wise laws, one must be a bit of an artist'. Cited from: Simonetta Falasca-Zamponi, *Fascist Spectacle. The Aesthetics of Power in Mussolini's Italy,* (Berkeley, CA: University of California Press, 2000), p. 15.

a stonemason in Geneva to the leader of the March on Rome, from unlimited dictatorial powers to an escape to the Apennine mountains, from nationally recognised leadership to a hanging in Milan's Piazza Loreto. Mussolini often presented himself in historical terms, comparing himself to Caesar, Napoleon, and Garibaldi. As well as the above, as Stewart rightly points out, another indicator of Nietzsche's influence on Mussolini is his frequent use of the term 'discipline' (Nietzschean *Zucht*) as well as words of similar meaning in his publications and speeches.

In addition, Mussolini was impressed by the Nietzschean understanding of freedom as 'freedom for' rather than 'freedom from' — the latter being the typical interpretation of freedom in left-wing political thought. 'Civil liberties', according to Mussolini, are not a goal-in-themselves — they are 'the newest invention of the nineteenth century'. According to Mussolini, it is not common for all people to want freedom — most are used to being governed, and this traditional order has been maintained for millennia. Service, understood as 'unfreedom' in a leftist frame of reference, was perceived by Mussolini as the highest good. He, incidentally, argued that he himself was 'unfree' in the liberal sense because he was the first servant of the state.[227]

Another important aspect of Nietzsche's influence is his attitude towards war. The German philosopher wrote in Zarathustra: 'Your enemy shall ye seek; your war shall ye wage, and for the sake of your thoughts! And if your thoughts succumb, your uprightness shall still shout triumph thereby! Ye shall love peace as a means to new

227 Although Mussolini's publications and speeches tend to use the word 'freedom' as a negative concept, pitting it against liberals and socialists, it is incorrect to apply this attitude to the political philosophy of Italian Fascism as a whole. As will be shown in chapters two and three of this work, freedom is perceived by Gentile and his associates as something necessary and inalienable. What can be difficult to understand is how exactly Fascist philosophers interpret freedom — freedom for a Fascist cannot lie outside the state to which he belongs and only a citizen who spiritually 'coincides' with the state, who is inseparable from it, can be truly free.

wars — and the short peace more than the long.[228] Mussolini wrote in *Il Popolo d'Italia* on November 9, 1918: 'War must have a social meaning. It must uplift people morally and materially; it must serve the rebirth of the nation, renewing the lives of its members'.[229] The admiration for war that Mussolini had developed during his National Syndicalist period was transformed during the *ventennio* years into imperial ambition and militarism. A certain Nietzschean influence can be seen at the root of this.

In 1910 Mussolini returned to Italy and for the next four years was extremely active among Italian socialists, both politically and as a journalist.[230] From 1910 he edited the journal *Lotta di classe* (*Class Struggle*) published in Forli, from 1912 the newspaper *Avanti!*, which was then the official publication of the Italian Socialist Party. During this period Mussolini was under the influence of the Syndicalists (especially Georges Sorel). The French philosopher showed the practical political value of myth in his writings, and Mussolini learned this lesson well. While broadcasting the Syndicalist myth of the 'work ethic' in his Milanese period, he readily adopted the national Syndicalist thesis, escalating it to radical calls for the restoration of the lost greatness

228 Friedrich Nietzsche, 'Zarathustra's Prologue: Zarathustra's Discourses. War and Warriors' in *Thus Spoke Zarathustra*, (originally published by Ernst Schmeitzner, 1883–1892).

229 Cited from: Piraino & Fiorito, *Fascist Identity*, p. 39.

230 In 1911 Mussolini spent five months in prison as punishment for organising a strike against Italy's colonial war in Libya. From the memories of Pietro Nenni (an associate of Mussolini) of that period: 'Our favourite thinker was Georges Sorel... Mussolini was not a fetishist, a Marxist fanatic. He was a socialist by instinct and by family tradition, but above all he was a rebel'. Cited from Jaime Nogueira Pinto, 'Benito Mussolini, the "Red" Years', in Erik Norling, *Revolutionary Fascism*, (Finis Mundi Press, 2011), p. 16. Interestingly, a few years later, Mussolini reversed his position. In an article entitled 'Courage!', published in *Il Popolo d'Italia* on 15 November, 1914, just three years later, he states, 'Today anti-war propaganda is propaganda of cowardice!' Quoted in Griffin, *Fascism*, p. 27.

of Italy as the direct heir to the Roman Empire.[231] Apart from the practical use of the new mythology, Mussolini borrowed three other important doctrinal aspects from Sorel, which he also applied in his realpolitik. The first is Sorel's anti-parliamentarianism, implemented in Italy in 1928, in which all political parties except the Fascist one were banned. The second is Sorel's justification of violence, which was taken literally by the Fascist Blackshirts.[232] The third is the belief that the trade unions (syndicates) play a significant role of in the modern state. Although Mussolini had claimed back in 1919 that 'socialism is dead', workers' unions were organically integrated both doctrinally (into the Fascist economic philosophy) and practically (through corporatist institutions).[233]

---

231 So-called 'Romanness', the 'Roman spirit' (*romanita*), is one of the most heavily exploited myths of the Fascist period, which was addressed by Mussolini and his ideologues using a typically Sorelian methodology. By identifying Fascist Italy with Rome, they drew direct parallels between the Roman military ideal and the Fascist ethic of discipline and obedience. The demonstration of 'Romanness' was meant to show the direct connection between a glorious past and a present that was full of fascinating possibilities and had the potential to leave a vivid historical memory, thus inspiring contemporaries to carry out heroic deeds for the glory of their homeland. For more details on specific ideological demonstrations of 'Romanness', see: Flavia Marcello, 'Mussolini and the idealisation of Empire: the Augustan Exhibition of Romanità', *Modern Italy*, 16, no. 3 (Aug. 2011), pp. 223–247.

232 The Blackshirts, Fascist Party combat units formed from World War I soldiers, were actively involved in street clashes with Communists and socialists in 1919–1922. The year 1924 saw the assassination of Giacomo Matteotti, a Socialist member of Parliament. This event precipitated a major political crisis, with all non-Fascist factions in Parliament appealing to King Victor Emmanuel III and demanding his resignation. The demand was not met. However, any involvement by Mussolini himself in the murder of Matteotti is still a matter of debate among historians.

233 Although some left-wing elements can be identified in Mussolini's policy during the *ventennio* period, the Duce himself actively disavowed them. His rhetoric since 1918 has been as hostile to the Left as possible. For example, in 1921, apparently recalling Saint-Simon, he reminded the Socialists that he had never shared the philosophical foundations of their beliefs: 'You socialists are witnesses to the fact that I have never been a positivist, not even when I was

Benito Mussolini, 1914

The third major influence on Mussolini's ideas, which he himself acknowledged, was Vilfredo Pareto and his elitist sociology, the basic principles of which have been discussed above. The teachings of Pareto, which Mussolini became acquainted with during the Swiss period of his life, contributed to the future leader's departure from the left-wing dogmas of economic determinism. Pareto argued that few things in people's lives can be so practically useful and authentically genuine as ideals. Mussolini fully agreed with this thesis: 'No one can achieve anything truly great without fervent love and religious mysticism'.[234] The influence of Pareto's political elitist doctrine can be seen in Fascist conservative-revolutionary modernism — by combining traditional-idealist aspirations with radical intolerance, Fascism gave the world its first 'Third Way revolution' set against both the conservative-religious order and the liberal-democratic one. In this respect, Mussolini appears as an attentive disciple of Pareto, practically fulfilling the sociologist's circulation of elites precept by squeezing the old-regime liberals out of politics.

in your party'. Quoted from Domenico Settembrini, 'Mussolini and the Legacy of Revolutionary Socialism', *Journal of Contemporary History*, 11, no. 4, Special Issue: Theories of Fascism (Oct., 1976), p. 251.

234 Cited from: Stewart, 'The Mentors of Mussolini', p. 860.

A fourth major influence on Mussolini that cannot be ignored is Niccolò Machiavelli (1469–1527). After coming to power, the Duce often referred to the great Florentine, whom he called 'a prophet of the pragmatic era in politics'.[235] For Mussolini, Machiavelli's *The Prince* was a handbook that all politicians should be familiar with. He asserted: 'I want to keep a direct link between Machiavelli's doctrine and my life, between his and my thoughts about people and things, between his and my public service'.[236] In this context, it is necessary to note the particular way in which the Italians perceived Machiavelli. While in the history of philosophy and political thought the Florentine is often seen as the model of political amorality, 'the first political scientist', in Italy, on the contrary, he is regarded as a great patriot and supporter of the unification of the country. Mussolini, who always considered himself first and foremost a politician, and who grew up in a culture of reverence for the Italian intellectual heritage, readily embraced Machiavelli's maxims.[237] The principles of the need to use violence in political struggle; the justification of immoral means to achieve an end by the importance of the end itself; the pessimistic view of man as a weak, greedy, ungrateful, and utterly false creature appealed to Mussolini. Machiavelli's Florentine patriotism[238] was also important.

---

235 Cited from: Ibid., p. 845.

236 Cited from: Ibid., p. 845.

237 For a discussion of how Mussolini followed Machiavelli's precepts in the early years of his dictatorship, see Arnold J. Lien, 'Machiavelli's Prince and Mussolini's Fascism', *Social Science*, 4, no. 4 (August, September, October, 1929), pp. 435–441.

238 In particular, Machiavelli was known to have a deep sympathy for Cesare Borgia, who was murdered twenty-five years before the first publication of *The Prince*. The image of Cesare inspired Machiavelli — Machiavelli saw him as a politician close to the ideal. For instance, in chapter 7 of *The Prince*, Machiavelli writes of Borgia: 'Reviewing his actions, I find nothing to reproach him for... For, with his great intent and lofty goal, he could not act otherwise: only the premature death of Alexander (Pope Alexander VI, father of Borgia) and his own illness prevented him from realising his intention'. Niccolò Machiavelli, 'The Prince' in *Selected Works*, (Moscow: Literatura Poetry, 1982), p. 323. Another reference to Borgia is in chapter 17 of *The Prince*: 'Many have called Cesare Borgia cruel, but

Of all the figures of the Italian Renaissance, in whom Italian patriots of the late nineteenth and early twentieth centuries were deeply disappointed politically, it was Machiavelli, combining an active political career with active intellectual work, who commanded the greatest respect and even admiration in Italy during Mussolini's maturity. Finally, Mussolini, a determined atheist and anti-clerical during his socialist youth, embraced Machiavelli's testament to the practical value of organised religion. During his *ventennio* years he politically capitalised on Rome's enormous potential as the spiritual capital of hundreds of thousands of Catholics by signing the Lateran Treaty with the Catholic Church in 1929. In addition to these four main influences, the pragmatism of William James (1842–1910)[239] and the reflections of the Italian intellectual Alfredo Oriani (1852–1909)[240] can also be noted as moderate influences on Mussolini's worldview.

---

this cruelty has put order in Rimagna, has united it, has pacified it, and has lead to obedience'. Machiavelli, The Prince, p. 348.

239 Stewart noted: 'The way in which pragmatists approach issues is essentially akin to Mussolini'. See Stewart, 'The Mentors of Mussolini', p. 862. Russian national-bolshevik Nikolay Ustryalov quotes Mussolini in his work on Fascism: 'When I was twenty years old, I was fascinated by Nietzsche, and it was he who strengthened the anti-democratic elements of my nature. The pragmatism of William James has also helped me a great deal in my political career'. Nikolay Ustryalov, *Италия — колыбель фашизма* [Italy — the Cradle of Fascism], (Moscow: Algorithm, 2012), p. 81. In general, James' influence on Mussolini, if anything, was rather weak. The Duce occasionally referred to James during his years as a pragmatist, but as another American researcher attests, during a conversation with a student of James, the philosopher Horace Meyer Kallen, he was unable to recall a single concept of the pragmatist, superficially referring to the titles of James' major works. John Patrick Diggins, *Mussolini and Fascism: The View from America*, (Princeton, New Jersey: Princeton University Press, 2015), p. 222.

240 A patriotic writer, Oriani rose to fame after the publication of *Political Struggle in Italy*, which Mussolini praised publicly more than once, including in his speeches in Parliament. The main pathos of his work is the glorification of self-sacrifice for an ideal. It is difficult to pinpoint Oriani as a precursor of Fascism, as he was more of a conservative who did not accept the modern world. However, the fact that Mussolini mentions him in an enthusiastic tone makes one note a

The intellectual impact of the thinkers listed above, as well as a rather dynamic, strife-ridden, exhausting existential experience (emigration, political struggle, World War[241]) shaped the core principles of Mussolini the politician, in turn forming the basis of the programme of the young Fascist movement. Upon coming to power on 28 October 1922 as a result of the March on Rome, Mussolini formed his own cabinet in addition to personally heading a number of ministries.[242] Now the state was under the control of the Fascists, it was necessary to give it a new myth, a new existential programme capable of inspiring innovative state-building. The need for a clearly articulated doctrine was evident, and this problem was solved by bringing one of the most famous Italian philosophers of the twentieth century into the cabinets of power and into the ranks of the Fascist movement — Giovanni Gentile.

certain influence the writer must have had on the Duce. Stewart, 'The Mentors of Mussolini', pp. 865–869.

241 Mussolini was drafted into the army in September 1915, shortly after Italy entered the First World War. Reflecting on this he wrote: 'This war is fought by citizens, not professional armies, so it will put an end to caste militarism, professional militarism. Thanks to the mobilisation a large proportion of Italian officers are being drafted from the civilian ranks. All junior officers, numerous lieutenants and warrant officers are fighting and dying as heroes'. Quoted from J. N. Pinto, 'Benito Mussolini, the "Red" Years' in Norling, *Revolutionary Fascism*, p. 21.

242 Mussolini immediately reserved personal leadership of the foreign and interior ministries for himself. During the Fascist *ventennio* he was at various times head of the ministries of labour, defence, industry, corporations, and colonies. In this way he was able to prevent the emergence of any competitors 'from within' the system for a long time.

CHAPTER TWO

GIOVANNI GENTILE'S ACTUAL IDEALISM AS THE FOUNDATION OF FASCIST POLITICAL PHILOSOPHY

§1. Gentile in the Context of the Era

1.1. Giovanni Gentile — 'Philosopher of Fascism'

THE MOST IMPORTANT thinker of all those who influenced the formation of the Italian Fascist doctrine was the academic Neo-Hegelian philosopher Giovanni Gentile. In many ways he anticipated Fascism in his idealistic philosophy and, after Mussolini came to power, he successfully put some of his conceptual work into practice (as a politician — the Italian Minister of Education) and finally, in 1932, helped the Duce formulate *The Doctrine of Fascism*. Moreover, Gentile nurtured a number of able pupils who applied their intellectual efforts to improving and refining both the system of actual idealism and Fascist political philosophy. In many ways, Gentile's work was shaped by the challenges of the time in which he lived. For this reason, it seems appropriate to preface an analysis of his philosophy with some biographical information, without which the perception of his philosophical and political ideas might be distorted.

Giovanni Gentile was born on 30 May, 1875, in the small Sicilian town of Castelvetrano, Trapani province, in the west of the island. After finishing primary school in Castelvetrano, Gentile continued his studies in Trapani, the provincial capital, where he graduated from high school and lyceum. In 1893 he enrolled at the École normale supérieure in Pisa, where the future philosopher's special talents in the humanities emerged. In Pisa he became the favourite pupil of the famous Italian writer and literary critic Alessandro d'Ancona (1835–1914), who taught Italian literature, and who foresaw a great future for Gentile in the field of philology. However, fate had a different plan for him: influenced by the philosopher Donato Jaja (1839–1914), the young humanitarian was immersed in the study of local intellectual traditions. Influenced by Jaja, a disciple of the neo-Hegelian Bertrando Spaventa, Gentile decided to develop the tradition of Italian idealist philosophy. He wrote his final thesis on the idealism of Gioberti and Rosmini. From Pisa the young philosopher headed for Florence, where he continued his studies for another year.

From 1898 Gentile began teaching philosophy at the Lyceum in Campobasso, then in 1901 he moved to Naples, where he worked until 1906. In Naples, he became acquainted with Benedetto Croce and was made assistant professor at the local university. In 1903, Gentile made his debut as a lecturer, presenting a course on the Renaissance of Idealism.[1] In 1907, Gentile took his first administrative position as Head of the History of Philosophy at the University of Palermo. In the same year he attended the Congress of School Teachers in Naples, during which he expressed the idea of teaching religion in primary school as preparation for the teaching of philosophy in high school, an idea which Gentile developed in 1920 in 'Lectures to Teachers of Trieste', which in turn would be organised into a work entitled *The*

1 It should be noted that Gentile published his first original work, entitled *The Teaching of Philosophy in High Schools*, somewhat earlier, in 1900. From that year onwards, he started to work on the concept of education, which largely determined his theoretical interests and his life's journey.

Reform of Education. While pondering the need for a reform of Hegelian dialectics, Gentile gradually developed an idealist concept of his own — Actual Idealism. His first work in the spirit of actual idealism was published back in Naples in 1912 under the title *The Act of Thought as Pure Act.*

In 1914, after the death of Donato Jaja, Gentile went back to Pisa to take his teacher's place. In 1916 he published a systematic, fundamental exposition of the theory of actual idealism — a work entitled *The Theory of Mind as Pure Act*, as well as *The Foundations of the Philosophy of Law.* In 1917, the philosopher joined the Sapienza University of Rome. From the same year, following the military defeat of the Italians at the Battle of Caporetto, Gentile became active in the public sphere, publishing patriotic articles in newspapers and magazines. In the early post-war years — after Italy had suffered a diplomatic defeat at Versailles despite being on the winning side in the First World War — Gentile focused both in theory and in practice on restoring national pride and national unity. He was convinced that this could not be done without a reform of school education, and came up with a plan for such reforms.

At the end of 1922, Gentile got a real chance to make a difference — after the success of the March on Rome, Italy's new Prime Minister, Benito Mussolini, offered Gentile the post of Minister of Education. The philosopher did not miss this opportunity to implement the reform plan he had long been formulating — Gentile accepted the offer.[2] In May 1923, Gentile joined the National Fascist Party. He remained a minister until June 1924, working hard to implement education reforms, and was very successful. In August of the same year, Gentile chaired a commission whose task was to draft constitutional reforms (the so-called 'Commission of the Fifteen', later the 'Commission of the Eighteen'). Between 1925 and 1928, Mussolini became dictator of Italy: all political parties except the Fascist Party were banned, and the power of the Duce was completely

2 Once a minister, Gentile was also appointed a senator, a post he retained until his death.

unchecked. During this period, Gentile acted as a consistent supporter of Mussolini, publishing *Manifesto of the Fascist Intellectuals* (1925). In 1925, Gentile founded and headed the National Fascist Institute of Culture (the philosopher would lead this institute until 1937). Gentile's social and political activities did not stop there; from 1923 to 1924, and later from 1925 to 1929, he was a member of the Great Fascist Council. Gentile's academic career was also on the rise — in 1926 he became Professor of Theoretical Philosophy at the University of Rome, and in 1928, following the appointment of Bernardino Varisco (1850–1933) as senator, he became head of the Department of Theoretical Philosophy (another post Gentile held until his death). In the same year, Gentile published an English-language article in the American journal *Foreign Affairs* entitled 'Philosophical Foundations of Fascism', in which he drew a direct line of continuity between the Italian idealism of the Risorgimento and his own social philosophy.

Fascist columns marching on Rome, 1922

From 1925 to 1944 Gentile concentrated his efforts on producing the *Encyclopedia Italiana*, giving overall scientific direction to the project. In 1932, in Volume XIV of the Encyclopaedia, a short article entitled

'The Doctrine of Fascism' by Mussolini was published, which was described as 'a fundamental and comprehensive basis for any historical and theoretical research on the development, understanding, and practice of Fascism'.[3] The Doctrine, in the writing of which Gentile took an active part, is the sum of the philosopher's political reflections and their most coherent and clear formulation. After the publication of the Doctrine, Gentile established himself as the official philosopher of the regime and the most influential public intellectual, with actual idealism as the philosophical basis of Fascism.

Despite this, relations between Gentile and the Fascist elite gradually began to cool. The Lateran Treaty concluded in 1929 between the Catholic Church and the Fascist government caused much dissatisfaction for Gentile, who rightly feared the growing influence of the Church not only in schools but also in universities. The situation was complicated by the fact that Gentile's successors as Minister of Education, Casati, Fedele, Belluzzo, Balbino, Ercole, de Vecchi, and Bottai, were making changes to the educational system constructed by the philosopher, which Gentile felt were totally inappropriate. The alliance between Fascist Italy and Nazi Germany also caused Gentile great apprehension, which was confirmed by a series of racial laws passed in the second half of the 1930s, totally inadmissible from the point of view of actual idealism. However, the philosopher continued to occupy a prominent place in society (in 1933 Gentile headed the Institute for Near and Far Eastern Studies, and in 1934 the Italian Institute for Germanic Studies) and academia (in addition to the aforementioned senior post at the University of Rome, he took up the posts of Director of the Higher Normal School in Pisa in 1932, and in 1934 Vice President of Bocconi University in Milan), and remained loyal to Mussolini and Fascism until his death.

---

3 Cited from: A. James Gregor, *Giovanni Gentile: Philosopher of Fascism*, (New Brunswick, New Jersey: Transaction Publishers, 2008), p. 3.

The young idealist philosopher Giovanni Gentile

On 24 June, 1943, Gentile delivered a fiery and patriotic 'Appeal to the Italians' in Rome, calling for national unity in the face of the advancing enemy. Exactly one month later, Mussolini was deposed by the Great Fascist Council and the National Fascist Party was officially dissolved. Mussolini was liberated by the Germans and taken to northern Italy, where he established the Italian Social Republic in Nazi-controlled lands in September 1943. Gentile was loyal to the Duce even in this disastrous situation, expressing his wish to serve the new republican regime by accepting the offer to head the Italian Academy. During this period, the philosopher resided in Florence, which remained in Mussolini's control until 1944. On 15 April, 1944, Gentile returned home from the police station where he had visited to clear a group of students suspected of having anti-Fascist sympathies. On the doorstep of his own house, he was shot dead by a group of four Red partisans. The philosopher was buried in the Basilica of Santa Croce, in Florence, along with Dante Alighieri, Galileo Galilei, Niccolò Machiavelli, and Michelangelo.

1.2. Italian Neo-Hegelianism. Gentile and Croce against Positivism and Pragmatism

Before examining the philosophy of Giovanni Gentile, we need to look at the historical and spiritual context of the era in which he created and implemented the theory of actual idealism.

In the last decades of the nineteenth century Italian philosophy underwent a gradual transition from idealism to positivism and pragmatism. Positivism was the most popular philosophical movement in Italy between 1870 and 1900. Italian positivists argued that their tradition was deeply rooted in the Italian national identity since the Renaissance, appealing to Telesio, Bruno, Leonardo, and Pomponazzi. The brightest chapters in the history of Italian positivism were associated with Roberto Ardigò (1828–1920). Ardigò, who was heavily influenced by the original positivism of Auguste Comte, argued that truth lies in facts. He divided facts into physical and mental, which, according to his doctrine, were essentially the same — the only difference lies in our experience of the facts. According to Ardigò, our sensations are proof of the reality of what is external to us. However, Ardigò also recognised an intermediate psychophysical reality, a substratum of the psychological and physical worlds. Ardigò's philosophy thus excluded both idealism and vulgar materialism.

Roberto Ardigò—positivist and one of the most influential philosophers of nineteenth-century Italy

Ardigò's introduction of the category of psychological facts into the positivist system led his contemporaries to talk about a new phase in the development of positivist philosophy. In particular, Salvadori writes that 'probably future historians of positivism will distinguish a naturalistic stage (Comte) in which psychology played no role and the subject dissolved in the object; an agnostic stage (Spencer) in which the relation between subject and object was accepted as fundamental, but the importance of psychology as an independent science was fully recognised—the subject appeared to have no activity of its own; a psychological stage (Ardigò) in which the attempt was made to explain all reality on the basis of the psyche alone; and finally, the realist stage in which the original elements of reality are seen as psychic and physical at the same time: the physical in their external relations and the psychic in their inner existence'.[4] The final, realist stage of positivism is attributed to the early philosophy of Bernardino Varisco (1850–1933). Varisco argued that 'positivism is the only true philosophy that ever

4 Guglielmo Salvadori, 'Positivism in Italy', *The Journal of Philosophy, Psychology and Scientific Methods*, 5, no. 17 (Aug. 13, 1908), p. 451.

was'.[5] According to this thinker, one can only philosophise on the basis of rigorous scientific data; any reasoning that is not supported by scientific knowledge is not philosophical. Varisco somewhat modified Ardigò's theory about physical and psychological facts. He argued that physical facts take place between subjects and psychological facts take place within a particular subject. In his later period Varisco switched to monadology, arguing that monads, the ultimate elements of reality, 'have a psychic potential which is the necessary substratum of consciousness'.[6] From this potential all intelligent life develops. According Varisco, the external physical world is essentially irrational and inexplicable. Science cannot reveal the laws of causality and answer the question 'why', it can only explain 'how' something happens. In Varisco's philosophical system, physical reality is not subject to reason, yet reason can help to order certain experiences we receive from the outside world.[7]

5 Ibid., p. 451.

6 Ibid., p. 452.

7 There are also alternative perspectives on Varisco's work. Despite his commitment to a typically positivist attitude to science and a strict empiricism in his theory of knowledge, some authors place Varisco in the camp of the idealists — in particular Giovanni Amendola emphasises the metaphysical aspect of his work, which emerged in his later years. See: Giovanni Amendola, 'La philosophie italienne contemporaine' [Contemporary Italian Philosophy], *Revue de Métaphysique et de Morale*, 16, no. 5 (September 1908), pp. 649–654.

Bernardino Varisco on the cover of a book covering his later period

Another popular philosophical movement in Italy at the turn of the century was pragmatism, which attracted a whole group of young intellectuals. The most active proponent of pragmatism at this time was Giovanni Papini (1881–1956), a poet, thinker, and literary critic. In addition to him, Italian pragmatism was developed by Giuseppe Prezzolini (1882–1982), Giovanni Vailati (1863–1909), and Mario Calderoni (1879–1914). Papini and Prezzolini founded the newspaper *Leonardo* in 1903, where Vailati and Calderoni also actively published. Pragmatists saw the need to free Italian intellectual life from the dogmatism of academic philosophy, both the old idealism of the nineteenth century, which presented man as a grain of sand in the games of the Absolute Spirit, and positivism, which chained the individual to facts in a deterministic manner. The vitality and vigour of the Italian pragmatists shocked one of the founders of pragmatism, William James, who visited Italy in the spring of 1905 to attend a philosophical congress.[8]

8 James, while at the Congress, wrote in a letter to his wife saying that a 'very serious philosophical movement is developing in Italy, truly inspired by Schiller

Giovanni Papini—poet, thinker, literary critic, and one of the leading representatives of Italian pragmatism

What did the Italian pragmatists believe? Papini argued that the task of philosophy was not to look for abstract truths, but to give man, who is by nature an active being, methods and tools of creativity. Knowledge of absolute truths is impossible because of human nature, which is sensual, emotional, and irrational. Philosophy should not be contemplative; it should be able to effectively improve man's nature and make him master of reality. By mastering reality, man gains peace in his soul. Furthermore, by becoming its master and co-creator, man becomes a de facto god.[9] Pragmatism, as interpreted by young Italian intellectuals, appeared to be a way of thinking by which man could become God—precisely a *way of thinking*, since Papini stressed that

and myself (I simply could not believe it before)... They show such enthusiasm, activity and literary scope, with which nothing can compare in our country'. Cited from: Giovanni Gullace, 'The Pragmatist Movement in Italy', *Journal of the History of Ideas*, 23, no. 1 (Jan.–Mar., 1962), p. 92.

9 Papini's concept of the human-God (*Uomo-Dio*) was greeted with great enthusiasm by William James. James wrote to Ferdinand Canning Scott Schiller: 'Papini is a treasure! To think this little Italian has beaten us all (even you, with his *Uomo-Dio*) by one leap. And what a writer! And how prolific!' Quoted in: Ibid., p. 93.

pragmatism was not a philosophy, but a way of living and thinking without any philosophy. Abandoning attempts to resolve 'eternal' philosophical questions and instead focusing on creating his own world, replacing metaphysics with aesthetic and moral pleasure, Papini centered his attention on three main problems: the problem of the relationship between the general and the particular, the problem of posing philosophical questions guided by the goal to be achieved, and the problem of the influence of faith and belief on people's actions. The latter was of particular interest to the Italian pragmatists — unlike James, who believed that faith did not have any direct effect on things, but only influenced attitudes, Papini and his associates were convinced that faith changed reality because faith and belief gave man the motivation to act. Papini called his pragmatism 'magical' and 'psychological'.

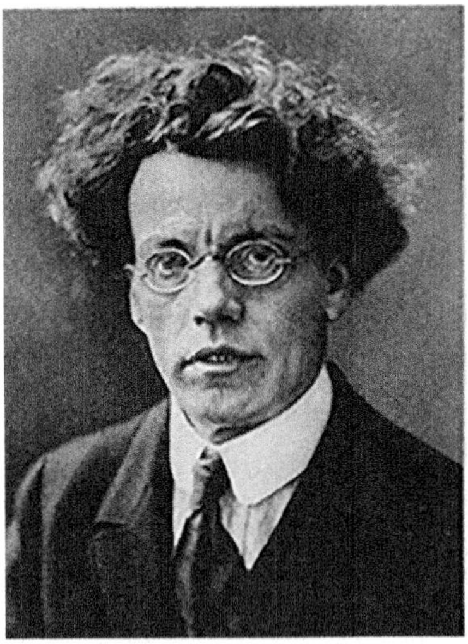

Papini argued that philosophy should not be contemplative — it should be able to actively improve human nature, to make man the master of reality.

Giuseppe Prezzolini focused on a critique of logic and logical thinking in general — his pragmatism was irrational but lacked the divine-human aspirations of Papini. Prezzolini's thought was closer to Schiller's 'humanistic' pragmatism, but when it came to the problem of truth he shared Papini's ideas — he saw all truths as subjective and concluded that the quest for absolute objective truth was pointless. In contrast, Vailati and Calderoni held a rational and logical view. The jurist Calderoni wrote that true pragmatism was a logical method by which one could separate true from false, while the mathematician Vailati insisted on the need to abandon the 'psychological' elements of Italian pragmatism. Both were closer to Charles Sanders Peirce than to William James.

The popularity of pragmatism in Italy was short-lived. After the newspaper *Leonardo* closed in 1907, pragmatists joined other schools of thought and social movements. In particular, Papini became one of the founders of the Italian Nationalist Association, while Prezzolini immersed himself in literary criticism and then emigrated to the United States. Vailati and Calderoni's fortunes were tragically cut short by early deaths.

However, a neo-idealism gradually gained momentum, inspired by the Neapolitan philosopher Benedetto Croce (1866–1952). Croce was the nephew of Bertrando Spaventa, who took the 17-year-old Croce from Naples to Rome, where the youth was introduced to Antonio Labriola and, through him, to Marxist philosophy. Unlike Labriola, Croce was never completely taken in by Marxism. For him, this early fascination was just an episode in the development of his own philosophical approaches. By 1900, it had practically disappeared. In November 1902, Croce founded the journal *La Critica*, simultaneously serving as editor-in-chief and energetic publicist. Disregarding the philosophical and literary orientation of the new periodical, Croce used its pages as a platform to participate in political polemics, criticising D'Annunzio, nationalism, clericalism, and Futurism. Many of Croce's columns in *La Critica* were reprinted in the major national newspapers, increasing his popularity and publicity. At this time, it was Hegel who had a fundamental influence on his political thought. Criticising the great German for excessive idealisation of the state,

Croce nevertheless completely shared his ideas on the evolution of the world spirit, dialectics, and the unity of opposites.[10]

Benedetto Croce, one of the fathers of Italian neo-Hegelianism

While working on La Critica, Croce became close to the young Giovanni Gentile, who was then beginning his academic career. The two Neo-Hegelians soon formed a close friendship. Croce and Gentile had years of productive intellectual interaction ahead of them.[11] The two philosophers were working towards the same goal of restoring the idealistic philosophical ethos that had inspired the '1860s generation' and been abandoned in favour of positivism and pragmatism.[12]

10 Denis Mack Smith, 'Benedetto Croce: History and Politics', *Journal of Contemporary History*, 8, no. 1 (Jan., 1973), p. 43.

11 For more details, see: Camille Schuwer, 'La pensée italienne contemporaine. L'idéalisme de Benedetto Croce et de Giovanni Gentile' [Contemporary Italian Thought. The Idealism of Benedetto Croce and Giovanni Gentile], *Revue Philosophique de la France et de l'Etranger*, 97 (January to June, 1924), pp. 351–401.

12 As we can judge from Croce's famous work 'What is alive and what is dead in Hegel's philosophy', first published in 1906, the main significance in Hegel for the Italian Neo-Hegelians lay in his closely related philosophy of spirit and philosophy of history, and in the Hegelian concept of state, which found

The joint efforts of Gentile and Croce significantly changed the philosophical climate in Italy. In the second half of the 1920s, Italian philosophy was divided into two camps, 'those who supported idealism and those who opposed it'.[13] However, during the Fascist years the scales were decidedly tipped in the favour of the idealists. The project of the revival of idealism, proclaimed by Croce and Gentile in 1903, was successfully realised. The latter confidently assumed the position of the country's leading philosopher, the most popular and most influential, and became the founder of a whole school of thought that developed in Italy until the last years of the Fascist regime. He created a coherent system capable of answering any philosophical question and, backed by the Fascist regime, became its chief philosopher.

§2. The Foundations of Gentile's Philosophy

2.1. *The Theory of Mind as Pure Act*: Gentile's System of Philosophy. Epistemology, Ontology, and Anthropology

Gentile detailed his system of actual idealism in *The Theory of Mind as Pure Act*, published in 1916. He wrote this work at a mature age (Gentile was forty-one at the time of publication, already a renowned scholar and head of the École Normale Supérieure in Pisa). In *The Theory of Mind as Pure Act*, Gentile presented his insights on almost all major philosophical problems.[14]

---

expression both in Croce and in the writings of Gentile. By developing these strands in a dialectical vein, they were both undoubtedly Hegelians. At the same time, of course, it is absurd to consider Hegel as a 'precursor of Fascism' on this basis (just as it would be with Plato, which has been attempted, for example, by Popper in *The Open Society and its Enemies*). Such 'accusations' are completely out of context for the era in which Hegel worked, a period in which Europe was gradually recovering from the shock of the French Revolution and searching for new justifications for the monarchical order.

13 Ruggiero and Allen, 'Philosophy in Italy', pp. 220–225.

14 It is worth noting here that Giovanni Gentile's philosophical legacy is extremely extensive, spanning fifty-five volumes in Italian. He wrote numerous

Beginning his philosophical exposition by looking at the subjectivity of reality, Gentile turned to George Berkeley. The English philosopher argued that to know reality meant at the same time to know the consciousness in which that reality was reflected. Because we can only reason about what we have understood and realised, the objects we have perceived are reflected in our minds as ideas. Hence the idea of a material substance external to consciousness, of bodies existing outside consciousness and spirit, seems contradictory. Noting the complexity and internally problematic nature of the concept of the idealism of the real, Gentile argues that Berkeley essentially rejected it, maintaining that reality was not an object of human reason and spirit, but a totality of ideas stemming from an objective and absolute Reason, whose existence is presupposed by the existence of human reason. 'From the empirical point of view, on which, as a pre-Kantian idealist, Berkeley insisted, it is obvious and seems irrefutable that our mind cannot conceive of all things conceivable, since it is a human mind, and therefore limited, and the mind of finite beings exists only within the limits of time and space',[15] Gentile continues the thought. In other words, Berkeley assumed the existence of the mind of God, free from all the limitations characteristic of the human mind. Thus, according to Gentile, Berkeley positions the human mind and the divine mind in opposition to one another. In Berkeley's reality, in which there is a pre-ordained, complete, and perfect world presented to cognition, cognition and contemplation essentially make little constructive sense. It is a static world, which excludes any possibility of knowing,

historical-philosophical, socio-political, religious, and logical works. Gentile's practical philosophy (his ethical, pedagogical, and political thought) is of primary interest for the purposes of this study, while epistemology, ontology, and the anthropology of actual idealism are important insofar as they constitute the fundamental groundwork for Gentile's political philosophy. Given the scope of this study, we are forced to leave out many of his other works.

15 Giovanni Gentile, 'Teoria generale dello spirito como atto puro' [The Theory of Mind as Pure Act] in *Works, Volume III,* (Florence: Casa Editrice Le Lettere, 1987), p.4.

becoming, or developing the new. Human thought is only a ray of divine thought. 'Modern philosophy, after exhaustive reflection, asserts the modest claim — thinking must be *something*',[16] Gentile writes. This *something*, according to the philosopher, is total and absolute reality.

Moving from Berkeley to Kant in his discourse on the nature of cognition, Gentile argues that the Kantian noumena has no foundation once we accept the notion of thinking as transcendental thinking, the understanding of reason as self-awareness, as the original apperception, as the prerequisite of all experience. 'In every act of thinking, and in our thinking in general, we try to distinguish two things: on the one hand, what we think, on the other hand, us, thinking, who are not the object but the subject of thinking',[17] Gentile explains. However, consciousness which is the object of consciousness, ceases to be consciousness, becomes not a subject but an object, not an ego but a non-ego. According to Gentile, this is the point at which Berkeley made a major mistake — his idealism was empirical.

Gentile explains that when we think, 'we do not see our thought as a perfect act, but as an act in progress. We can never transcend this act, because it is our subjectivity, our self, something that we cannot objectify in any way'.[18] Thus, Gentile brings the reader to a key underlying thesis — the actuality of the self, 'the point of view from which the self can never be presented as its own object'.[19] According to Gentile, any attempt to objectify the self, which is 'the inner activity that constitutes our spiritual nature'[20] is doomed to failure. He concludes: 'Genuine thought activity is not that which is defined, but that which defines'.[21] According to the Italian philosopher, if we try to understand something of spiritual value, a fact of spiritual life, we must regard that

16 Ibid., p. 6.

17 Ibid., p. 7.

18 Ibid., p. 8.

19 Ibid., p. 8.

20 Ibid., p. 8.

21 Ibid., p. 9.

something as identical with our own spiritual activity. That is how we understand, evaluate, agree, argue — we carry out what Gentile calls 'spiritual penetrations' (*penetrazione spirituale*), without which there can be neither cognition nor any kind of orientation in the world. An indispensable prerequisite for a genuine understanding of the other, a condition for productive communication, is the union of our reality and the reality of the other. Moreover, at such moments, the spiritual unity of reason is not enough; what really counts is a good spiritual disposition (*la buona disposizione spirituale*), namely goodwill, love, sympathy, openness, and other warm feelings. Gentile asks: what is this, what is the significance of this spiritual unity behind all meaningful spiritual communication?

In seeking an answer to this question, Gentile derives the law of cognition of spiritual reality, which implies the necessity of dissolving the object into the subject. In other words, to know something, one has to merge with it. He distinguishes two kinds of spiritual objects. The first are 'subjects of experience, human beings, sentient beings'[22] and the second are 'spiritual facts or the work of reason as realised by the subjects of experience'.[23] Gentile goes on to argue the following thesis: 'The moment we examine the nature of the spiritual facts, which we distinguish from true and proper subjects of experience, we see that the distinction is inadmissible.'[24] Gentile explains this by giving the example of language, which we separate from those who speak it, making it an ideal fact. The reality of language is contained both in the person of the individual who speaks it and in the language itself, even if no one speaks it. The language spoken by a person is inseparable from the speaker's mind — 'the spiritual fact which we call language is mind itself in its concreteness'.[25] According to Gentile, the function of language is 'the reconstruction of the moment of our

22 Ibid., p. 14.

23 Ibid., p. 14.

24 Ibid., p. 16.

25 Ibid., p. 15.

own consciousness, our spiritual experience'. We separate the *Divine Comedy* from Dante and from ourselves reading it. But Gentile insists that even when we make this distinction explicit, the *Divine Comedy* remains with us, in us, in our minds, despite the divisions we make. In this way, the poem becomes one with those who read it.

Gentile states: 'When we speak of a spiritual fact, we speak of spirit, and to speak of spirit is to speak of a concrete, historical individuality; of a subject that we do not think of in this way, but that is actualised in this way'.[26] Spiritual reality is thus reduced to pure spirit as a subject which can only be known by dissolving its objectivity into the subjectivity of the knower. It follows that there is no 'other' outside of us — by being known to us and being in communication with us, the 'other' is in us. 'To know is to identify, to overcome the otherness as such',[27] Gentile writes. Thus, the spiritual world is knowable only as the reality of the spiritual activity of the subject.

Spiritual reality is always the reality of becoming. The facts of nature are always the same, they take place, they are final, their development is impossible. Gentile claims: 'In the world of the spirit nothing is ever finished or accomplished; everything is in the process of becoming'.[28] From this thesis he draws an ethical conclusion: since we are spiritual beings and the life of the spirit is becoming, no noble deeds and accomplishments of the past can cancel our duty and necessity to perform new deeds and accomplishments.

The philosopher goes on to say that the actualist view of the spirit differs significantly from that of previous spiritual theories. Previously, spirit was opposed to matter. Gentile explains that it was then relegated to a state of matter because it was proclaimed to be a substance. According to actual idealism, the spirit cannot exist outside of its manifestations, in which it finds its realisation. At the same time, the philosopher states: 'We can say of spiritual reality what the great Christian

26 Ibid., p. 16.

27 Ibid., p. 16.

28 Ibid., p. 24.

thinkers said of God: "He who seeks Him will find Him.'"[29] The unity of spirit, which is the epistemological basis of Gentile's philosophy explaining the process of knowledge, has two fundamental properties in his system: the unity of spirit is immultiplicabile (*immoltiplicabile*) and infinite (*infinita*). It is immultiplicable because spirit is indivisible into separate parts, independent of each other; infinite because the reality of spirit cannot be limited to any other reality and still retain itself. Hence the infinity of the horizon of our consciousness, which contains all other things and consciousnesses that we can conceive and imagine.

Despite the unity, inexhaustibility, and infinity of spirit, there is a multiplicity of different things, objects, entities. Gentile sets out to understand the nature of the relationship between the unity of spirit and the multiplicity of things. The solution is the synthesis (*sintesi*) of unity and multiplicity, without which all things become exclusively themselves, without any connecting thread to anything else. Things are plural insofar as they are the objects of the ego, of the subject. For the multiplicity of things to become an object of consciousness, the multiplicity must be absorbed into the unity, fused with it. 'We perceive the difference between us and things when we perceive the relatedness of things to each other, and we become silent when we regard our self as a grain of sand on the shore of a gigantic ocean, this self being the experiential self, not the transcendent self, which is the only true subject of our experience, and thus our only true self',[30] Gentile explains.

The philosopher also points out as a crucial characteristic of the spirit that in the spirit it is impossible to make a clear distinction between the theoretical and the practical. 'There is no theory or contemplation of reality that is not at the same time an action and thus a creation of reality',[31] Gentile writes. He refutes the notion that we are

29 Ibid., p. 27.

30 Ibid., p. 35.

31 Ibid., p. 36.

only responsible for our actions, and not for our thoughts. 'Every spiritual act, then (including that which we regard as simply theoretical), is practical in as much as it has a value, practical in being or in not being what it ought to be. It is therefore our act and it is free',[32] he explains. Gentile concludes that the laws of nature and the laws of the spirit are fundamentally different from each other, and while in nature facts do speak for themselves and the laws of necessity apply, in the realm of the spirit, which implies freedom, the laws of the ideal apply. The laws of nature answer the question 'what is it?', the laws of the spirit answer the question 'why?' Gentile concludes by saying: 'If the spirit is free, its restriction to the laws of the spirit can only mean that the laws in question are not a different, distinct reality, but the same reality'.[33]

Gentile had already pointed out earlier in *The Theory of Mind as Pure Act* that our human experience cannot be called purely theoretical — because our world is a world in which we encounter other living souls, other personalities, our experience is conditioned by the non-self to the same extent as it is by the self.[34] Insofar as, as mentioned above, spirit is the synthesis of unity and multiplicity, this, according to Gentile, implies the dynamism of spirit. Thus, spirit is not a static being; spirit is an infinite creative process, something evolving. In other words, there is a 'development of the spirit'.

Gentile explains what he means. According to actual idealism, it is equally erroneous to assume both the primordial perfection of the spirit and a certain finite perfection. Spirit has neither beginning nor end because it is becoming, and its nature is this infinite process of becoming. The spirit cannot be a unity alone, without plurality, because

32 Ibid., p. 37.

33 Ibid., p. 38.

34 As Roger Holmes observes, it is rather odd that Gentile does not refer to Fichte more often than to any other German philosopher — his constant reference to the 'self' and the 'non-self' might make one think that it is 'Fichte who is his brother in spirit'. Roger W. Holmes, *The Idealism of Giovanni Gentile*, (New York: The Macmillan Company, 1937), p. 4.

plurality is necessary 'for the very concreteness, the very dialectical reality of the one'.[35] The plurality, according to Gentile, reinforces the unity of the spirit, the infinity of which is realised through the unity. The plurality of the spirit thus appears in his philosophy as an actualisation of the real, presupposed by the necessity of the dialecticality of the spirit. Yet spirit never confronts itself with the other, alienating it: 'What is different from us is not different enough not to be us'.[36]

In discussing the development of the spirit and its dialectical dynamism, Gentile considers two notions of dialectics, the Platonic and the Aristotelian. Neither of them fully satisfies him. Gentile notes that dialectics for Plato is philosophical enquiry itself, that which allows philosophical reflection to take on systematic form. Plato's dialectic is the negation of all dynamism and all development, because it belongs entirely to the sphere of the infinite and eternal ideal. Plato's ideas are eternal and unchanging. According to 'modern dialectic' (in other words, the dialectic of Gentile himself) 'a thought which can be conceived (*pensiero pensato*) implies the act of thinking (*pensiero pensante*); its life and truth are in the act'.[37] The act, in turn, consists in actualisation, that is, in becoming and developing.[38] Thus, Plato's dialectic, according to Gentile, is not quite dialectic. And Aristotle was no more successful in his eyes. Becoming is for him only a postulate, since something conceivable cannot be becoming, and something becoming cannot be conceivable; there is no substance that is not a unity of form and matter. Ultimately for Aristotle there is no science which would

35 Gentile, 'Teoria generale dello spirito como atto puro', p. 42.

36 Ibid., p. 34.

37 Ibid., p. 44.

38 Modern scholars note that the *pensiero pensante* in Gentile's dialectic is an assertion that the only true reality is the act of thought existing in the present. The past, expressed by *pensiero pensato*, is realised through its actualisation in the present. History becomes a reality by bringing it into the present through an act of actualisation — this is how Rick Peters sees Gentile's ontology. See Rik Peters, 'Actes de présence: Presence in Fascist Political Culture', *History and Theory*, 45, no. 3 (Oct., 2006), pp. 362–374.

not be an act of the intellect — knowledge is realised as a relation of the human intellect to the eternal.

According to Gentile, the whole world of ancient philosophy is static; dynamism is inaccessible to it. Equally inaccessible are notions of history and progress. What is more, both medieval and modern philosophy, according to him, did not pay enough attention to it. The Italian philosopher singles out only one exception, Giordano Bruno, who was the first to suggest the development of the spirit, which consisted of increasing its powers and capacities, and thus allowing for more genuine self-realisation.[39] According to Bruno in Gentile's account, we can trust the experience of previous generations and the 'wisdom of the ancients' in the sense that we have the opportunity to study the account of their experiences and reflections, thereby strengthening ourselves. Gentile argues that this is the first indication of the importance of history in modern philosophy. Continuing the idea of the importance of history, he argues that 'the dialectical conception is possible only on the sole basis that in history we see not the past, but the actual present'.[40] The mistake of the positivists is that they view history as one studies the facts of the natural world, missing the organic spiritual side of history. The historian must understand his object — as Gentile argues, 'they must speak the same language'.[41] This means that the historian and the object he studies must belong to the same reality, the same process. Thus, history is studied and learned as our spiritual act. History is part of a dialectical process when the

39 It should be noted that Bruno occupies a special place in Gentile's historical and philosophical explorations. The Italian philosopher devoted his life and work to the book *Giordano Bruno and Renaissance Philosophy*, first published in 1920. Gentile attributes a prominent place to Bruno in the history of philosophy. He writes that, for Bruno, the knowledge of the divine is not a direct ecstatic union with the world of the spirit but a rational process — intellectual reasoning, true and pure philosophy.

40 Gentile, 'Teoria generale dello spirito como atto puro', p. 51.

41 Ibid., p. 51.

individual can identify with history, continue and concentrate it in his consciousness. History is seen as the activity of the historian.

Gentile then pays tribute to Hegel as the first to recognise the need for dialectical thinking about the real in its particularity.[42] According to him, Hegel convincingly proved the impossibility of dialectical thinking about reality when the latter is separated from the act of thinking itself and viewed as something presupposed by the act of thinking. Gentile draws attention to the Hegelian distinction between the intellect, which comprehends things, and reason, which comprehends the spirit. Reason grasps all things in the unity of the spirit. Yet Gentile points out that in developing this distinction, Hegel makes the important mistake of resorting to abstract, non-dynamic definitions. Gentile calls for a rejection of the view that reality is what we think; that which does not exist outside the conceivable. He calls for the genuine and concrete reality of thought to be seen in the act, in action. This is, in his view, the only way to recognise and consider the dialectical character of reality, to know the law of dialectical thinking in action, in other words, the law of actual thinking.

Gentile continues his discussion on dialectics by looking at the problem of nature. He again turns to Hegel, in whose system the natural world does not develop, but appears only as an unfolding of the Absolute Spirit and, accordingly, the philosophy of spirit itself only begins where we go beyond nature. Gentile raises the question of whether this contradicts the thesis of the infinite unity of spirit. In Plato's system of Idealism we are confronted with thinking outside of

42 Evelyne Buissière is quite right to point out that whichever of the great philosophers of the past Gentile mentions, be it Berkeley, Kant, or Hegel, they all appear in *The Theory of Mind as Pure Act* as precursors of actual idealism. The 'errors' of Hegel that Gentile identifies in *The Theory of Mind* were expounded and justified in detail by the Italian philosopher in *A Reform of Hegelian Dialectic*, published three years before *The Theory of Mind*, in 1913. See Evelyne Buissière, 'Giovanni gentile réformateur de la dialectique Hégélienne' [Giovanni Gentile, Reformer of the Hegelian Dialectic], *Les Études philosophiques*, no. 4, Philosophie Italienne (Oct.-Dec. 1994), pp. 521–542.

which there is nothing. In Hegel's system there is something beyond the Logos, but it is nonintelligible. If we try to know nature by means of the Logos, we fail, because the Logos excludes nature, and spirit occurs as a self-rejection of nature.

Another unresolved problem of classical philosophy to which Gentile refers is the scholastic argument about universals. The philosopher considers this problem very important—how we interpret universals determines how we know the individual. Gentile criticises the nominalists, calling nominalism 'a naturalistic and materialistic theory'.[43] According to Gentile's nominalists, the form of each individual, because it is not identical with the form of all other individuals, because we know the form of each independently of the others, is not universal but particularistic, exclusive. Reality is thus conceived as a purely abstract mental supposition. Gentile concludes: 'The individual, as a pure individual, is not an individual: he is nothing'.[44] Realists, according to Gentile, make the opposite mistake: if the universals are real in themselves and the individual can add nothing to them, what is the individuality of the individual? 'We return to the great Platonic problem, where [Plato] found himself imprisoned in the circle of ideas, without any possibility of returning from them to the world, even though he conceived of ideas in order to understand the world'.[45] According to the Italian philosopher, eclectic theories (such as Avicenna's) were no more successful in solving the problem of the universals. Gentile believes that the problem of the universal had gradually begun to be solved in the philosophy of the Modern Age—Descartes was the first to free himself from the problem, by asserting the particularity of the 'I', the thinking individual. The ensuing argument between rationalists and empiricists seems to the Italian philosopher to be a choice between 'a metaphysics of empty shadows and the inclination of reason towards the unknown and unknowable

43 Gentile, 'Teoria generale dello spirito como atto puro', p. 69.

44 Ibid., p. 70.

45 Ibid., p. 70.

Absolute'.[46] Gentile notes that Kant made a determined effort to understand the immanence of the universal in the individual and to clarify the very possibility of individuation. However, by separating the phenomenon and the noumen he constructed an essentially scholastic system, changing the terminology, but failing to bring us any closer to a solution to the antinomy of the universals. Gentile maintains that this problem is not resolved by contemporary epistemology, the heir of medieval nominalism, which is in fact a form of naturalistic scepticism. Thus, according to Gentile, modern philosophy does not solve the problem that has been topical since Aristotle's time — the problem of the concreteness of the real. Philosophy has still not moved beyond the choice between empty concepts and blind intuition.

What does Gentile himself propose to solve this problem? How can 'the individual be preserved without drowning in the bottomless ocean of thought and its schemata, devoid of any theoretical meaning'?[47] Returning to the Aristotelian critique of Plato's theory of ideas, Gentile argues that we think of ideas as a principle of reality, without the ideas themselves possessing any reality. The idea of a house conceived by an architect is not a real house, and may never become one if the design for the house is not approved. At the same time, we do not need the house itself to understand the architect's house plan. What is the relationship between the ideal and the real? Gentile says that when we think of ideas, we do not think of a house. We think of the idea as the origin and the cause of the house. Thus, when we think of ideas themselves, we think of them as some principle of the real, which means that the very concept of the ideal is integrated into the concept of the real.[48]

He reaches the following conclusion: '*ideas are not real; realised ideas are real*'.[49] The ideal and the real are united *when the ideal exists and the real is existence*, in other words, concrete being. For Aristotle,

46 Ibid., p. 72.

47 Ibid., p. 81.

48 Ibid., p. 82.

49 Ibid., p. 82.

nature and the individual are what really is, not what should or could be. In other words, the individual is the positive, which is not a process, but a consequence of a process, a shaped and finished creation, a result. Like historical events and natural phenomena, it is something that is already imprinted, that is (or was) there, that leaves no choice and no scope of action for the spirit. The true positive, according to Gentile, *already exists* when it is presented to the individual. It is presented to us, but not by us. 'Universals, therefore, are either whatever we call a universal, as empiricists claim, or, since their reality is independent of us, they exist solely insofar as we reconstruct them, as the apriorists would say',[50] Gentile writes. In the end the philosopher agrees with Vincenzo Gioberti, who claimed that the intuitive has to be absorbed by reflection, whereby the subject gains an awareness of this intuitive as a result of his consistent work. Thus, the activity of the subject plays an auxiliary but necessary role in the process of knowing, both universal and positive. Gentile concludes that the positive is ultimately postulated by ourselves when we confront it. But is it possible for such a positive, confronted by the subject into becoming a realised reality, to not in fact be a creation of the subject?

Gentile notes that at first glance, the idea of the individual as a true positive seems absurd. The philosopher believes that there must be a limit beyond which the individual ceases to be a springboard enabling the subject to leap from the realm of pure ideas into the realm of the subjective, and to maintain a connection to the real, positive world. This limit is in the subject's consciousness, linked to his ego, beyond which something ceases to be an object for the subject. Without such a link, the object as object loses any meaning for the subject. It follows that the positive individual cannot be understood other than through a connection (*relazione*) with the subject. What, in turn, does the fact of connection itself mean? 'To say that two concepts are related is to acknowledge their difference, but at the same time to assume

50 Ibid., p. 85.

the existence of an identity', Gentile explains. If the concepts are connected, even though they are distinct, then at least by thinking of one we are also thinking of the other. In the case of a connection the idea of one also contains in some form the idea of the other. If we pit the individual against the universal, how do we understand the universal? And how do we bring the universal closer to a substantive reality? Is all this 'chasing empty shadows'?[51]

As a result of extensive discourse, Gentile comes to the conclusion that the individual and the universal, in their antagonism to one another, are two abstractions. We universalise the individual by thinking about it. In turn, when we think of the universal, we individualise it.[52] Through thinking, we either individualise abstract categories or realise universal ideas. By reasoning in this way, we leave the concreteness of the very process of thinking as an act, which is itself the unity of the universal and the individual, outside the brackets. By directing his reasoning towards the problem of 'grasping' thought as an act, Gentile hopes to find an answer to the above question on the possibility of the genuine positive.

'The distinction between abstract and concrete thought is fundamental. Translating a problem from the realm of abstract thought into the realm of concrete thought is the key to our whole doctrine',[53] Gentile

51 Ibid., p. 90.

52 Here Gentile again turns to Plato's theory of ideas, in particular to the dialogue Phaedrus. He writes that if we ascend to a heaven in which we can behold the real horse, which is the idea of the horse, whose reflection we see in mortal, earthly horses, we realise that we can only contemplate the idea by defining it, by making it the subject of judgement — just as we would do with an ordinary horse that we would see outside the window. Without saying 'this is an authentic horse', without using definitions, we cannot arrive at any inference as to the nature of the contemplated. The idea of the horse in this example is a universal concept, with a specific ontological meaning in Plato's system. However, without individualising this universal we cannot conceive of it. As a result, Gentile arrives at the conclusion that we cannot in principle conceive of the 'pure universal'. See Ibid., p. 92.

53 Ibid., p. 94.

argues. He calls for an elevation of the speculative basis of doctrine above the limitations implied by other philosophical concepts (particularly empiricism and Kantianism). He believed that all judgements are acts of the thinking 'I', whose form is unchanging. All judgements of the Kantian classification ultimately take the form of an 'I think' that is outside any categories. In criticising Kant, Gentile showed that the giant of German philosophy did not categorise judgements, but empty abstractions. 'Judgements are spiritual acts, but both judgements and all spiritual acts become natural facts (*fatti naturali*) when they are thought of in the abstract, outside their concrete actuality',[54] argues the Italian philosopher. Returning to the problem of the genuine positive, Gentile makes the following thesis: the genuine positive is the realisation of reality, whose principle is in the idea, and which complements the idea itself by what is inherent in it. 'Thought, which is genuine thought, must generate the being of that which is conceivable, and this is the meaning of the Cartesian *cogito*. I, this reality which is 'I am', the most unquestionable reality that I can access and which, even if I let go of all possibilities of convincing myself of the existence of any reality, remains the only stable point to which I can attach the world I can conceive — this 'I am' exists insofar as I think. I am aware of it in the process of thinking, thinking of what I am thinking. 'I am', as will be made clear later, is there insofar as it is self-consciousness. The 'I' is not consciousness that presupposes identity as object, but consciousness that postulates selfhood',[55] Gentile explains.

In his discussion of Plato, Gentile has already shown the complexity of the transition from the ideal to the positive individual in intellectual philosophical doctrines. Actual idealism tries to overcome this complexity: 'The individual is the opening which thought makes, when it suddenly realises it has derived from a starting point, and instead of having before it ideas created by itself, has before it the self confronting

54 Ibid., p. 96.

55 Ibid., p. 98.

its own self. The individual is the realisation of a process in which ideas arise and reside at the moment when we turn the abstract into the concrete. It is in the concrete that we must look for the positive basis of all reality'.[56] The universal and the multiple merge in the self. If the uniqueness and the self of the individual thus depends entirely on his thinking, it is thinking that must be the highest universal: 'The thinking with which I think of myself is the same thinking through which I think of everything'.[57] In this way, Gentile is convinced, the problem of the universals is solved, and both realists and nominalists are right in their own way: the universals are not only real, but also nothing except them is real; moreover, there is nothing outside the individual, as the nominalists claimed. 'The universal, not presupposed by thought, but really posited by it, is all that can be thought real. When, then, we make distinctions, as indeed we must, all distinctions fall within it'.[58] Thus, nothing conceivable can be outside of thought, but everything conceivable is contained in concrete thought, which includes everything.

Giovanni Gentile (left) at his desk

56 Ibid., p. 99.

57 Ibid., p. 99.

58 Ibid., p. 100.

Gentile arrived at the conclusion that the individual is positive. Moreover, it is the only true positive; it is believed by the subject itself, and is the very subject that believes it. Gentile illustrates that our positive subjectivity is an inherently necessary fact of our 'I' with the example of sleep. When we sleep, we dream. If events happen to us in a dream that are not too out of our ordinary experience, we often fail to realise that we are dreaming. When we wake up, what do we do to make sure that we are awake? We immediately try to validate the surrounding external reality through some bodily sensations. We authenticate ourselves through acts, which confirms for us the positivity of everything around us as well as of ourselves. The genuine and uniquely positive is therefore the act of the subject. This brings Gentile to a final judgement on the universal and the individual. As the philosopher has shown before, the genuine universal is universalisation, the process of the accomplishment of the universal, 'or rather, as the universal is the thought that creates it, the self-emergence of the universal (*farsi dell'universale*)'.[59] Gentile concludes on the theme of the universal and the individual: 'We can speak of the universal and the individual insofar as we have in mind the subject, the "I" who thinks and in the process of thinking is universalised through individuation and individualised through universalisation'.[60]

The discourse on the individual and the universal in *The Theory of Mind as Pure Act* plays an important role as it brings us closer to an understanding of Gentile's ontology, which he sets out in chapters 9 to 13 of this work ('Space and Time', 'Immortality', 'Causality, Mechanism and Contingency', 'Freedom and Foresight', and 'The Historical Antinomy and Eternal History'). However, the philosopher already makes the transition to ontology in chapter 8 ('The Positive as Self-Created'), stating that by opposing nature to spirit, we limit the spirit. The spirit is universal, nature is its individualisation. Spirit

59 Ibid., p. 104.

60 Ibid., p. 105.

is the expression of the one, nature is the expression of the many. Positivity as such is integrated in plurality and realised through plurality, while ideality arises as the knowability of plurality. 'To overcome pure ideality, therefore, it is necessary to "grasp" not just the real, but the real multiplicity',[61] Gentile writes. Using examples from ancient philosophy, he shows that human thought has always strived for unity and order, without wanting to destroy the multiplicity of individual and positive things. But he observes that pure multiplicity is of course incognisable (indeed *unthinkable*).

Gentile goes on to write that most philosophical concepts portrayed the world in space and time, and every positive individual was imagined as existing in space and time — for as long as they existed. What is space and time? These are two systems of multiplicity, understood as 'the great repository of everything that is positive, genuinely real, concrete, particular'.[62] The two main questions we ask when confronted with the presumed existence of something are 'where?' and 'when?' What is real in a positive sense exists in space and time. Nature thus appears as the 'realm of the existing' (*regno dell'esistente*), contrasted with the 'realm of thought'. Thought, in this case, is effectively outside the spatial categories. Gentile schematically presents space and time as two lines intersecting at one point — 'a unique point of space that cannot be a point of space without being one of the infinite points in time'.[63] Next, let us imagine the multiplicity of such points of unity in space. Space appears as an absolute multiplicity, each element of which is itself a multiplicity. This is a directly given pure multiplicity. Time, in turn, 'spatialises the unity of space' (*spazializzazione dell'unita dello spazio*). Without time we cannot 'remove' any element from space and perceive it. Gentile notes, however, that such an understanding of space and time is insufficient — in fact, at this stage of reasoning he has arrived at absolute multiplicity, which, as noted above, is fundamentally

61 Ibid., p. 106.

62 Ibid., p. 112.

63 Ibid., p. 115.

unknowable. We, on the other hand, use the categories of space and time to refer to the very concrete, the positive, the individual.

Gentile asserts that 'space and time are unknowable as pure forms to be filled in by the perceptions of sense experience, just as we would fill up empty vessels'.[64] If this were the case, they would constitute a multiplicity independent of the activity of the spirit. In fact, as Gentile is convinced, it is the spatialising activity of the spirit that creates multiplicity. By acknowledging the existence of the activity of the spirit, instead of a multiplicity (*molteplice*), we get multiplication (*moltiplicazione*). By multiplying, the spirit does not destroy. Moreover, what is multiplied does not cease to be the multiplicity of the one. This is the essence of the synthesis of the life of spirit. What is more, the acts of spirit are amenable to analysis, which only strengthens and enriches reality. Space, then, appears as 'a harmonious wholeness of the world, which we designate spatially, and which appears as one with the horizon of our consciousness'.[65] Gentile writes that space is as infinite as we can imagine, but 'it is contained in us as an object of present experience, a given (insofar as we make it so) and constrained by the seal of time'.[66] Every element of space, and space itself in its totality, is 'articulated in the series of its states, connected together and forming an adamantine chain within which all that is positive in the facts is stretched out in the reality of the world'.[67] 'Everything is in us, and we are everything',[68] Gentile concludes. This 'everything' which 'is us' includes both space and time, which are expressions of the activity of the spirit.[69] 'We' are thus not an empirical but a transcendental ego.

64 Ibid., p. 120.

65 Ibid., p. 121.

66 Ibid., p. 122.

67 Ibid., p. 122.

68 Ibid., p. 122.

69 As the thinker's contemporaries note, Gentile in his ontology 'unlike other Hegelians, does not even presuppose a rational world. There is nothing in his

Gentile notes, however, that all processes of the development of the spirit are conditioned by time, pointing out that chronology is a necessary element of history in its spiritual understanding. Yet it is essential to distinguish between a positive fact (such as good or bad weather on a given day in the past) and a spiritual act (a meaningful historical event). The essence of the distinction is the presence of a spiritual act through which the temporal becomes positive. The philosopher also notes that space and time have two fundamental properties. For space, this property is the coexistence (*coesistenza*) of elements, for time the co-presence (*compresenza*) of elements. The latter is the convergence of all moments in time in the present, which thus turns out to be the negation of temporal multiplicity (not duration, but eternity). The former, in turn, negates the multiplicity of spatial points, centring all the elements of space around the 'I'. Gentile sums up: 'This merely ideal, or as we should say transcendental point, by its spatialising activity posits all the points of space and all the moments of time, thus generating the positive character of the real in space and time'.[70] Spatiality and spirituality appear as thesis and antithesis, through the synthesis of which the knowledge of a particular spiritual process is possible. The pre-natural and pre-mental spirit acts as a pure act through which understanding and awareness of the spatial as spiritual is possible.

Space is not infinite, but indefinite. It has no tangible limits. As defined by spirit, it has no existence of its own. But because it is an act of the spirit, it is never infinite, so the limits of space can be compressed and expanded — in other words it is flexible and mobile. Being thus an object of the spirit, space has a certain finality, but this finality is not final. According to Gentile, the indeterminacy of space is a consequence of the infinity of spirit. Spirit overcomes all limitations and restrictions, its activity is capable of transcending and pushing the boundaries of space. Since time can also be thought of as a kind of

world that does not emanate from the pure act of thought.' George de Santillana, 'The Idealism of Giovanni Gentile', *Isis*, 29, no. 2 (Nov., 1938), p. 368.

70 Gentile, 'Teoria generale dello spirito como atto puro', p. 125.

space, the relationship of spirit and time is analogous to that of spirit and space. Spirit is infinite in time, existing outside of time.

The timelessness of the spirit leads us to the question of immortality. According to Gentile, everything we hold dear (he cites as examples children, parents, God, the possessions we have acquired as a result of our work) has value for us insofar as it transcends our natural, physical, material life; has an immortal character. Gentile writes: 'The man who seeks to be reunited with God and his departed loved ones in another world different from this world of experience, in this world is united with those who remain behind, with his heirs, to whom he leaves the fruits of his labour, with his successors, to whom he entrusts what he created with his spirit, because his whole identity becomes immortal in what he values as the reality of his own life'.[71] As we see, for Gentile the question of immortality is closely linked to the question of values; moreover, it has a direct bearing on the problem of truth. Truth is one and absolute; in its unity it is opposed to a multiplicity of opinions. In actual idealism it is transcendental. Truth is not subject to the categories of space and time and regards itself as immortal. The immortality of truth in turn presupposes the immortality of the thought that reveals it. In this way truth bestows immortality on our spirit, on our individual souls; through the experience of truth in our self, in our 'I', in our subjectivity, we feel in ourselves the eternal—in fact we participate in it directly.

Immortality is the spirituality of the spirit and the rationality of the mind; belief in it is intrinsic to our subjectivity. It is characteristic both of values, which have an absolute character, and of the corresponding spiritual activity. Immortality is a property of the spirit that transcends nature and its limits. When we are conscious of ourselves, we often identify ourselves with our natural existence, confined within the boundaries of time and space beyond which we do not seem to exist. But our origins, according to actual idealism, lie in a higher

71 Gentile, 'Teoria generale dello spirito como atto puro', p. 139.

subjectivity which has genuine authenticity. This higher individuality, according to Gentile, is on the other side of all 'before' and 'after', in other words it is eternal. Thus it is our transcendental individuality that is immortal and eternal, and not the natural individuality (this is an important difference between actual idealism and mysticism of any kind).[72] He arrives at the conclusion that the part of us that can die is the material, which was never alive. Gentile ends his discourse on immortality with the following extended thesis: 'So is the individual mortal or immortal? The Aristotelian individual, which is individual in the ordinary sense of the word, is mortal; his immortality is his mortality, because his reality lies within the immortal spirit. But the individual as a spiritual act (*individuo individuandosi*) is immortal. The act of the spirit as a pure act, outside of which there is nothing that is not abstract, is the realm of immortality. If man was not this act and did not feel, however vaguely, that he was immortal in his very essence, he could not live, because he could not escape absolute practical scepticism, which is not merely an attempt not to think — as theoretical or abstract scepticism always was, which often encroached on human souls — but a valid arrest of thought; the thought by which alone we can grasp the truth in the eternal world. Can we be and not think, if being is essentially thinking or rather thinking oneself? The energy which sustains life is precisely the consciousness of the divine and eternal (*consapevolezza del divino e dell'eterno*), so that we always look down on the death and vanishing of everything perishable from the height of the immortal life'.[73]

72 In the course of his discussion of immortality Gentile makes another interesting remark on the theme of time: 'between the two opposing concepts of "past" and "future" there is no "present". The present is the eternal, the negation of time' (Ibid., p. 146). Horace, as a man who was born and died, is certainly dead. However, the Horace whose poems we read is not assumed by us as something different from ourselves; the moment we read his poems, he merges with our identity. Thus, what is truly alive is co-created by us in the timeless eternity of the present, in which there is neither past nor future.

73 Gentile, 'Teoria generale dello spirito como atto puro', p. 147.

Continuing the ontological problematics, Gentile delves into an examination of the problems of causality, mechanism, and contingency. The philosopher distinguishes between a metaphysical and an empirical understanding of causality. In this context he refers to metaphysics as 'the intuition of the real, striving for unity', and to empiricism as 'the intuition of the real, striving for the multitude'.[74] Gentile criticises both approaches to causality. According to his vision, to speak of causality in the metaphysical sense is to refer to something that has no meaning. An empirical view of causality leads to mechanism — for example, as it exists in the modern natural sciences. In such sciences the factor of chance plays an important role — even though they do not abandon the understanding of reality as contingent. A philosophy that presupposes randomness[75] is, according to Gentile, more empirical than any empirical mechanicism. It does not bring us any closer to an understanding of freedom. 'Contingency, in fact, does no more than affirm the reality of the differences, but not the multiplicity of the real',[76] he writes. According to Gentile, just as being does not derive from the possible, freedom does not derive from the contingent. Thus, according to actual idealism, the 'philosophy of contingency' is no better than Hume's empiricism with its critique of causality.

Gentile moves on from his discourse on chance to the question of foresight. The natural scientific point of view assumes the existence of natural laws. Referring to Auguste Comte, the philosopher notes that empiricists, mechanising nature, formulate natural laws, through the knowledge of which it is possible to foresee future events. The changes we observe are facts. We do not presume them, they are independent of us. Anticipation is therefore knowledge like any other if the past is for us a finished, known fact. Gentile cites the example of astronomy, where we are able, through mathematical calculation, to predict the

74 Ibid., p. 151.

75 The philosopher cites as an example the work of Emile Boutroux, *The Contingency of the Laws of Nature*, first published in 1874.

76 Gentile, 'Teoria generale dello spirito como atto puro', p. 167.

trajectory of comets. But what is true of the natural world is not true of man, as man is not created by external conditions and events, but creates himself. And if his birth in this or that place from specific parents is a fact, his intellectual life, for example, cannot be a fact. In such a context, all that we can call fact is presumed to be an act of the spirit. Anticipation of the human future is difficult to imagine because it completely nullifies the significance of our actions and the freedom of our spirit. The notion of divine foresight, in turn, according to Gentile, is a sign of a naturalistic understanding of God.

Developing his discourse on freedom, Gentile argues that 'the *a priori* synthesis of condition and conditioned is dialectics and, from our point of view, it is obvious that dialectics outside thinking is incomprehensible'.[77] He writes: 'The first unconditioned we may call Being, the second unconditioned, Spirit. The one is the unconditioned of abstract (and therefore false) thought, the other is the unconditioned of concrete (and therefore real) thought'.[78] If being is the result of a finished process, this implies the necessity of the future as an object of divine foreknowledge. The act of the spirit, in turn, is a free action in which nothing is presupposed, but everything is supposed. 'Freedom is absoluteness (infinity of the unconditioned), when the absolute is the cause of itself (*causa sui*)',[79] Gentile explains. According to actual idealism, this *sui* relies on the free self-consciousness of the subject, in which freedom is not opposed to the necessity of being, which, in turn, in its concrete expression is the dialectic of the spirit. The philosopher notes that this understanding of the dialectic of the spirit does not allow for any conditionality.

Here, on the horizon of Gentile's thought, emerges the main problem that actual idealism seeks to solve, namely the historical antinomy of the spirit. In other words, the problem arising from 'the understanding of the spirit as a pure act in its inherent connection with the notion

77 Ibid., p. 186.

78 Ibid., p. 187.

79 Ibid., p. 188.

of history'.[80] Gentile formulates the antinomy as follows: 'Spirit is history because it is a dialectical development'; which is countered by the antithesis 'Spirit is not history because it is an eternal act'.[81] According to Gentile, we cannot understand man without history, as history is where man realises his essence. Man, unlike nature, belongs to the realm of freedom ('nature is, spirit becomes'[82]). The state, society, culture, art — all this exists as a reality of the spirit, created by the minds and souls of people. And every great creator, be he a philosopher or a poet, exists in two qualities — eternal and historical. Eternal existence is the creator's spiritual legacy. By engaging with it (by reading a poem or a philosophical treatise), we come to know it as spirit. Historical existence is empirical existence in a concrete space and time, limited by factuality and cultural features. Thus, the historicity of spirit is the naturalisation of spiritual events from which we are separated by space and time. On the contrary, when we come to know the spiritual content of a spiritual fact, we come to know it in its eternal ideality. The problem, as Gentile defines it, is to understand reality as being both eternal and historical. The Italian philosopher clearly shows that this problem is typical of the history of thought, and precisely because of its complexity Plato denied any value to history and contained all being in the upper world, while all empiricists since Protagoras have denied the absolute value of anything over and above the casual and specific. Gentile solves this antinomy by bringing spiritual reality, values, and history from abstract thought to concrete thought.

As Gentile has noted, one can look at history in different ways. It is possible, for example, to see nothing in history but facts in their multiplicity, which is a view that prevents us from seeing history as a manifestation of the spirit. On the other hand, we can look at it from the position of actual idealism, which presents history as 'the spiritualisation of the One (*spiritualizzazione dell'Uno*), which assumes the

80 Ibid., p. 192.

81 Ibid., p. 192.

82 Ibid., p. 192.

fact as an act, and thus assumes it in time.'[83] The dialectic of history, according to Gentile, consists precisely in this, in the actualisation of multiplicity as unity. The historical antinomy of the spirit thus finds its resolution 'in the idea of a process as a unity which multiplies, but remains unified: history as ideal and eternal at the same time.'[84] Gentile finds support for this in the concept of the 'solid circle' (*circoli solidi*), according to which philosophy is inseparable from its history. Philosophy implies the necessity of its own history because philosophy as such is an outcome that requires a certain preparation and development that takes place over time. The history of philosophy, in turn, implies philosophy as a result of its own flow over time and development. 'Philosophy and its history, taken together, are a single process of the spirit',[85] explains Gentile.

Gentile also points out that the history of philosophy is made up of what has been philosophised — in other words, it is the history of acts of philosophising. Awareness of this brings us closer to understanding Gentile's argument that 'the identity of philosophy and its history is the typical form and climax of the transformation of temporal history into eternal history, or rather of the facts of spirit into concepts or spiritual acts — the climax because philosophy is the highest and most concrete form of spiritual activity, which can judge all others, and yet is not subject to anything.'[86] Gentile claims that 'to evaluate philosophy is to philosophise.'[87] Although the facts of philosophy belong to the past, when we think of them, they are inevitably transformed into acts. When we, in studying someone else's philosophy, immerse ourselves in the structure of arguments, we, by our spiritual efforts, live them anew with those by whom they were created. These acts, directed by

83 Ibid., p. 198.

84 Ibid., p. 199.

85 Ibid., p. 202.

86 Ibid., p. 204.

87 Ibid., p. 204.

us towards the comprehension of philosophy, are timeless — in other words, they are eternal.[88]

To show the uniqueness of the example of the history of philosophy, Gentile examines four kinds of other activities of the spirit, which the thinker argues have no history. These are art, religion, science, and 'life' (*la vita*), understood as 'the will and practice'.[89] What are the fundamental differences between philosophy and these spiritual practices? The key difference between art and philosophy is that art expresses only the world of the artist, completely detached from the real world and created by the will of the creator of the artistic work. Art strives for subjectivity (as opposed to philosophy, which strives for objectivity). The essence of art is the free creativity of the artist, poet or writer. It has a lyrical character. Gentile offers this striking example: 'Try to remove Leopardi's soul from his world, try to read his poems and prose, not to immerse yourself in his feelings and emotions, but to learn his philosophy through rational arguments, and Leopardi's poetry is destroyed'.[90] Such an understanding of art makes any construction of the history of art as such problematic, since art, as a maximally individual act of the spirit, hardly lends itself to any logical categorisation and typification according to one or another feature. It should be clear here that Gentile is by no means trying to belittle art,

88 A clear illustration of the fundamental character of philosophy in Gentile's framework is the definition given by him in his late work (published in 1933) *Introduction to Philosophy*: 'Philosophy could be defined as the effort made by reflective thought to attain the critical validity of truths which are the domain of reason, those truths which everyone naturally feels and which constitute the solid structure of the mentality which serves to support everyone in order to live'. Giovanni Gentile, *Introduzione alla filosofia* [Introduction to Philosophy], (Florence: G. C. Sansoni, 1952), p. 1.

89 Camille Schuwer, Gentile's French contemporary, in his analysis of Modern Idealism presented a classification of Gentile's spirit activities in terms of the traditional Hegelian dialectic: art as absolute object, religion as absolute subject, philosophy as synthesis of absolute subject and absolute object. Schuwer, 'La pensée italienne contemporaine L'idéalisme actuel: Giovanni Gentile', p. 86.

90 Gentile, 'Teoria generale dello spirito como atto puro', p. 212.

which is an important element in the dialectical life of the spirit. He only tries to make the case that art as a type of spiritual activity can never be historical in any other way than as an exhibit in a museum or a gallery (categorisation by genre, in the case of works of writing). 'When we look at art, we do not see its history; when we look at history, we do not see art,'[91] Gentile concludes.

A similar reasoning is applied by Gentile to religion, which, he argues, 'is the exact opposite of art'.[92] Religion presupposes the absolute unknowability of the object, which is intolerant not only of the presence of an active subject, but also of the presence of objects.[93] In the actualist understanding, its history is as impossible as the history of art.[94] History is a process of the development of the spirit, and this process requires a subjectivity that develops. As Gentile argues, in the case of religion, the subject plays no role, has no value. The spirit, however, cannot completely abstract from its own subjectivity. According to Gentile, 'in its religiosity the spirit is immovable; it is set in motion only through the continuous overcoming of its own religious aspect and its absorption in philosophy'.[95] According to actual idealism, the history of religion, in its rational reading, devalues the religious content of religion itself by striving towards philosophy. On the other hand, when considering religion in terms of its specificity, we cannot

91 Ibid., p. 216.

92 Ibid., p. 216.

93 Here Gentile stipulates that only a monotheistic confession can be a truly religious feeling, but not polytheism in any way. The philosopher realises that his argumentation does not apply to polytheistic cults, but according to his reasoning they are not quite religion, because in them the object is not opposed to the subject with all certainty and the possibility of differentiating objects is allowed.

94 Gentile returns to the discourse on art and religion in an article of the same name in 1923: 'Art and religion are two opposite poles: on the one hand an infinite subject; on the other, an infinite object. One infinity excludes the other. A poet finds peace in his heart; a saint finds there only emptiness and turns his gaze to the distant sky'. Giovanni Gentile, 'Art et religion' [Art and Religion], *Revue de Métaphysique et de Morale*, 30, no. 4 (Oct.-Dec. 1923), p. 491.

95 Gentile, 'Teoria generale dello spirito como atto puro', p. 217.

speculate about its history, because the religious worldview does not presuppose development. If we approach art and religion from the point of view of the dialectical development of the spirit, we find ourselves in the sphere of the influence of philosophy. A truly dialectical history of art and religion is a history of philosophy.[96]

Having separated philosophy from art and religion, Gentile goes further and examines the specificity of science. It would seem that science should be closer to philosophy than the previous two spheres of spiritual activity because, like philosophy, it is a strictly rational endeavour. The key difference between science and philosophy, according to Gentile, is that science is not universal. 'Every science is one of many, and therefore specific',[97] the Italian philosopher writes. Once science begins to go beyond its own subject field, it becomes philosophy. Since modern science is naturalistic, it gravitates towards materialistic philosophy. Another important difference is the fact that science assumes its own object, which is assumed to exist before it is studied. Any change in the above-mentioned state of affairs (for example, a shift to the position that the object is created by the subject) transforms the scientific worldview into a philosophical one. Gentile also notes that science is dogmatic: 'It cannot prove its two fundamental premises: 1) that its object exists and 2) that perceptions, the primordial and substantive fact of cognition, which are in direct relation to the object, are undeniable'.[98]

96 As Evelyne Buissière rightly points out, in Gentile's actualism 'the history of philosophy is not the same history as all the rest; it is the truth of the historical feeling for everything that has a history'. By means of the *circoli solidi* Gentile closes the history of philosophy and philosophy itself in one infinite process of mutual understanding. Ultimately, the process of philosophising throughout the history of philosophy is contained in the act of philosophising 'here and now'. See Evelyne Buissière, 'Éternité de l'esprit et actualité de la pensée de Hegel à gentile' [The Eternity of the Spirit and the Actuality of Thought from Hegel to Gentile], Les *Études philosophiques*, no. 3, Emmanuel Lévinas (1996–2006) (July 2006), p. 391.

97 Gentile, 'Teoria generale dello spirito como atto puro', p. 219.

98 Ibid., p. 220.

Philosophy, unlike science, is genuinely critical — it explains reality in its totality, checking every position and every aspect. Science is thus 'the weakest and most naive form of philosophy'.[99] What Gentile writes about science is not just about the natural sciences. According to actual idealism, any scientific approach suffers from the above-mentioned defects. All sciences work with presumed reality, not with presumed spirit, so they do not understand the higher order of spirit, which consists in the synthesis of unity and multiplicity. Their reality turns out to be a chaotic multiplicity. This is why the history of science is impossible — if only because there is no 'science' as such, there is only a plurality of different sciences with different subject areas. There is, as a rule, no connection between the sciences. The history of science, in turn, is only possible when it 'does not regard science as science in its particularities and dogmatism'.[100] According to Gentile, the history of science, like the history of art and the history of religion, is possible only in the form of a history of philosophy. He draws a number of parallels between science and religion, pointing out that science bows to the reality assumed before it with the same sense that religion bows to its mysterious God. There is also much in common between science and art, in particular the pure phenomenality of the subjective, 'as fragmentary as the poet's imagination'.[101] A true synthesis of all these kinds of spiritual life can only be achieved by 'an act of the spirit, which alone is real as the inseparable unity of subject and object, the unity whose process is philosophy in its history'.[102]

The final important concept, distinct from philosophy, that Gentile examines is 'life, practical activity, the will'.[103] The philosopher argues that the opposition between theoretical and practical origins is not only unproductive, it is not useful at all. The main mistake of

99 Ibid., p. 221.

100 Ibid., p. 223.

101 Ibid., p. 224.

102 Ibid., p. 225.

103 Ibid., p. 225.

all pre-Christian philosophy was precisely the opposition of spirit to nature, theory to practice. Christian philosophy, for all its profound spiritual intuition, which Gentile acknowledges, introduced the notion of grace, which made it impossible to comprehend the spirit as will. From the point of view of actual idealism, all this seems an outdated perspective. According to Gentile, life, which can be understood both from a spiritual and a natural point of view, is a reality that generates both the will and the intellect. Will and intellect are identical with each other, they are inseparable.[104] The division into the practical and the theoretical, the vital and the scientific, is explained by Gentile as comprehending the concrete in one case and the abstract in the other. 'To speak of death and to die are different things',[105] the philosopher explains. Spiritual life, being distinct from philosophy,

104 This discourse on *la vita* might lead the reader to a suggestive analogy between Gentile's actualism and Henri Bergson's 'life force', which for our purposes is not quite correct in view of the fact that Bergson introduces an opposition between intellect and instinct according to his theory, intellect by its very nature is not adapted and not meant to comprehend life. Much closer to this comprehension is the instinct, which is an operational, non-intellectual capacity of the spirit. Accordingly, philosophy, in Bergson's view, relies predominantly on the sphere of intuition, which is an instinct conscious in relation to itself that has no practical concerns. Gentile's picture of the world is essentially rational (and in this he follows Hegel) — thought is the absolute form, spirit is the act, assuming itself in the multiplicity of objects. Bergson wrote that the philosopher 'must sympathise' — he has an essentially artistic model of knowledge, and Gentile has a scientific-rational model (albeit essentially idealistic, derived from the premise about the absolute reality of the spirit). Another analogy the reader may ponder is the irrationalism of Arthur Schopenhauer, yet there are few parallels here as well — his 'World as Will' is illogical and unconscious, and, moreover, the concepts of 'spiritual' and 'material' cannot be applied to it, it is a kind of spontaneous urge and aspiration. When Gentile speaks of *la vita*, of life, he points out that the practical and the theoretical cannot be opposed. The will and the intellect are inseparable — this is the fundamental difference between Gentile and Schopenhauer, whose will is irrational. The apprehension of life is the apprehension of the concrete and the apprehension of the scientific-theoretical is the apprehension of the abstract, but, in any case, both are apprehended consciously-intellectually.

105 Gentile, 'Teoria generale dello spirito como atto puro', p. 227.

exists in the form of philosophy. Placed before the mind as a reality external to its experience, it can only be perceived in philosophical form. 'Philosophy is thus the immanent substance of every form of spiritual life',[106] concludes Gentile.[107]

Having clarified the exclusivity of philosophy as a form of spiritual activity, Gentile comes to formulate the key points of the doctrine of actual idealism. The following are the resulting propositions of *The Theory of Mind as Pure Act* and the foundation for Gentile's social philosophy, which is crucial to the opening of our study and the justification of its key theses. 'We can summarise our doctrine as a theory according to which spirit, the spiritual reality, is an act that assumes its object in a plurality of objects, reconciling their plurality and objectivity in its own unity as a subject. A theory that derives every limit of space and time and every external condition from spirit',[108] writes Gentile. History plays a key role in the system of actual idealism — the role of reality in its concreteness, of the basis for the absolute freedom of the spirit. Thus, Gentile's fundamental ontology presupposes a single reality, a single primordiality in the concreteness of which multiplicity is possible. The subject who knows and is aware of the whole, knows and is aware of itself as a whole, as a reality, as one. In addition, the system of actual idealism assumes an absolute formalism (*formalismo assoluto*). Genuine science, according to Gentile, must rise to the recognition of reality as spirit. If we consider the transcendental activity of spirit as a form, then there is nothing outside this form, including matter as external and inherently assumed in relation to spirit. Spirit

106 Ibid., p. 228.

107 A British contemporary of Gentile interprets this statement of actual idealism as the claim that 'philosophy is the highest form of self-consciousness, the perfect form of experience, and since experience is all that can be real, philosophy is the only reality'. J. A. Smith, 'The Philosophy of Giovanni Gentile', *Proceedings of the Aristotelian Society, New Series*, 20 (1919–1920), p. 74. This seems, however, to be too radical an interpretation.

108 Gentile, 'Teoria generale dello spirito como atto puro', p. 230.

as an act supposes everything.[109] Thought turns out to be the absolute form. Grounded in these positions, Gentile comments on a number of philosophical problems.

If one proves a theoretical position to be incorrect, no one will support it. Gentile applies the same logic to practical (in other words, moral) errors, because the will is identical to the intellect, moreover the former is a concreteness of the latter. From the position of actual idealism we cannot perceive the world as external to us. Its laws are therefore our laws, which is where Gentile deduces the notion of duty (*dovere*), so central to his social philosophy. He poses the questions: 'What is duty if not the unity of our law and the universal law?'[110] The separation of the self from the whole, egoism, is a manifestation of the absence of morality in man. As moral consciousness strengthens in the process of self-knowledge and self-consciousness of the spirit, so does the spiritual understanding of life. Evil, pain, egoism, errors, immorality are not something that must completely disappear from the world in the process of revealing reality as a concept-in-itself (*conceptus sui*), but rather they must be eternally present in the world, because without them it is impossible to know good, pleasure, truth, and morality; they

109 Here it seems important to comment on the fundamental difference between Gentile's actual idealism and the German 'philosophy of life' (*Lebensphilosophie*). The latter arose in opposition to the traditional idea of 'reason' and thus to German classical philosophy. Dilthey, Scheler, Spengler, and Simmel all rejected traditional metaphysics. For example, Simmel believed that life follows not a rational, but a 'vital' logic; it is impossible to define life precisely, but it can be understood as 'constantly transcending boundaries'. It is in this that the meaning of life lies, which life cannot possess in itself. Dilthey sought to 'get closer to the mystery of life' using methods of descriptive psychology, comparative psychology of personality, the method of analysis of human life objectivation. Spengler's philosophy of life attempted to 'cast a more open mind' on world history, to see 'the spectacle of a plurality of cultures', each with 'its own form, its own idea, its own life, its own death'. Gentile's actualism, by contrast, is largely derived from the German classical tradition. It has its own unique characteristics, which make it a philosophical concept in its own right, but in fact its main historical and philosophical source is Hegel's rational Idealist philosophy.

110 Gentile, 'Teoria generale dello spirito como atto puro', p. 235.

play the role of the non-existence of the good reality. The goodness of spirit, by virtue of the latter's activity, is derived from the spirit's inner absorption of its own 'inner enemy'. A spirit which has stagnated, petrified, ceased to develop, is not the spirit in full—it becomes nature, the immovable world. Thus, there is no absolute good and no absolute evil. Evil acts as a means for the absolutely formal realisation of good.

Postage stamp from the Republic of Italy in memory of Giovanni Gentile, 1994

Gentile then draws a series of conclusions regarding the 'I', the 'self'. The 'self' is a spiritual reality, an identity of self with itself. The 'self' duplicates itself and finds itself in the other. From this dialectic of the 'self' and the other Gentile deduces the reality of the subject as pure subject, the reality of the object as pure object, the reality of spirit as the unity of the subject and the immanence of the object in the subject. The philosopher poses these questions: 'If there is no subject, then what can think? If there is no object, then what will the thinker think about?'[111] Indeed, our thinking presupposes subjectivity as such, the 'I' as a person. At the same time, as Gentile showed in the beginning of *The Theory of Mind as Pure Act*, cognition is impossible without the

111 Ibid., p. 239.

identity of subject and object. Plurality in the anthropological sense thus derives from the self-differentiation of the 'I'. Hence, the real synthesis in the actualist dialectics is not the synthesis of the subject and object (as thesis and antithesis), but 'only the subject, the real subject realised in the process by means of which it overcomes the ideality of the pure abstract subject and the accompanying ideality of the pure abstract object'.[112] 'This synthesis as a concrete reality of self-consciousness is a process which appears not as a fact, but as an act, a living and eternal act: to truly reflect on something is to realise it',[113] Gentile concludes.

Deepening the anthropological aspect of *The Theory of Mind as Pure Act*, the philosopher questions the self-realisation of the creative spirit, which appears as the realm of man (*regnum hominis*), which in turn is the fullness of freedom and dominion over nature. For us, nature appears as 'the eternal past in our eternal present (*l'eterno passato del nostro eterno presente*), the iron necessity of the past and the absolute freedom of the present'. The world appears to us as an eternal history in which man's ever-evolving triumph over the forces of nature is recorded. We subjects, the plurality of the 'I', are not inherently what we are supposed to become, but we become what we are supposed to become by supposing ourselves in our acts. In the acts we perform. The 'deep breath of the universal'[114] is in our self-awareness.

Gentile concludes with an answer to a crucial question for our study, namely the distinction between actual idealism and mysticism. Fascism in general, and its intellectual and ideological side in particular, has been characterised by some scholars as irrational, placing emphasis on religious and mystical foundations. If we take Gentile's actual idealism as the philosophical basis for the doctrine of Fascism,[115] then

112 Gentile, 'Teoria generale dello spirito como atto puro', p. 239.

113 Ibid., p. 240.

114 Ibid., p. 242.

115 This, it should be recalled, is one of the main hypotheses of this work.

this statement is false, at least with regard to the intellectual foundations of Fascism.

In fact, the actualist thesis of the world as a spiritual act (or act of thought) that synthesises multiplicity in the one, may seem mystical. Considering Gentile's philosophy, we can easily arrive at the same conclusion that Benedetto Croce came to: the supposed unity of the human and the natural, in which the human is divine and the divine is human, is a mystical concept. Gentile agrees that both actual idealism and mysticism claim that everything is one. However, the mystic loses the individual in the 'dark night of the soul' (*notte oscura dell'anima*), and enthuses about the infinite. The action becomes inexplicable. The mystic's absolute reality is devoid of subjectivity—it is an absolute object. 'Idealism reconciles all differences, but, unlike mysticism, does not erase them, it accepts the finite no less decisively than the infinite, and differences no less firmly than the totality',[116] Gentile explains. Actual idealism proceeds from the self, the spirit manifests itself through the acts of the subject. 'I am not I, without being "I think"; and that "I think" is always unified insofar as it is "I". Plurality always belongs to the abstractly assumed content of consciousness; in reality it is always reconciled with the unity of the "I". Genuine history is not that which unfolds in time, but that which is eternally assembled in the act of thinking in which it truly manifests itself',[117] the philosopher concludes.

2.2. The Practical Philosophy of Gentile. Ethics and the State. The Role of Science and Philosophy. Political Philosophy

Having reviewed Gentile's epistemology and ontology, as well as the introduction to the philosopher's anthropology in *The Theory of Mind as Pure Act*, we move on to an analysis of the Italian thinker's practical philosophy, which we need to understand in order to proceed to a

116 Ibid., p. 255.

117 Ibid., p. 265.

consideration of his political philosophy. The key work of Gentile's to which we will turn in this context is *Genesis and Structure of Society*, written by the philosopher in August-September 1943 and published after his death. It is one of the last texts written by Giovanni Gentile. In many ways it can therefore be seen as the sum of his convictions regarding practical philosophy.

As has been demonstrated earlier, actual idealism presupposes a unity of thought and action, knowledge and will, theory and practice. In our everyday lives, we think and make decisions that enable us to cope with certain problems. However, because everything is one, we cannot see our reality as external to us. Thus, all our actions have a moral and ethical character, and can be judged in terms of the categories of responsibility and duty. 'The essence of ethics lies in the act of thought, in which the whole moral world resides',[118] Gentile writes. By an 'act of thought' the philosopher means the self-consciousness of the individual, 'the *a priori* synthesis of opposites (subject and object)'[119] which is the nature of the individual human being, his 'I'. The individual is only fully revealed in interaction with others, only through the other can he rise above the self-personal to the self-ideal. What then is his 'I', his ego in a practical sense?

Gentile agrees with Aristotle's famous dictum that man is a political animal. Some thinkers imagine man as the ultimate paragon of the individual as the singular, the sum of which constitutes human society. According to Gentile, such social atomism, which conceptually does not recognise society as a whole but presents it as a mechanical agglomeration of atomic individuals, is the embodiment of a materialistic spirit that kills all values, all ethics, all morality. This kind of social ontology inevitably places the individual in the position of being controlled by external conditions, and thus essentially deprived of freedom. 'The human experience of humanity is the experience of his

118 Giovanni Gentile, *Genesi e struttura della società* [Genesis and Structure of Society], (Florence: Editore Arnoldo Mondadori, 1954), p. 37.

119 Ibid., p. 37.

Ego, which speaks and sings, thinks and feels, desires and wills, and altogether constitutes its own reality through its continuous activity',[120] Gentile writes. He argues that man's spiritual life is unique and deeply individual, but at the same time always, where there is an 'I', there is also a 'We'. In the values we share. In the language we speak. In the art we admire. Furthermore, according to Gentile, the 'we' always precedes the 'I': 'The community to which the individual belongs is the foundation of his spiritual existence, it speaks with his mouth, feels with his heart, thinks with his brain'.[121] This is the intrinsic law of man's existence in society. The inner voice, with which we check our intentions and our feelings, is the voice of the ideal, the inner 'voice of the people' (*vox populi*). When we perform acts, we act not only in our own name, but as 'interpreters' of the collective: 'The Italian, who feels that he is Italian, speaks for all Italy; the man speaks for humanity; the father for all fathers; the son for all sons, the soldier for all soldiers, and so on — everyone for everyone'.[122] How can this not contradict the uniqueness of human individuality? Gentile, in his social philosophy, applies to man the same argument as he does to spirit in ontology — man combines unity and multiplicity. We are given a plurality of individuals as individuals and, at the same time, the ideal 'we' of the community. In the individual, these two elements, universality and individuality, coincide and manifest themselves in acts.[123]

120 Ibid., p. 42.

121 Ibid., p. 44.

122 Ibid., p. 47.

123 In this context, it is worth recalling Gentile's attitude towards the Renaissance, as a historian of philosophy. He noted that there was certainly much in the Italian Renaissance that was bright and filled the souls of Italians with pride, but that all aspirations, both philosophical and practical, were highly individualistic. This was the reason why strength deserted the Italians — Italy at the time, not being a nation in the full sense, not having a single state, did not meet the actualist requirement of the unity of the individual and the state, as the necessary social component was absent. Hence the contrast between 'old Italy' (pre-Risorgimento) and the 'new Italy' that emerged during the Risorgimento period and continued during the Fascist period. It is for this reason that Gentile, for all his

When Gentile talks about the human being, he does not talk in empirical categories of space and time; the human being in actual idealism is always a manifestation of the spirit. When he speaks of community, he does not speak of a community as an empirical fact, the accidental cohabitation of individuals in a particular locality, but of an ideal community, the essence of which lies in shared values, principles, language, and identity. Extending the scope of the discourse, Gentile argues that the dual ideal nature of the individual gives rise to civilisation, which manifests itself in human consciousness and self-awareness. Self-awareness is not given to us as a natural attribute of the mind — it is always the result of working on oneself. The individual gravitates towards the ideal, the universal, and through work (through acts) advances towards the comprehension of universal truths and values. The individual is not born human to the fullest extent, he develops in the process of his life. Gentile says that we only see new-born babies as individuals with rights because we expect them to become free creative individuals in the future — so we give them certain advances. Sometimes they let us down and do not live up to expectations. 'Sometimes it is worth limiting the rights of adults as well, limiting to the necessary extent society's recognition of their individuality',[124] notes Gentile. The essence of the Italian philosopher's discourse on the individual in society is that simply being born in space and time is not enough to be considered an individual. To become fully human, we acquire a self-consciousness, gaining through it a sense of self and subjecting reality to ourselves. We rise above multiplicity to universality. If

admiration for Dante and Bruno, draws a direct line of historical continuity to Fascism from the Risorgimento, but not from earlier. For him it is the Italy conceived by Mazzini that is authentic. For more details see section 'Humanism Reborn and Fulfilled: From Positivism to Giovanni Gentile's Actualism' of chapter 'Philosophy and Revolution: Italian Vichianism and the "Renaissance Shame"' in Rocco Rubini, *The Other Renaissance. Italian Humanism Between Hegel and Heidegger*, (Chicago, IL: The University of Chicago Press, 2014), pp. 84–104.

124 Gentile, *Genesi e struttura della società*, p. 51.

we do not do this, then we do not deserve the rights that are ascribed to us. As individuals with our own particularities, in the process of actual universalisation we make an effort to dissolve our non-ideal particularities into the morality and legitimacy of the human as a whole, which in turn manifests the immanence of community to us. 'Man cannot stand firmly on the solid ground of the private without having ascended to the free air of the universal and of the affirmation of himself in the world of freedom',[125] Gentile concludes.

The next notion, important for Gentile's practical philosophy, is character. He redefines it as such: 'Character is the constancy of the will (*constanza del volere*): the constancy that endows human volition with unity, necessity, rationality, universality'.[126] Our character gives us the strength to not change our beliefs, to not contradict ourselves, to overcome difficulties and not abandon our goals before they are translated into action. Character is of a spiritual nature — it allows us to manifest a unity of will in individual acts. It is the organic unity and completeness of the individual will. To be human is to live consciously, in other words, to manifest character. By virtue of its ideality, character has a timeless nature, anticipating actual existence. One of the most important corollaries of character which Gentile stresses is civic courage (*il coraggio civile*). It is a necessary quality for life in society. It consists in 'Unshakable fidelity to the dictates of the conscience, in word and deed, and in assuming full responsibility for one's actions and one's relations with others'.[127] The characterless man betrays not only himself but also society, rejecting the truths that are the source of life and values.

As has been described above, our human ego has an alter intrinsic to it, namely *socius*, which, according to Gentile, is for the ego not an object but a subject like itself. In the practical philosophy of actual idealism, the ego-in-itself and the non-ego-in-itself are nothing. They

125 Ibid., p. 53.

126 Ibid., p. 53.

127 Ibid., p. 60.

cannot presuppose each other. We without the world and the world without us are a void in which there is no creative potency. But the synthesis resulting from the dialectic of the ego and its alter *socius* allows us to rise to our subjectivity, to true humanity and conscious freedom. Uniting with the *socius*, the ideal inner community, our ego takes on a shared spiritual life with it. This manifests itself even in the process of our thinking, for in the inner dialogue there is always a 'speaker' as well as his invisible 'interlocutor'. A man without an interlocutor is only half a man, and therefore he is nothing. Our inner companion is the voice of our 'We', the transcendental society. The dialectical essence of society is not the mechanical physical coexistence in a particular territory, but precisely this mutual dialogue, a constant exchange between the bearers of consciousness. 'A flock of sheep is not a society',[128] Gentile gives the example. 'The genuine beginning of society is thus ideal. It is generated by the immanent dialectic of the spiritual act as a synthesis of subject and object'.[129] According to Gentile, before the transcendental society is established, the human being is unconscious and unknowable. Just as it is impossible to look at that which precedes self-consciousness, so it is impossible to consider the human before the point of formation of transcendental society. Before an 'awakening' we can only discover a dormant and lifeless universe.

According to actual idealism, to be human is to think. In a broad sense, it means to understand oneself, to understand the world around oneself, to understand the ultimate foundations of things, to understand God. It is something that all human beings strive for, consciously or unconsciously. Genuine understanding consists in 'the reduction of external otherness to inner otherness'.[130] This genuine understanding is 'the unbreakable chain of love that connects us to our fellow man'.[131]

128 Ibid., p. 68.

129 Ibid., p. 71.

130 Ibid., p. 77.

131 Ibid., p. 77.

It requires 'fidelity, commitment, acceptance',[132] in other words, it is not a detached state of consciousness, but a constant practical action. 'Love is not a consequence, but the finished perfection of knowledge',[133] Gentile stresses. What we love, be it a person, an activity, or a thing, is the centre of our attention, the object of a permanent active concern. 'It is absolutely true that it is necessary to love in order to understand, but we must add that it is equally necessary to understand in order to love',[134] the philosopher asserts. Gentile thus deduces that our thinking is a necessary component of our ethical experience. What the philosopher calls moral reasoning in turn generates a sense of duty — it is not the reflection on duty that is true, but rather the feeling. Duty in Gentile's system is an imperative category. The whole multiplicity of duty (if we approach it as external to us) is ultimately reduced to one unique and at the same time unified duty for all of us — duty as our inner reality and inner obligation; good as the reality we can achieve through our creative activity; values determined by the actuality of the spirit; overcoming the eternal evil that is nothing ('the unknowable chaos of a violent nature, mechanism, spiritual darkness, ugliness, falsehood') against which humanity has been struggling throughout history. Evil is the pressure of the material, 'which clips our wings and prevents us from flying to the heaven to which the spirit calls us'.[135] What, then, is good? 'If we want to call the good by a name that will shine before the gaze of humanity, let us call it freedom',[136] Gentile sums up the ethical digression.

Turning directly to social philosophy, Gentile provides definitions of state, nation and law. 'The State is a general and universal will',[137] the philosopher writes. The state is the manifestation of the concrete

132 Ibid., p. 77.

133 Ibid., p. 78.

134 Ibid., p. 79.

135 Ibid., p. 88.

136 Ibid., p. 88.

137 Ibid., p. 88.

will of the nation. What is a nation? It is not a common land, some community with its own customs, language, and traditions—all of which, according to Gentile, are the 'matter' of the nation, but not its 'form'. A nation exists only when 'people are aware of its "matter", accept it in their hearts as the substantive content of their own spiritual basis, the real object of the national will'.[138] The state, whether it is only 'conceived' and ideal or already present, is a concrete manifestation of this will. Nationality, in its turn, is a secondary consequence of the existence of the state. Thus, in the social philosophy of actual idealism, nation is primary as form and the state is its concrete expression which allows nationality to exist in a civic sense. So, what is law? For Gentile, it is 'the will of the State'.[139] Law exists insofar as there is a State, for outside the State there is no State will, and therefore no law. In law, the citizen 'finds his boundary, the assumption of his existence, and the condition of his freedom'.[140] Law is a decision already made by the State as a universal will. It does not limit the absolute freedom of human spiritual acts, but affirms it.

Gentile goes on to argue for the contrast between the government (*governo*) and the governed (*governate*—citizens who do not participate in decision-making at the level of public administration), which is falsely interpreted as a dualism between the state and its citizens. The fallacy of this opposition is that it is essentially an abstract rule devoid of concreteness: the state makes the laws and oversees their implementation, the citizens, who fall under the authority of these laws, are subject to them. However, without the moral consent of the governed to the fairness of the laws which are established and enforced, no government can stand. The fact of consent and public approval removes this false opposition. The rule is universal, whether the government

138 Ibid., p. 88.

139 Ibid., p. 89.

140 Ibid., p. 90.

is democratic or absolutist, liberal or authoritarian.[141] These oppositions also seem to Gentile to be very arbitrary: 'The philosopher must always stress that power must not destroy freedom and that freedom must not claim to operate outside of power. Neither of these notions can exist on its own; the need for their synthesis is a consequence of the essentially dialectical nature of the spiritual act'.[142]

All political forms, according to Gentile, are only responding to certain challenges of the time, solving historical problems. The problems set before Syndicalism and Communism are essentially the same as those that liberalism tackled a few centuries before them. Ultimately, they must all arrive at the same thing — an affirmation of the plurality of individuals in the spiritual unity of the state. The struggle against the state, falsely enforced by individual political ideologies, is a road to nowhere, to emptiness, to 'nothingness'. The origin of this ideological error is clear — it is a materialist ontology, according to which there is only a mass of individuals, but never a whole. There is nothing in this that has anything to do with freedom; referring to Mazzini, 'a liberal who understood what freedom is',[143] Gentile shows that a man who understands his own nature is free as part of a whole if the whole is free, and unfree as part of a whole if the whole is unfree. The whole pathos of the emancipatory struggle of the Risorgimento era derives from this conviction, which Gentile borrows from the liberal idealists of the nineteenth century: 'the individual can only be free in a free state. Or, more precisely, the free individual is a free State, since

141 In his *Introduction to Philosophy*, Gentile expounds this thesis more firmly: 'The State in its essential interiority is not only an ethical will, but also a self-consciousness in general; and hence a complete and perfect humanity. On the contrary, the State is often supplanted by the government and, moreover, by the physical persons in whom this government is embodied. And what people fail to see is that these persons and the government itself are not the State, but only elements of the form in which the State is realised'. Giovanni Gentile, *Introduzione alla filosofia* [Introduction to Philosophy], p. 163.

142 Gentile, *Genesi e struttura della società*, p. 92.

143 Ibid., p. 98.

the State is not a relationship between individuals, but is contained in individuals, in the unity of the private and the universal that constitutes their individuality'.[144] The state, if it is indeed the concrete actuality of the will of the individuals, has the same limitations as the individual — in this sense it is ethical. It is only then that the universality of the laws relied upon by the State has authority. Thus, Gentile concludes that there is an inherent, intrinsic ethics in the state. From the thesis that the ethical state is a value, theocracy can be deduced. The Italian philosopher urges that we should not shy away from this, for if we accept the state as an actualisation of our will, we, in a sense, ascribe to it a divine nature. Ethics and morality are key attributes of the spirit. The state, embodying the spirit of the nation, cannot help but be moral. 'The spirit is morality, freedom',[145] Gentile argues. State institutions must protect manifestations of freedom — this is the moral duty of the state as a whole.

From the definition of nation, state, and law, Gentile moves on to an analysis of the interaction between the state and forms of social and spiritual life: economy, religion, and science. The philosopher starts from economics, which is a necessary practical activity of men and therefore of the State. Gentile understands the economic as practical in a broad sense, as an activity guided by the principle of utility, the success of which can be judged in terms of efficiency. His criteria of efficiency apply to animals as much as to humans, but with the difference that animals do not have the same understanding of freedom as humans alone have. Furthermore, animals may appear to be more 'utilitarian' than humans, driven by hedonistic principles, perceived mechanically (that is to say, instinctively). Generally speaking, this is true for economic activity as well — its purposive nature is also mechanical in its search for the best solution to this or that practical problem. However, the utility obtained by man and the utility obtained

144 Ibid., p. 98.

145 Ibid., p. 102.

by the animal are still essentially different. In the specifically human perception of utility, utility is *causa sui*—utility is not the surrounding objects, not the concrete results of labour, but the process through which we derive satisfaction. 'Happiness and joy in life lie in us, not in things',[146] Gentile writes.

Things do, however, have a role to play because human beings are simultaneously both souls and bodies. We work on our body to make it a better mechanism for actualising spiritual goals, to educate and spiritualise it. The body is thus a necessary element in the synthesis that is man as a creative subject. At the same time, the body still belongs to the pre-human, the realm of necessity, the realm of nature that knows no freedom. Along with it comes the realm of utility, coordinated mechanically. Without the body, immanent existence is impossible, but it still holds a subordinate state in relation to the spirit, is its instrument. 'Natural means mechanical, and mechanical means mathematical',[147] Gentile continues his reasoning. In fact, it is from here that the mechanical character of modern mathematical economics, with its strict determinism, its rigid causal relations, derives. 'Economic theory is pre-human; it is characteristic of the genuinely human will to constantly strive to intervene in this mechanism, to deviate from strict mathematical formulas in order to bring this mechanism in line with the changing demands of political life, governed according to the principle of freedom',[148] Gentile argues. The phrase 'political economy' has no meaning at all in terms of actual idealism—politics is the realm of spiritual freedom, economics is the realm of natural necessity. However, Gentile is not totally against all utilitarianism and hedonism, only against the baser natural drives. Utility and pleasure can also have a spiritual character, such as an understanding of utility based on freedom or the pleasure of knowledge. Ultimately, the Italian philosopher argues that the will of the state, like the human

146 Ibid., p. 108.

147 Ibid., p. 116.

148 Ibid., p. 116.

will, has a certain economic component, but 'it must be transcended, transformed in the light of freedom, endowed with ethical and spiritual values'.[149] Just as man is not a slave of nature, the state must not be a slave to economic processes.[150]

Turning to the relationship between the State and religion, Gentile argues that any power always balances between two opposites — a theocracy and a total separation of church and State in the spirit of pseudo-liberal democracy. The political life is in close relationship with the spiritual life, therefore the State cannot ignore the religious issue (namely the faith, beliefs and customs of the people), it has to find a solution. How to achieve this? Gentile sees a very natural alliance between the State and the Church. Because of the divine nature of the just state in the system of actual idealism there is in fact much in common between the two. However, Gentile makes an important distinction between positive and negative secularism. The latter is a consequence of base forms of utilitarianism and hedonism, whereas the former, by accepting the religious, transcends it and rises above it. Religion is a constructive element of the collective will that the state embodies. It cannot be absent, just as art and morality cannot be absent. State policy devoid of religious feeling is soulless and mechanistic. The religious is intrinsic to the moral.

The last important question on the nature of the State that Gentile addresses in this work is that of the relationship between the State and science. As has been shown in the consideration of questions of knowledge in *The Theory of Mind as Pure Act*, science, in order to overcome empirical particularities and its own dogmatism, must necessarily take a philosophical point of view. Philosophy, as the most perfect form

149 Ibid., p. 120.

150 Continuing Gentile's logic, one could argue with the same degree of certainty that the state should not be enslaved by economists who proceed from abstract mathematical schemes and dictate their vision of public policy from the theoretical prescriptions of neoclassical economics. In actual idealism, they are strictly subordinated to politicians and to those who understand 'science of spirit', who are able to consider political problems historically and philosophically.

of the actual manifestation of the spirit, permeates everywhere — in the air we breathe and in our thoughts, it shapes our worldview and our faith. 'Everyone is philosophical; philosophy runs in the streets as 'common sense', as man's awareness of himself, and of the world to which he belongs,'[151] Gentile writes. Thus, philosophy must inevitably be in some kind of contact with the state as the absolute form of the nation's self-awareness. As a rule, however, the relationship between the State and philosophers has been quite cool throughout history. The reason is that 'philosophy is the conscious pursuit of absolute knowledge and because, above all else, it requires unqualified freedom'.[152] According to Gentile, philosophy can criticise, control and judge any thought and any sphere of thought. Philosophers in the State tend to be the main critics of public policy. One could wonder why the State should not in principle dispense with philosophy, like religion, and deal with its own worldly problems? The answer, according to Gentile, is that the worldly affairs of the State include education and culture.[153] This plays a crucial role in the self-awareness of the whole. Indeed, Gentile glorifies the critical role which the philosopher plays: 'The philosopher should always be an apostle of the ideal, never a guardian and protector of the status quo'.[154] The Italian thinker even suggests that the phenomenon of 'state philosophy' is intrinsically harmful.[155]

Gentile also acknowledges that 'the essentially critical activity of philosophy includes the obligatory recognition of a certain positive

151 Gentile, *Genesi e struttura della società*, p. 128.

152 Ibid., p. 128.

153 This is where Gentile places education, grouping it with the sciences he criticised earlier such as economics and mathematics, as all these have their place in the system of sciences and human cognition in general.

154 Ibid., p. 132.

155 It is worth noting here that although Gentile's actual idealism was recognised as a state philosophy during the *ventennio* years, to which his *Doctrine of Fascism* stands as a monument, the philosopher himself never sought to personally benefit from the numerous public positions he held within the Fascist state; indeed, he rejected any attempt at direct material reward for his active public work.

content in every regime or specific organisation of the State in its historical actuality'.[156] The state, governed by specific public servants with their own philosophical convictions, is concrete in a particular space and historical time. The government makes decisions based on specific problematic situations. Even if the philosophy held by some officials is wrong, there cannot be nothing positive about it. 'In any case, whether we think philosophy is inside or outside the state, it remains indispensable to the state, because it is indispensable to human life itself. Without it, there can be no state, no religion, no art, no science, no morality... Philosophy is a constant vigilance and reflection on who we are and what we make of ourselves; a burning anxiety, a dissatisfaction that does not allow us to accept ourselves as we are and things as they seem',[157] Gentile concludes.

Having tackled the nature of the State, the philosopher moves on to international politics. He is immediately confronted with a conceptual problem: it would seem that an understanding of the state, identical with self-determination, free and infinite, should contradict the plurality of states. The freedom of the state seems absolute only in matters of domestic politics but not in matters of international politics. The infinity of the state also runs out the moment it finds its counterpart — another state.

In fact, according to Gentile, a plurality of states only exists if we view them in the abstract and in theory. Our relation to our State is comparable to that of a foreigner to his State, but not to our relation to a foreign State, which is for us the object of theoretical knowledge. There is only ever one true 'our' state — our own; only this state is given to us to the fullest extent of practical experience. Since we are a unique individual, we have one state. Gentile draws an analogy between the state and parents, whom we also do not choose. We, as a state, can recognise a foreign state by an act of our will. International

156 Gentile, *Genesi e struttura della società*, p. 133.

157 Ibid., pp. 134–135.

politics is always a never-ending process of self-realisation of the state as a unique entity. International agreements and normative acts of international law recorded on paper are 'decisions of the past', in other words, dead. The power of the state, its spiritual potency, is revealed in its active actuality, in its endless flow of life, in the 'eternal history of human social life'.[158] When one state impedes another in achieving its goals, states are engaged in conflicts — wars, which have many facets and can be fought by different means. Victory in a war is the recognition by one state of the will of another. 'The cause of war is dissension (*dissenso*), and its end is nothing less than the overcoming of dissension',[159] notes Gentile. When peace is restored, the citizens of the warring states resume cooperation and, in their solidarity, enrich their spiritual life through each other. The aspirations of the various warring countries, which want to expand their territories and resolve all future controversies without going back to war, are, according to Gentile, a grand illusion — 'sooner or later, all empires are in ruins'.[160] A 'universal state' cannot be built — 'unity is good, but it must take place in a plurality that includes all differences'.[161]

Returning to the question of history — not from the perspective of fundamental ontology, but from the perspective of practical philosophy — Gentile argues that the State, as a process in development, is at the same time history, because only in the State does the spirit manifest in its concreteness. 'The history of the State is the history of humanity as a true individuality, a unique universal subject; it is a process of the development of the unique,'[162] he writes. The state in the idealist sense is never finished — having a spiritual quality, it is always in the making. It is never immanent 'to the fullest extent'; moreover, 'the transcendence of the state is the reason why it belongs to the realm

158 Ibid., p. 138.

159 Ibid., p. 139.

160 Ibid., p. 139.

161 Ibid., p. 139.

162 Ibid., p. 140.

of freedom'.[163] As transcendent it has a divine character, but to worship it as purely immanent is nothing but idolatry. Specific historical eras do not deserve this reverence, because the state is in constant self-creation, sometimes reaching the extreme point of self-criticism, which finds its expression in revolution, defined by Gentile as 'the changing of state structure'.[164] Conservatives have always insisted on adherence to the existing norms, on stasis, and this, according to Gentile, is their fundamental error, because the political consciousness of citizens cannot be static, it is always developing, renewing and striving for something new. Political life is 'an eternal self-critique, an eternal revolution'.[165] This revolution happens invisibly, every day, with every new act taking place within the state.[166] Of course, in certain moments of crisis, uprisings and outbreaks of violence are possible, but they are rare. 'It is quite true that the history of the state is the history of its continuous revolution, the history of the process which truly constitutes the state',[167] Gentile concludes.

In the practical philosophy of actual idealism, the state cannot be a product of the human will. If the individual wants to create the state, he must 'possess' it, to ' be' the state in the idealist sense. It is inherent in us to feel that we belong to the State, that we share a common destiny, a unity of *res publica* and *res sua*. The latter, according to Gentile,

163 Ibid., p. 141.

164 Ibid., p. 142.

165 Ibid., p. 143.

166 Curiously, in 1919, in response to an accusation of conservatism by the liberal Mario Missiroli, Gentile replied that he wished to be 'more liberal than Wilson and more socialist than Lenin'. This harsh statement suggests that already at that time Gentile was in search of a kind of 'third way', not finding complete satisfaction in either liberalism or socialism. Sergio Romano, 'Giovanni Gentile, philosophe du Fascisme' [Giovanni Gentile, Philosopher of Fascism], *Vingtième Siècle. Revue d'histoire*, no. 21 (Jan.–Mar., 1989), p. 73. The constant readiness for new historical stages and accomplishments is characteristic of Gentile; in *Genesis and Structure of Society* he justifies it theoretically.

167 Gentile, *Genesi e struttura della società*, p. 144.

is the feeling of the political which contributes to the development of civilisation. He praises the 'new Italian system of representation' as a product of a 'new humanism', a humanism of culture that clears the way for a humanism of labour. For Gentile, the field of culture covers all forms of human activity—all intellectuals, scientists and artists need to develop a common consciousness with people of simpler, uncomplicated labour. 'The value of man must be judged by the quantity and quality of his work,'[168] Gentile sums up, withdrawing with his Syndicalist principles.

Giovanni Gentile at work, 1940s

The individual, in turn, is never a social atom—he is one with his family. The state must in every way support family policy—the human desire to have heirs, to produce a new generation. 'The love which creates a family is eternal; and this love is fully manifested in posterity',[169] writes Gentile. It is through the institution of the family that the moral sense in man manifests itself; it is essential for a healthy, living state.

168 Ibid., p. 147.

169 Ibid., p. 148.

Finally, Gentile's thought moves into the realm of the political. 'Politics is the activity of the spirit as a state'.[170] In order to understand politics as an actual experience immanent to human consciousness, he calls for the avoidance of all possible abstractions: laws imposed on the will; understanding the state as being outside the individual and not within the individual; treating self-consciousness not as an act of will and vice versa; separating theory and practice. For Gentile, the concrete experience of the political act is identical to the concrete experience of the ethical act. He draws this connection from the properties of the will which, in an infinite self-completion, encompasses the whole world of social relations. The political act is performed in eternity — being an act of the spirit and an act of conscious life, it has no empirical beginning and no end, no boundaries it cannot cross. The unchanging ideal goal of political life is the self-awareness of the spirit. Reaching this goal is an ethical task. Gentile presents ethics as the limit of the political, immanent in itself, but never fully uncovered. Ethics, as 'the form of conscious activity most appropriate to the nature of the spiritual act',[171] precedes politics — we cannot perform genuinely political actions without reference to ethics. Ethics is also a spur to political action.[172] According to Gentile, the avoidance of politics can only be explained by laziness and the absence of the ethical in man, and not by a desire to devote oneself to some 'higher realms' like art. Politics certainly requires courage, without which no 'realm of the spirit' can be built, and our awareness of the ethical gives us that courage.

Gentile explores in detail the logic of the individual's detachment from politics. Its origins lie in the division of life into 'private' and

170 Ibid., p. 149.

171 Ibid., p. 151.

172 As one of Gentile's English-speaking commentators very accurately pointed out, in the system of actual idealism, the free will of man is not 'the freedom of indifference'. We are free only when the will of our 'I' merges with the will of 'We', in which a truly ethical attitude towards the world is manifested. Valmai Burdwood Evans, 'The Ethics of Giovanni Gentile', *International Journal of Ethics*, 39, no. 2 (Jan., 1929), pp. 205–216.

'public' space. This division stems from the idea of the individual as an atomic individual with private interests that do not coincide with those of society. 'The truth is that in the state, everything abstractly "private" becomes "public" in a concrete situation',[173] the philosopher claims.[174] There is no sphere that the State does not concern itself with, as evidenced by the branches of law that regulate the norms of the relations of individuals with each other. The state, according to Gentile, is universal and transcendental — being in us from the beginning, it does not allow flight from itself. This unity of the individual with the state is presented in actual idealism as the natural order of things, characteristic of the spirit. Hence the natural link between politics and ethics.

In essence, according to Gentile, the exclusion of the individual from politics and the division of life into 'private' and 'public' was dictated by the desire to hide private interest from the state, thus reducing the scope of its powers. The philosopher gives the example of Catholic 'private' schools, which in many countries at the time were an 'alternative' branch of education alongside mainstream schools. Such a demand for exclusive, uncontrolled powers and opportunities is always a latent revolution against a particular state.

Thus there remains nothing truly 'private', nothing beyond the bounds of state intervention. If one takes this intermediate conclusion literally, one can imagine a tyrannical state that leaves no stone unturned in human freedom, completely crushing any expression of individuality. Yet Gentile notes that this is a one-dimensional, false conclusion.

173 Gentile, *Genesi e struttura della società*, p. 153.

174 Here it is possible to draw a parallel between the thought of the Italian Hegelian Gentile and the German 'philosopher of life' Oswald Spengler (1880–1936), who noted in his *Prussianism and Socialism* (1920) that in a genuine state (that is, in the German state, contrasted in this work with Great Britain) a 'private person' living exclusively in his own interests and not participating in political life is impossible. Furthermore, the subject participates in the life of the state as an inalienable part of the organism, not as a 'voting citizen'. For more details see: Oswald Spengler, *Preußentum und Sozialismus* [Prussianism and Socialism], (London: Arktos, 2021).

The truth is that one can say with the same degree of certainty that the individual completely absorbs the state, which is his will, universalised and absolutised, acquiring all the power of law himself. How is this possible? It is possible through a conscious active participation in the life of the state via institutions of representation — in other words, by actualising the political dimension of the individual.

In Gentile's system, the opposite of this understanding of politics is not even liberalism, but anarchism: the most consistent doctrine of denial of the state. Where the liberal languishes in halftones, the anarchist asserts emphatically his opposition to the existence of any social superstructure over the 'private'. The anarchist's 'no' to the state also means 'no' to the law, a logic that leads exclusively to violence as a method of interaction between individuals. Liberalism, on the whole, follows the same path, but less confidently. Ultimately, in both liberalism and anarchism there is no spiritual bond between individuals, no bond with the 'other' which is essentially intrinsic to the human spirit. The victory of one becomes a misfortune for the other, war becomes a norm of life. The two ideologies are a monstrous violation of the spirit that aspires to a conscious harmony of eternal unity, rather than to the unending conflict of its manifestations. Gentile reminds us that the highest manifestations of the human spirit have created the myth of the one Father, to whose reunion we painfully seek as we progress through human civilisation. War is not acceptable as a way of life, but only as a means to a new type of peace. Peace is always a social product; its maintenance is the task of the state. It is not possible to achieve peace by the police alone, it is not possible to achieve consensus by violence. Peace within a social organism is always the result of the successful functioning of a politics that gives a state the vitality that emanates from the caring hearts of its citizens. This vitality is the 'political feeling' (*sentimento politico*) that drives us to political action. It is not enough to understand the necessity of this action intellectually, theoretically; one must feel it, just as a mother feels love for her child, as something deeply immanent to our 'I'. 'The State is born in the transcendental rhythm of self-consciousness',[175] Gentile explains. When political feeling dries up, political action ceases to be sincere — it is emptied, the strength of the state wanes, and eventually the particular state dies.

It follows from such an understanding of politics that the genius of a single politician is closer to that of an actor, a philosopher, a saint, a hero. It is not the result of training, but a natural gift. Gentile agrees that training and experience are also necessary, but that the key to political achievement lies in intuition and creative power, often hidden. Usually, the first glimpses of this power emerge in the future politician as a child, in the relationships within the family. The child searches from an early age for his 'politics', a system of behaviour to achieve a goal, the need for which he feels innately. The political aspect, according to Gentile, manifests itself in all forms of human interaction. The role of the father in the family is a political role because within his home he embodies the 'state'. The creativity of artists also has a political character: rising from their pure subjectivity to the whole, their acts then return to themselves again, resulting in a work of art, a process, according to Gentile, entirely analogous to the political process. Politics manifests itself also in the work of the scientist, the researcher, the philosopher who conducts a transcendental dialogue with himself, setting concrete meaningful goals and achieving theoretical and practical results. The study of the scientist, his inner dialogue in which, according to Gentile, there is a mutual permeation of subject and object, in the course of which one gradually comes to understand the only true path of action — what is this if not politics? The results of research only matter when they are published — in other words, when they are manifested in society, when they resonate, when they have had an impact. This eternal aspiration towards the ideal, through which the self-consciousness of the spirit develops, also has political overtones (remember what was mentioned above about ethics

175 Gentile, *Genesi e struttura della società*, p. 161.

as the ideal limit of the political). The political also manifests itself in religious faith — not in the lower practical sense of popularising individual beliefs and flooding the state with popes, but in the higher, actual sense. 'Pure religious faith, in its essential content, is a form of conscious life in which the spirit aspires to an absolute object, which is the second moment of self-synthesis. This moment, taken by itself, is abstract, but in synthesis, in the unity of the opposites, it becomes real concretely',[176] Gentile explains. The object of religious faith is infinite and absolute. Faith itself is an irrelevant, abstract aspiration, but it is concretely embodied. The believer is never completely subjective, his aspiration to the universal is always alive within him, without which he is nothing. He feels complete when he receives the response of his God in his heart. The relationship between the believer and his God has a political, social model, because sincere faith always implies an inner law and an inner dialogue.

Unfortunately, the religious community is not always limited to acts of pure faith. As a rule, religions try to popularise their doctrine and actively engage in propaganda. Religious dogmatism often becomes a cause of intolerance. Theoretical and philosophical distinctions between truth and opinion do not play any role here — being sure of the steadfastness of his own truth, the believer seeks to convey it to everyone else. If the unbeliever cannot be 'saved', then his life has little value — all religious extremism grows out of this belief. Gentile is convinced that truth cannot be found in dogma — only in free thought. Of course, not all people have matured to the point of understanding the need for intellectual inquiry, but this does not mean that they need not be enlightened. To make his thought clear, the philosopher writes, 'Children are not adults yet, but they will become them'.[177] Unthinking people behave like children, but we love children and we teach them

176 Ibid., p. 167.

177 Gentile, *Genesi e struttura della società*, p. 173.

with patience. The same should be done with those who have not yet discovered all the qualities of the spirit.

Concluding his theoretical discourse on the political, Gentile argues that politics is our duty and our right. Without political participation our existence is essentially incomplete. As human beings, we are free to exercise our humanity in interaction with others. Moreover, it is our duty — not only because of the natural properties of human nature, human conscience and the state, but also because it is the duty of each of us to respect the right of the other. 'Participation in politics can be understood as a right that cannot be denied to anyone; but only because political life is a duty from which no one can escape',[178] Gentile argues. He fully agrees with his revered Mazzini: 'Life is neither a pleasure nor a right, but a duty'.[179]

The ideas discussed above give an insight into Gentile's practical philosophy in its theoretical form. However, the thinker would be inconsistent if he did not try to implement his ideas in practice, if he himself withdrew from political life and did not engage in a struggle for his ideals — for further movement towards the ideal limits of the ethical, towards the heights of the spirit, towards new forms of statehood. Being a man of consistency, Gentile undertook acts of a practical nature aimed at implementing the conceptual — he formulated and attempted to implement an educational reform and then, after leaving his ministerial position, he proposed a political doctrine in which many of the points of actual idealism are evident.

178 Ibid., p. 174.

179 Ibid., p. 174.

§3. Gentile and the Fascist Regime

3.1. The Pedagogical Aspect of Gentile's Philosophy. Educational Reform[180]

In 1917 Gentile was appointed professor of the history of philosophy at Sapienza University of Rome. In this role as a renowned Italian scholar, he gave a series of lectures in 1920 to schoolteachers in Trieste, which had been ceded to Italy under the 1920 Treaty of Rapallo. Gentile published his book *The Reform of Education* the same year, the contents of which was made up of a series of lectures on the subject inspired by the philosophy of actual idealism.

Gentile begins his argument with the necessity of developing education for the real formation of the Italian nation by referring to Giuseppe Mazzini, who called on 'the Italians of the future' to fight for 'independence, which is freedom and unity, and is what constitutes a nation.'[181] The nation, according to Gentile, is one with the ethical essence of the individual, and is embodied in the Absolute Will — in the State. The continued prosperity of the Italian nation depends on people with a strong self-awareness, the bearers of the destiny of the State.

Science, in turn, is national science — the notion that ideal science resides outside human life was vehemently denied by Gentile. 'Today's

180 For the main ideas of Gentile's pedagogical philosophy see Dmitry Moiseev, 'Педагогическая наука в философии Джованни Джентиле' [Pedagogical Science in the Philosophy of Giovanni Gentile], *Социальная философия науки. Российская перспектива. К юбилею В. С. Степина. Материалы конференции* [Social Philosophy of Science. Russian Perspective. For the Anniversary of V.S.Stepin. Conference papers], volume 5, section 4. STS — Epistemological Specifics of the Social Science, ed. I.T.Kasavin, A.Y.Antonovski, K.K.Momdzhyan, (Moscow: Alpha-M, 2014), pp. 30–33.

181 Giovanni Gentile, 'La riforma dell'educazione. Discorsi al maestri di Trieste' [The Reform of Education. Speeches to the Trieste teachers] in *Complete Words of Giovanni Gentile*, Volume VII, p.12.

science is not an indifferent object of the pure intellect'[182] but a self-consciousness produced by man through the actualisation of his own humanity, his culture, and the formation of his mind. If something called science does not shape one's identity, then it is not real science. Since the practice of science and education in schools is a spiritual activity, it is inseparable from the higher life of the nation, 'the spiritual breath of the glorious fatherland'.[183] For Gentile, a reformation of the educational system in the spirit of an actual idealism was a necessary step on the road to the further prosperity of Italy.

The philosopher notes that a person called a political or social animal 'must also be called the educatable animal'[184] (*animale educatore*). Making up a single social set (nation), individuals must educate each other, not only children, but also adults, because, according to Gentile, it is impossible for a person not to want to expand his intellectual load — learning is inherent to human beings. People are eager to learn, to search, to explore, to reach new heights of knowledge and skill. Teachers working with children, seeing in them fresh souls curious about the world, must find inspiration from this, must free themselves from the mechanical routine, from 'repeating the same story';[185] a teacher remains a teacher only when his work is a series of new events, new ways of presenting the universal to his students. Gentile's task in education is to form and educate free people, because 'a man is worthy to be called human when he owns himself, is capable of acting for which he is responsible, assimilates and develops ideas, when what he believes, accepts, and does truly comes from him'.[186] The teacher does his job well when the pupil learns from him and starts to think for himself and to think originally. This can be called the basis of freedom, which, in turn, is the result of education. The teacher awakens in the

182 Ibid., p. 15.

183 Ibid., p. 16.

184 Ibid., p. 28.

185 Ibid., p. 29.

186 Ibid., p. 30.

pupil an interest which, before the act of education, had been unknown to the pupil. The teacher imbues the student with his soul, and shapes his character, his will, his intellect. The problem Gentile identifies in this context is this: How do we find the balance between the teacher's desire to turn the student into a free spiritual subject, and the desire to control his development? This contradiction between freedom and control is what Gentile calls the fundamental antinomy of education.

How does Gentile address this problem? If the school is a true 'forge of freedom'[187] (*fucina di libertà*), the problem does not exist, because good teachers can achieve a unity between the subject matter discussed and the souls of the students: listening to Leopardi's poems in the classroom, the students should gradually lose the sense that they are students — rather, nothing but the meaning of Leopardi's words should exist for them at that moment.[188] If the teacher cannot communicate his subject matter to the students in this way, the process cannot be called education and such a school is lifeless.

What link must exist between teacher and pupil to achieve the total understanding of education described above? According to Gentile, it is culture — the content of education, which should pass from the teacher to the pupil. It is the transmission of information, life experiences, and norms of behaviour; it is the shaping of the pupil's personal

187 Ibid., p. 47.

188 In this context, it is relevant to remember that all of Gentile's historico-philosophical work, based on the immanent activity proposed by the actualist doctrine, was centered on the inseparable unity of thought and action, the theoretical and the practical. Gentile's historico-philosophical approach can also be seen as a kind of hermeneutics (as Emilio Betti thought, in particular). A simple example: we know something about Dante, we have read him and about him, we have formed some opinion and idea. For Gentile this is not enough — it is too abstract, not a living Dante, just a product of our thinking. The real Dante is revealed when, when we read his works and understand what is behind them, we immerse ourselves in his world, in his thoughts, and think of them as our own. When we read a thinker's work and become immersed in his text, we become him; his thoughts are our thoughts, even if temporarily. In this way, history itself is actualised — through *individual* actualisation.

abilities. Figuratively speaking, education fulfils its task when the life of the *Divine Comedy* does not end once it has left Dante's pen, but the poem is incorporated into us to form part of the infinite life of the spirit, which can be called culture — an idealistic culture that exists not in heads and libraries, but in our souls. Culture is never finished; it always lives in its bearers. 'This is why human life has value, this is why education is a mission',[189] Gentile concludes his thought. Gentile's detailed discourse on culture returns to the notion that man is not a human being by virtue of natural laws. Man needs to be earned — he needs to become man. Man is free to make an effort, to carry out a spiritual act of becoming wherein his freedom is expressed. Culture experiences a similar becoming in the spirit and the state of 'becoming'[190] (*divenire*), i.e. dynamic life, is natural for it. Culture is never an 'object' or a 'thing' — it is rather our thoughts. Culture is killed when it is reduced to concrete, sterile material expressions, as it is essentially an ethical *process*, an active life of the spirit, the liberation and perfection of our human essence.

Gentile's idealist understanding is very far from the realist perception of the 'modern school', on which the philosopher dwells separately. Apologists for the 'kingdom of man', which claims to control the forces of nature, see school as a temple of abstract and objective Science, administered by special priests. Gentile proclaims the struggle against the torpor of the mind and the laziness of the heart, against the lifelessness of the educational process. By reading the textbook, the student must *make it his own*, and the teacher must animate the process. A textbook becomes a 'spiritual guide for the mind' when its author, teacher, and pupil form a unified spirit capable of bringing the content of the text to life.[191]

Gentile argues that education must become one — it cannot be divided into physical, intellectual and moral. The 'moral insufficiency' of

189 Gentile, *La riforma dell'educazione*, p. 63.

190 Ibid., p. 94.

191 Ibid., p. 116.

the school is only an indication that the educational process is poorly organised. Putting a special emphasis on humanities, the philosopher argues that reading is the most powerful tool for shaping a person and his beliefs. The library is the first thing a school should take care of to raise and educate children. Unsuccessful reading that does not touch the reader's soul is extremely damaging — we must recognise our world in what we read, our interests and our personal experiences. Education should not be an abstract intellectual exercise — the student should be able to extract the spiritual values of living culture from it.

In addition to developing the moral and intellectual qualities of the student, the school should also, according to Gentile, pay attention to his physical cultivation. The philosopher pays tribute to the Greek principle of athletic training, which he believes should be taken into account in the unified concept of education. Gentile notes that in ancient times there was almost no separation between physical and spiritual education — many Greek philosophers saw exercises such as gymnastics and music as complementary. We owe the division and opposition of the spiritual and the natural to Christianity. Actual idealism opposes the limitations of the spheres of activity of the free spirit and consequently proclaims that 'our science is the science of man, of man in the universe, and therefore of nature'.[192] According to Gentile, physical education is also an education of the spirit, as much as is intellectual and moral education.

What, according to Gentile, is the ideal of education? Moral and intellectual education should be united. It is equally necessary to ensure the education of a culture of the mind and a culture of the body. Pedagogical routine must be replaced by an awareness of a new educational duty — to work not in the physical space of the school but in the soul of students. The pedagogical problem is a problem of the spirit, and is a problem of philosophy. Nothing but philosophy is capable of unifying the various concepts into a single, coherent and

192 Ibid., p. 149.

contradictory one. Thus, 'education that seeks true unity, which is the life of the spirit, must always be moral, spiritual, philosophical'.[193]

Two years after Gentile delivered a lecture on education to teachers in Trieste, he was given a real opportunity to put his ideas into practice. In Benito Mussolini's first Fascist government, formed in October 1922, just after the success of the March on Rome, he was given the position Minister of Public Education and immediately set about educational reform. Gentile updated both school and university teaching standards.

It should be noted that the situation in which Italian education found itself by the time the Fascists came to power was utterly deplorable. It was the twentieth century, and in Italy there were fewer secondary school students than in the tiny Belgium and Netherlands.[194] A large part of the population was illiterate. There was only three years of compulsory education, and the main cadres of the future elite came from public schools with widely differing curricula.

Gentile took up the challenge very vigorously: the first decree to reform education was issued on December 31, 1922, and four more royal decrees were issued the following year. Gentile took actions aimed at achieving several objectives: creating mechanisms for the speedy formation of an educated elite, adapting the population to the new political reality, implementing the principle of giving priority to liberal education, and developing state schools.

Gentile achieved a number of practical results in a short period of time. First of all, universal compulsory education was extended — it now continued until a young Italian citizen reached the age of fourteen. Children attended five years of compulsory primary school,

---

193 Ibid., p. 176.

194 T. p. Nesterova, 'От реформы Джентиле к реформе Боттаи: образовательная политика Италии в 1920–1930-х гг.' [From the Gentile Reform to the Bottai Reform: Italian Educational Policy in 1920–1930s] in *Известия Уральского государственного университета. Сер. 2, Гуманитарные науки* [The Proceedings of the Ural State University. Series. 2 Humanities], (2008), p. 119.

then either three years at a technical institute, five years at a grammar school, seven years at a teacher training institute, or three years at a supplementary school.

A new educational standard was introduced, setting the principles of course content and required learning outcomes, allowing Italian teachers to experiment with educational programmes and enabling the creative principles of 'free education' described by Gentile to be implemented. The humanities component of school education was significantly strengthened, with the introduction of compulsory teaching of the Law of God in the lower grades and philosophy in secondary schools.[195] Teaching in languages other than Italian was abolished in schools, which caused some dissatisfaction in the German, Slovenian, and Croatian communities.

According to Gentile, higher education was to be elitist and he achieved this goal by allowing only the best and brightest applicants to pursue university studies. At the same time, a system of vocational schools was established to provide practical training. Only graduates of grammar schools, one of the four types of school, had the opportunity to enter university.

Gentile introduced a system of unified state exams aimed at objectively assessing the knowledge acquired by pupils. The standardisation of education dealt a blow to corruption in the education system. Moreover, Gentile established a vertical power structure: the post of principal was no longer an elected position and the head of an

195 Such an approach lacked initial support: Catholic priests argued that religion must be taught throughout schooling, while freedom-loving philosophers categorically rejected the very need for religion to be taught in school. Gentile replied to his opponents that Italian children born in a Catholic country had to understand the environment in which they were growing up — which was impossible without an awareness of religion. But at a later age children must be led to a deeper understanding of moral truths which is only possible by teaching philosophy — the science of the spirit. See Valmai Burwood Evans, 'Education in the Philosophy of Giovanni Gentile', *International Journal of Ethics*, 43, no. 2 (Jan., 1933), p. 215.

educational institution was appointed by ministerial decree. Gentile also catered for children with disabilities: the foundations were laid for special education for children with disabilities (including the blind and deaf).

After a series of reforms, Gentile resigned from his post on 1 July, 1924, to concentrate on the development of Italian culture, a year later heading the National Fascist University of Culture.[196] He remained among the important protagonists of Fascist policy, but from this point the fate of Italian education began to be decided by other men: Balbino Giuliano and Giuseppe Bottai.[197]

To Gentile's credit, even after the defeat of the Fascist regime due to the military collapse, most of the reforms he carried out remained in force in the new, democratic Italy. Inspired by his fight against positivism in education, the idealist Gentile achieved a qualitative improvement in the Italian school system and a balancing of the educational system as a whole, eliminating the overproduction of intellectuals and achieving a significant elevation of the humanities. Many of the ideas underlying his reforms are still relevant today.

196 For more on Gentile's role in the organisation of Italian culture during the Fascist period, see: Albertina Vittoria, 'Giovanni Gentile e l'organizzazione della cultura' [Giovanni Gentile and the Organisation of Culture], *Studi Storici* [Historical Studies], 25, no. 1, Louis Gernet e l'antropologia della Grecia antica (Jan.-Mar., 1984), pp. 181–202. As well as leading some pre-existing cultural and educational institutions, Gentile often initiated bold new intellectual projects, as in the case of the Italian Institute for Near and Far Eastern Studies (ISMEO). The project itself was prepared by Gentile's Orientalist student Giuseppe Vincenzo Tucci, but it was Gentile who proposed it to the Duce (on behalf of a 'group of friends, experts in Oriental affairs') and who became the first president of the new institute. Gherardo Gnoli, 'Giovanni Gentile Founder and President of ISMEO', *East and West*, 44, no. 2/4 (December 1994), pp. 223–229.

197 Italian education policy since Gentile has somewhat eroded the progress he made. In particular, during Bottai's tenure as Minister of Education there was an intensified 'Fascisation' of schools, aimed at increasing social mobility. Bottai's actions were aimed at bringing schools closer to the 'world of work'. For more details see: Edward R. Tannenbaum, *The Fascist Experience. Italian Society and Culture, 1922–1945*, (London/New York: Basic Books, Inc., 1972), pp. 151–177.

3.2. Gentile in Big Government. Breaking with Croce. Manifesto of Fascist Intellectuals. Philosophical Foundations of Fascism

In 1924, Gentile's last year in office, Mussolini considerably strengthened his position both in the foreign policy arena and in domestic politics. His cabinet succeeded in streamlining the economic life of the country and creating conditions for the development of industry and agriculture. As for foreign policy, he obtain the annexation of Fiume to Italy, conclude a peace treaty with Yugoslavia, and was one of the first to establish diplomatic relations with the USSR. By the time of the parliamentary elections scheduled for April 1924, the Fascist Party's popularity had reached unprecedented heights.[198] The result was a landslide victory for the Fascists, with 65 per cent of the vote. Their closest pursuers, the People's Party, garnered only 9 per cent. With a turnout of 63%, up 5% from the 1921 election, the Fascists' success looked even more remarkable.

Gentile joined the Fascist party as early as 1923. For him this was 'a natural consequence of the liberal-conservative political aspirations derived from his concept of an ethical state'.[199] Gentile's resignation as Minister of Education can be seen as a political move to support the Mussolini cabinet, which was largely criticised for its unpopular

198 In this context, it is useful to explain some of the nuances of Italian electoral law at the time. In 1923, Parliament passed a law stipulating that at the end of elections two-thirds of the seats should go to the party that had obtained the most votes, provided that it had received at least 25% of the total number of votes cast. The remaining one-third of mandates must be distributed proportionally among the remaining parties. So, in the election of April 1924 the winning party would have had to get 25% of the votes to win 355 seats out of a possible 535. As a result of this law, many liberals compromised with the Fascists in order to secure a guaranteed place on the large electoral list of the Fascist party, whose victory in the elections, under the above described formula, few doubted. Dieter Nohlen and Philip Stöver, *Elections in Europe: A Data Handbook*, (Baden-Baden: Nomos, 2010), pp. 1033–1047.

199 Gabriele Turi, 'Giovanni Gentile: Oblivion, Remembrance, and Criticism', *The Journal of Modern History*, 70, no. 4 (December 1998), p. 929.

education reform as well. After leaving his ministerial post, the philosopher concentrated on his work in the Commission of Fifteen and then in the Commission of Eighteen, entrusted with the preparation of Fascist constitutional reforms, and from 1925 he headed the project for the Italian Encyclopaedia.

Gentile's popularity in the second half of the 1920s was as high as ever. During this period, Gentile openly claimed to have become 'the philosopher of Fascism'. In the autumn of 1924, Croce broke off relations with him, accusing Gentile of betraying freedom and Italian science.[200]

In January 1925, Mussolini crushed all hopes of the Liberals for a return to the old order. The coalition government was replaced by a purely Fascist government which immediately set about dismantling the liberal institutions of administration. There was no doubt in anyone's mind that Mussolini intended to create a dictatorship.[201] Gentile, who remained loyal to the Duce, delivered a fiery speech in defence of the regime at the Conference of Fascist Cultural Organisations[202]

200In a letter to Gentile dated October 24, 1924, he argued that the disagreement between them was no longer philosophical, but practical and political, making their friendship henceforth impossible. The rupture of relations between two of Italy's most influential intellectuals was a sign that Fascism had divided Italian science and culture into two sides — its supporters and its opponents — a vivid manifestation of which were the two opposing manifestos of the intellectuals.

201 A contemporary scholar notes that the Fascist regime underwent a number of significant transformations in its little over two decades of existence. We can distinguish six distinct phases of its life: 1) 1922–1925, the formal continuation of the parliamentary regime in Italy; 2) 1925–1929, the creation of a Fascist dictatorship; 3) 1929–1934, the 'lull', the absence of radical change; 4) 1934–1940, the intensification of Italian international relations, aggressive imperial foreign policy, rapprochement with Nazi Germany; 5) 1940–1943, the war; 6) 1943–1945, the 'Salò period'. Payne, *A History of Fascism*, p. 212.

202The term 'Fascist culture' itself has recently attracted a great deal of scholarly interest. Modern scholars tend not to support Norberto Bobbio's famous thesis 'Where there was Fascism, there was no culture. Where there was culture, there was no Fascism. Fascist culture never existed'. For example, Roger Griffin notes that 'Fascist culture certainly existed, but it was extremely heterogeneous

held in Bologna in March 1925. The conference resulted in the *Manifesto of Fascist Intellectuals*, authored by Gentile but signed by Gabriele D'Annunzio, Filippo Tommaso Marinetti, Curzio Malaparte, Margherita Sarfatti, Ugo Spirito, Gioacchino Volpe, and many other famous people[203] besides him. The document was published on 21 April, 1925, the anniversary of the founding of Rome.

The manifesto is structured into four parts: 'Origins', 'Fascism and the State', 'Youth and Squadrism', and 'Fascist Government'. 'Origins' argues that Fascism originated in the trenches of the Great War, in which Italy was victorious but was then betrayed by its own individualist and utilitarian 'demosocialist' (*demosocialista*) government. 'The individual who opposes the state is a typical expression

and instrumental, shaped by a modernist socio-political ethic'. Roger Griffin, *Modernism and Fascism. The Sense of a Beginning under Mussolini and Hitler*, (London: Palgrave Macmillan, 2007), p. 233.

203 Despite the fact that in this particular case, Gentile, Curzio Malaparte (real name Kurt Suckert, 1898–1957) and many other right-wing Italian thinkers found themselves on the same side of the barricades, and Gentile in the story of the *Manifesto of Fascist Intellectuals* appears in the role of the undisputed leader of the Fascist 'intellectual guild', one should nevertheless note the somewhat ambiguous nature of Gentile's relations with other Fascist intellectuals, many of whom deemed the philosopher 'not radical enough'. Gentile, true to the neo-Hegelian spirit of actual idealism, was always in favour of the normalisation of public life. The March on Rome, according to Gentile, was necessary, but a further radicalisation of the situation was excessive. The correspondence dispute between Gentile and Malaparte is particularly revealing—for example, their disagreement on the 'church question' is very telling. Gentile insisted on the compulsory teaching of Catholicism in junior schools as 'the most natural religion for Italians', while Malaparte, in *Viva Caporetto!* (1921), was highly critical of the possible alliance between Fascism and the Catholic Church. See: Sergio Luzzatto, *Padre Pio: Miracles and Politics in a Secular Age*, (London: Picador, 2011). In addition, Malaparte criticised Gentile for continuing the Hegelian line of philosophising by embedding rationalist, German aspects in Fascism. According to Malaparte, the Fascist revolution had to go on. Some of Gentile's other opponents among the Fascist intellectuals are discussed in more detail in the third chapter of this work.

of a spiritually decomposed political camp',[204] Gentile writes in the manifesto. Fascism, on the other hand, is ascribed a moral and spiritual character, according to which the individual is sacrificed for the collective, for the Fatherland, for history. Fascism sees the tradition of history and civilisation as a mission.

This, according to Gentile, demonstrates the religious character of Fascism. In the section 'Fascism and the State' he asserts that from 1919 to 1922, Fascism waged a fierce struggle against socialism and liberalism, inspired by the idea of Italian unity — the very idea handed down from the heroes of the Risorgimento. In the next paragraph, 'Youth and Squadrism', Gentile calls Fascism 'the party of youth', likening it to Mazzini's 'Young Italy'. It attracted the youth in the same way that the bright religious ideas that demand sacrifice do. It gave inspiration to all Italians who wanted a renewal of their state. It provided an outlet for the energy that had been languishing in the nation since the Great War. Organised militarily, the squadrists took up arms against the decrepit left-wing government. Their last decisive action was the March on Rome, which awakened Italy and brought Fascism to a resounding victory — as a system and as a doctrine of life.

The final, fourth section of the Manifesto glorifies the actions of the Fascist government after the success of the March on Rome. The revolution ended there, but the renewal was just beginning — the Fascists began to prepare reforms. Gentile notes that the Fascists overhauled the law, the army, science, and education. The new Fascist social institutions were a manifestation of the new spirit and new life. This, the author notes, attracted the interest of intellectuals in other countries, to whom the manifesto is addressed. Gentile goes on to give a purely actualist definition of the state as an 'inner fatherland' contained in

204Giovanni Gentile, 'Manifesto degli intellettuali Fascisti agli intellettuali di tutte le Nazioni, dai giornali italiani del 21 aprile' [Fascist Intellectuals' Manifesto to Intellectuals of All Nations (*Manifesto of Italian Intellectuals* in English, from Italian newspapers of 21 April] in E. p. Papa, *Fascismo e cultura* [Fascism and Culture], (Padua: Marsilio, 1974), p.187.

the individual. He asserts the need to subordinate private interests to common ones, in order to achieve an ideal social state in which 'word becomes deed'. Thus, Gentile imbues the manifesto with the basic tenet of actualist philosophy—the unity of thought and action, theory and practice.[205]

The Manifesto finally cemented Gentile's reputation as the regime's chief ideologue, arousing contradictory feelings among Italian intellectuals.[206] In the following years he acts as an 'intellectual ambassador' of Fascism, publishing texts in defence of the regime in Italian and other languages.

Towards the end of the 1920s, the firmly established Fascist government gradually began to implement a plan to export ideology. The key theoretical product that the Fascists decided to export abroad was the social and philosophical writings of Gentile, who by that time had already fully associated his actual idealism with the Fascist regime and was not only comfortable with such activities, but supported them

205 Some scholars (e.g. A. James Gregor) have suggested that in the manifesto Gentile presents Fascism as 'the end of the Risorgimento', the end of the state-building of the new Italy. Given that Gentile always insists on the essential incompleteness and temporality of any political form, it is difficult to agree with this. See A. James Gregor's position: Gregor, *Giovanni Gentile: Philosopher of Fascism*, pp. 60–61.

206 For example, Croce, who had already severed all relations with Gentile, responded to the *Manifesto of Fascist Intellectuals* with a counter text published on 1 May, 1925. In the *Manifesto of the AntiFascist Intellectuals* Croce argues that the intellectual can of course join a political party and serve it faithfully, but it is his civic duty to promote the spiritual and intellectual growth of the entire political sphere. According to Croce, Gentile and his associates impose unnecessary restrictions on Italian culture and science. They act as apostles of a new aggressive faith, fomenting a new religious war in Italy. Fascist intellectuals, according to Croce, see all Italians who disagree with them as 'enemies in wartime'. Fascism, meanwhile, has said no new word on state-building, and its 'new faith' is demagoguery without clear answers to key questions. According to Croce, Fascism betrayed the liberal ideals of the Risorgimento, building a new absolutism in Italy. Benedetto Croce, 'Manifesto degli intellettuali antiFascisti' [Manifesto of the AntiFascist Intellectuals] in E. p. Papa, *Fascismo e cultura* [Fascism and Culture], (Padua: Marsilio, 1974), pp. 212–214.

in every possible way. One of the most interesting publications from that period is Gentile's article 'Philosophical Foundations of Fascism', which appeared in the January 1928 issue of the respected American magazine *Foreign Affairs*. In this article, Gentile draws a number of conclusions about the genesis of Fascism as a political and philosophical doctrine.

Fascist poster celebrating the 'March on Rome'

The philosopher begins by saying that 'for the Italian nation, the World War was the resolution of a profound spiritual crisis'.[207] The crisis lay in the essential division of the country into two camps of opposing values and views on politics and history. Some were militant and insisted that the young Italian nation had to be tested by blood. Others, on the contrary, were opposed to going to war and the risks involved. 'The neutralists favoured material advantages, tangible, palpable, appreciable; the interventionists favoured moral advantages, intangible, impalpable, inestimable',[208] the philosopher defines the parties. The confrontation almost led Italy into civil war, but the king intervened and decided the situation in favour of joining the World War.

Fascist units approach Rome, crossing the legendary Ponte-Salario bridge, 1922

According to Gentile, this conflict is historical and dates back to the unification of Italy. At the time of the Risorgimento there was no 'Italian people'—there were just isolated individuals, inspired by

207 Giovanni Gentile, 'The Philosophic Basis of Fascism', *Foreign Affairs*, 6, No. 2 (Jan., 1928), p. 290.

208 Ibid., p. 290.

idealistic ideas, acting of their own free will. The new Italy, 'its new soul',[209] was created by Mazzini and Gioberti, Leopardi and Manzoni, Alfieri and Foscolo. According to Gentile, the key difference between this 'new Italy' and the old was that the former 'took life seriously',[210] unlike the latter. By 'taking life seriously' the philosopher means, first and foremost, the transformation of thought into action, of theory into practice; the perception of life as mission.[211] The Risorgimento was a characteristic manifestation of the effectiveness of the idealist worldview—how thought precedes action, paves the way for action and finds its culmination in action. Italian idealist intellectuals created a soul-searching doctrine which inspired the great politicians of the unification era—Garibaldi, Cavour, Victor Emanuel. All of them, as Gentile writes, were followers of Mazzini. Rosmini and Gioberti devoted their talents and intellect to the same goal—to prove that 'true life is not only the life that is, but also the life that can be',[212] a religious and anti-materialist truth.

The struggle between these two poles in the following period of Italian history was transformed into a struggle between right-wing and left-wing factions in the parliament of the united Italian kingdom.[213] The Right reigned unchallenged over Italy from 1861 to 1876, and the Left from 1876 to 1919. Gentile points out that the concept of freedom itself has been interpreted differently by the Right and the Left: the Right ponders from the State to the individual and the Left from the

209 Ibid., p. 291.

210 Ibid., p. 291.

211 In particular, he reminds us of Mazzini's famous slogan: 'Thought and action!' Ibid., p. 292.

212 Ibid., p. 292.

213 The irreconcilable struggle between the 'Historical Left' and the 'Historical Right' took place in the Italian Parliament for over half a century, from 1861 to 1922. The Left was anticlerical, democratic and progressive, defending the principles of protectionism in the economy; the Right was centralist and militarist, defending the principles of free trade. In 1922 both the Historical Left and the Historical Right merged with the Italian Liberal Party.

individual to the State. On the Left, the individual and his inalienable rights were central, while the 'nation' was the mechanical sum of the individual. For the Right, on the other hand, the authority of the State, above and beyond any private interests, was fundamental.

Gentile, while sympathetic to the Right, still finds arguments for the historical justification of the Left's takeover of power in 1876; he notes that over-regulation leads to stagnation and people, tired of the pressure of the Right, needed a breath of fresh air. The left-wing government had lived up to expectations — the last decades of the nineteenth century had been successful for Italy. The country had been revitalised by private initiative. However, destructive tendencies developed under left-wing rule: Marxism began to raise its head during the rapid industrialisation of the country, Freemasonry spread, the authority of the state declined, and public life in general gravitated spontaneously towards materialism and anti-clericalism.

Giovanni Gentile (far right) and Benito Mussolini (middle)

'From 1876 until the Great War we had a materialistic and anti-Mazzinian Italy, even if it surpassed in every respect both the Italy of the Mazzini era and the Italy before it',[214] Gentile writes. This materialist era in the country's history took place under the banner of positivism in science and the perception of reality in general. 'Everyone wanted "facts", "positive facts". Everyone laughed at "metaphysical dreams", intangible realities. It seemed to people that the truth was right in front of them. All one had to do was to open one's eyes and see it',[215] Gentile recalls the times of his youth, when even touching on patriotism was a sign of bad taste.

The situation was transformed by the next generation, to which Gentile describes himself as belonging. Young people rebelled against 'demosocialist' Italy by resurrecting their grandfathers' idols — the works of Italian idealists from both the Risorgimento era and the deeper past were actively re-read. Vico, Mazzini, Rosmini and Gioberti became even more popular with the young generation of Italian intellectuals in the late nineteenth and early twentieth centuries than they had been in their day. Positivism and materialism were losing ground; even Marxism yielded to Sorel's Syndicalism, which had gained greater popularity with the Italian Left. In Sorel's doctrine, Italian radical leftists discovered both purely idealistic aspirations for a more moral world order and a departure from the Left's characteristic betrayal of national interests.[216] The Syndicalists extolled such virtues as duty and self-sacrifice, which before them had been regarded as typically right-wing, idealistic. Radical sentiment was also growing on the Right, where a young nationalist movement emerged, springing, according to Gentile, from the Italian statist tradition. 'The Syndicalists, the nationalists, and the idealists succeeded in returning the majority of Italian youth to the spirit of Mazzini',[217] the philosopher asserts. Italy,

214 Ibid., p. 295.

215 Ibid., p. 295.

216 In addition to the betrayal of national interests, Gentile, faithful to the precepts of Mazzini set out in *On the Duty of Man*, reproaches the Marxists for betraying the interests of the proletariat.

217 Ibid., p. 297.

led by Giovanni Giolitti, tried to paralyze this vital spirit. The conflict was resolved by the Great War.

In the early 1920s Benedetto Croce, like many Italian liberals, supported Fascism as a force capable of resisting Bolshevism, but then changed his mind and became one of the leading critics of the regime and its philosophy.

After the war, however, as Gentile rightly points out, the scales seemed to tip again in the favour of materialist Italy. As a result of the victorious war, the country gained little or nothing of what it desired. Domestically, tensions were growing and left-wing radicalism and anarchism were gaining strength. Yet, a new Italy was emerging, whose spirit was strengthened in the trenches of the First World War.[218] A Fascist movement was emerging which, as Gentile writes, was frankly lucky to have a leader. 'Mussolini was a pure-blooded Mazzini, of the kind that Mazzini always found in the province of Romagna',[219] the philosopher draws a direct line of continuity. Gentile uses unsparing

218 In the first post-war years, even before the rapprochement with Fascism, Gentile argued that a return to the pre-war order was not only undesirable but also impossible — the war had awakened a new vitality in Italians, which had to find its appropriate political form. Daniela Coli, *Giovanni Gentile*, (Bologna: Il Mulino, 2004), pp. 116–118.

219 Gentile, *The Philosophic Basis of Fascism*, p. 298.

words of admiration for Mussolini: he moved away from socialism, was deeply aware of the need for order and a strong state, and supported the aspirations of revolution and violence in contrast to parliamentary lethargy and corruption. Furthermore he was a man of action: 'From the beginning the Fascist party was not a party of faith, but a party of action. It was not in need of a platform or a principle, but an idea that gave it a goal, a way to reach it'.[220] Fascism sought to build a true nation-state; moreover, Fascism was the force of that state—a new state that was just emerging but had not yet been created.[221] Because the Fascists were firmly entrenched in the legal field, the Fascist revolution effectively ended with the March on Rome, giving birth to a new Italy of idealists.[222]

220 Ibid., p. 298.

221 In 'The Philosophy of Fascism', published in *Italia Today* in 1941, Gentile identifies three factors that influenced the creation of the Fascist State: '1) the Sorel-Syndicalist critique of parliamentarism and social-democracy, 2) a weakened structure and authority of the State due to the constant conflict between parliamentary forces and political parties, 3) the experience of war'. Cited from Piraino and Fiorito, *Fascist Identity. Political Project and Doctrine of Fascism*, p. 221.

222 Gentile's thesis about the opposition between the 'Italy of the materialists' and the 'Italy of the idealists' is fruitfully developed in some modern theories on the interpretation of Fascism—for example, by George Mosse and Stanley Payne. In their works, Fascism is, first and foremost, a cultural revolution against nineteenth-century pragmatism, liberalism and materialism. See Stanely Payne, *A History of Fascism, 1914–1945*, pp. 450–451.

Painting depicting the Duce in the company of the Quadruplets during the commemoration of the sixth anniversary of the March on Rome. From right to left in the foreground are Michele Bianchi, Cesare Maria De Vecchi, Benito Mussolini, Emilio De Bono, and Italo Balbo.

Turning from his own view of historical events to a more explicitly political philosophy, Gentile argues that in Fascism — as in the social philosophy of Mazzini, to which he actively refers throughout the article — it is extremely difficult to find the 'purely political', separated from morality, religion, ideas on living, and other spheres of spiritual life. Fascism's strength is that it is totalitarian,[223] which means that it embraces human life in its totality, 'the whole will, thoughts, and feelings of a nation'.[224] The second point Gentile makes is that Fascism is neither a philosophy, nor a religion, nor a political theory; its true meaning cannot be formulated in short theses or in large texts. 'The Duce's true views are those that he formulates and immediately puts

223 Gentile actively introduced the term 'totalitarianism' into intellectual discourse in 1925 to positively denote the all-encompassing conception of life attributed to Fascism. Totalitarianism referred to the organic unity of all processes within the state: economic, political, cultural and social. See: Payne, *A History of Fascism*, p. 121. We may add to this that in a philosophical sense it was indisputably derived from an actualist vision of the unity of the consciousness of the state and the individual.

224 Gentile, *The Philosophic Basis of Fascism*, p. 299.

into practice',[225] Gentile expounds. Fascism, for him, is the art of making perfect use of the moment, of seizing the right time for action. Through his life and political deeds, Mussolini reinterprets Mazzini's 'Thought and Action!' Fascism can only be perceived as an anti-intellectual movement if one separates 'thought from action, knowledge from life, brain from heart, theory from practice'.[226] He views all utopias extremely negatively by virtue of the fact that they are unrealisable; everything abstract insofar as it remains a game of words. The culture that Fascism resists is that of aesthetes and pedants who contribute nothing to the development of man and the state. 'If by a system of philosophy we mean living thought, a universal principle which daily demonstrates its own intrinsic significance and fruitfulness, then Fascism is an ideal system whose development has solid foundations and an inexorable logic',[227] Gentile writes. The third point noted by the philosopher is that Fascism is more than just a political system. It certainly gravitates towards politics and presents itself as a political methodology, but to perceive it in this way is not sufficient to fully understand it.

Finally, the philosopher outlines the main features of Fascist politics. Its key concept is the nation state, which is the foundation of every right and every value for the individuals within it. 'The state is not a consequence — it is a principle',[228] Gentile stresses. Fascism, however, does not limit individual freedom by making the individual dependent on the state. In Fascist political philosophy, the state and the individual are one; they are indivisible components of a dialectical synthesis. The nation-state is a spiritual organism, because the nation as such is a creation of the spirit and not of nature. Therefore, the Fascist state is not static — it is never complete, but always in the process of being created. Unlike nationalists — for whom the authority

225 Ibid., p. 300.

226 Ibid., p. 300.

227 Ibid., p. 301.

228 Ibid., p. 301.

of the state (especially its educated ruling elite) is always preordained and presupposed, and whose state has, in Gentile's eyes, an aristocratic character — the Fascist state is the people's state: its eternal fulfillment is the consequence of the development of the self-awareness of its members. According to Gentile, the popular character of Fascism is also proved by its constitutional reforms — most notably by the introduction of syndicate corporations that discipline and order the trade union movement. The final important characteristic noted by Gentile concerns the Fascist understanding of freedom. Freedom, according to the philosophy of Fascism, is concrete freedom, resulting from the interaction of state authority and the will of citizens. Gentile contrasts this understanding of freedom with liberal freedom which is abstract and illusory, opposing the will of citizens and the will of the state.

During the *ventennio* years Gentile wrote many ideological works like the one discussed above. The basic principles set out in them did not change from year to year, from decade to decade: the unity of ethical thought and political action; the essential unity of the individual with the state; the active vital character of the state (as a consequence, the state as an eternal accomplishment); Fascism as a new historical form in an endless cycle of social transformations, originating from the spirit of the Risorgimento idealists; and rebukes to liberals and Marxists. In other words, Gentile imbued Fascism as an ideology with all the basic principles of his own actualist political ontology. Nothing proves this better than a look at *The Doctrine of Fascism.*

3.3. The Doctrine of Fascism as an Actualist Work

Having looked at the ideas presented by Gentile in the works discussed above brings us closer to understanding the main ideological text in the political philosophy of Italian Fascism — *The Doctrine of Fascism*, co-authored by Gentile and Mussolini. The work is in two parts, each containing thirteen theses. In the first, philosophical part of this work, called 'Fundamental Ideas' (*idee fondamentali*), we can see a clear reflection of all the key points of actual idealism,[229] while in the second, 'Political and Social Doctrine' (*dottrina politica e sociale*), in which Mussolini had a hand, we see the influence not only of Italian idealists, but also those who shaped the Duce's thought, namely Sorel and Nietzsche. Let us examine this work in detail.

The first thesis of Fundamental Ideas defines Fascism as an integrated political concept which is at the same time a thought and an action: 'action in which doctrine is immanent, and doctrine arising from a given system of historical forces in which it is inserted, and working on them from within.'[230] The reality of the private has, at its base, a higher, eternal, immutable reality. Continuing this thesis, Gentile argues that a conception of the State which would not be in its essence a conception of life is unthinkable. This conception of life (*concetto della vita*) is the philosophy that is expressed in organic doctrine.[231]

In the next thesis Gentile argues that Fascism must be understood as a spiritual concept of life. Fascism perceives the individual as a

229 When the Catholic dignitaries learned that Gentile would write the philosophical part of the Doctrine of Fascism, they caused a real scandal — in their eyes, actual idealism was nothing more than heretical pantheism. Given the Lateran Agreements between the Holy See and Mussolini's government, the Church clearly planned to play a role in writing the regime's main ideological text. However, the Duce was adamant. On this incident, see A. James Gregor, *Giovanni Gentile: Philosopher of Fascism*, p. 63. This is not the first time that Gentile clashed with Catholics. Alessandra Tarquini gives a detailed account of Gentile's confrontation with the 'neo-scholastics of the Catholic University of Milan' who radically rejected both his educational reforms and his actualist philosophy. For more details see the chapter 'Cattolici contro Gentile' in Alessandra Tarquini, *Il Gentile dei Fascisti. Gentiliani e antigentiliani nel regime Fascista* [The Gentile of the Fascists. Gentilians and Anti-Gentilians in the Fascist Regime], (Bologna: Il Mulino, 2009).

230 Benito Mussolini, *La dottrina del Fascismo* [The Doctrine of Fascism], (Rome, 1941), Idee fondamentali. I.

231 Gentile asserted in a lecture entitled 'What is Fascism?' which he delivered in Florence on 8 March, 1925: 'Gentlemen, Fascism is a party, a political doctrine. But above all, Fascism is a total conception of life.' Quoted in Griffin, *Fascism*, p. 54.

moral individual, united with the nation and the state, striving to assert higher values, aware of his duty and mission. Thus, in its doctrine, Fascism takes into account not only and not primarily the issues, problems, and concerns of the material world, but also seeks a purely spiritual existence (*esistenza tutta spirituale*).

Giovanni Gentile, 'the philosopher of Fascism'

The philosopher writes that all 'negative doctrines', to which he includes positivism, scepticism, pessimism, and agnosticism, believe that the centre of life is outside the individual. Fascism, on the contrary, 'wants the active man' (*vuole l'uomo attivo*), i.e. a man of action, ready and eager to fight. From this Gentile deduces the utmost importance of education, upbringing, and culture as the spiritual spheres of life which shape the individual, as well as the placing of great value on work, through which man subdues the world to his will.

The fourth and fifth theses of Fundamental Ideas are devoted to the definition of Fascist morality and ethics. 'The positive conception of life is obviously an ethical one',[232] writes Gentile. This ethical, 'serious' conception is that everything in the world has a moral side. A

232 Mussolini, *La dottrina del Fascismo*, Idee fondamentali. IV.

person who perceives the world in this way lives immanently within a higher law, by virtue of which Fascism can be perceived as a religious concept.[233]

Fascism is also a historical concept, in which the individual is a participant of the 'spiritual process to which he contributes as a member of the family, the social group, the nation, and in function of history to which all nations bring their contribution'.[234] Fascism, according to Gentile, opposes everything abstract and utopian; it is realistic and concrete. Fascism is a response to the challenges of time and intends to 'solve only the problems posed by history'.[235]

In the remaining seven theses of the Fundamental Ideas, Gentile reveals and articulates the philosophical foundations of Fascist political philosophy. He asserts the anti-individualist character of Fascism, recognising only the individual united with the state, which is its only possible reality. Fascism, according to Gentile, defends freedom, but understands it differently than liberalism. Freedom in Fascism is not freedom from the state, but freedom in the state, because nothing spiritual or valuable is possible outside of the state. 'In this sense, Fascism is totalitarian, and the Fascist state, the synthesis and unity of all values, interprets, develops and strengthens the life of the people',[236] the philosopher writes. In addition to denying the liberal understanding of freedom, Fascism also denies the socialist understanding of class struggle. Fascism's corporate system is the optimal mechanism of class representation in the state, which eliminates such antagonisms. Fascism is also opposed to the traditional understanding of democracy, which equates the people as a mass, but at the same time, Fascism

233 Modern scholar Emilio Gentile notes that it was Fascism that was essentially the first political religion of the twentieth century, with all the attributes typical of an institutionalised cult. Emilio Gentile, *Politics as Religion*, (Princeton, New Jersey: Princeton University Press, 2006), p. 36.

234 Mussolini, *La dottrina del Fascismo,* Idee fondamentali. VI.

235 Ibid., Idee fondamentali. VI.

236 Ibid., Idee fondamentali. VII.

'is the purest form of democracy if one understands the people as it should be, qualitatively rather than quantitatively, as the most moral, consistent, true idea, which is realised in it through the consciousness and the will of a few, even one, and as an ideal seeks to be realised in the consciousness and the will of all'.[237]

Giovanni Gentile (second from right) at a public event

Gentile gives an idealistic definition of the nation as 'a multitude united by one idea'[238] which is a 'supreme personality'[239] (*personalità superiore*) when it is a state. The philosopher argues the opposite of the prevailing view of the relationship between the state and the nation — classical political theory held that the nation creates the state;[240] Gentile argues that the state creates the nation by giving it a will. The State, in turn,

237 Ibid., Idee fondamentali. IX.

238 Ibid., Idee fondamentali. IX.

239 Ibid., Idee fondamentali. X.

240 This statement also applies to the majority of modern socio-political scientific theories. For example, the following definitions of the concept 'nation' are given by our colleagues, modern Russian scientists: 'A nation is an aggregate of people who have one common fatherland' (Yuri Semenov), 'A nation is a special form of ethno-cultural community' (Vladimir Sergeevich Krzhevov). See: Dmitry

creates law by acting as a universal ethical will (*volontà etica universale*). Understood in the Fascist sense, the state is profoundly moral and ethical as it is 'an ethical reality which exists and lives insofar as it develops. The moment it stops, it dies'.[241] It is from this dynamism that the state' outward aspiration, the will to expand, is derived. According to the Doctrine, the Fascist state is a spiritual force, 'an inner form and norm that disciplines the individual, penetrating the will and mind'.[242] Fascism, for its part, is not just an institutional form, but 'an educator and engine of spiritual life',[243] seeking to improve the entire inner content of the individual.

In the Fundamental Ideas of the *Doctrine of Fascism* we can recognise all the fundamental positions of actualist idealism outlined by Gentile in *The Theory of Mind as Pure Act*, or direct references to them, as well as the basic theses of Gentile's practical philosophy that he later outlined as universally applicable in *The Genesis and Structure of Society*. The theses on the unity of thought and action and the immanent connection between doctrine and its corresponding historical being, fundamental to actualism, are taken as the starting point of the discourse outlined in Fundamental Ideas, which immediately moves to the ontological plane with a statement on a spiritual (essentially idealistic) understanding of life, from which follows the great synthesis of the one and the many — citizen and state — the path to which appears in the form of the Fascist doctrine.

The fundamental importance of activism, of an active relationship to the world, as advocated by Gentile in Fundamental Ideas, also follows from the anthropology of *The Theory of Mind as Pure Act*.[244]

Moiseev, 'Этнос. Нация. Ценности' [Ethnos. Nation. Values], *Вестник Российской нации* [Herald of the Russian Nation], 39, no. 1 (2015), p. 254.

241 Mussolini, *La dottrina del Fascismo*, Idee fondamentali. XI.

242 Ibid., Idee fondamentali. XII.

243 Ibid., Idee fondamentali. XIII.

244 Some commentators on Gentile even suggest calling actual idealism 'activist idealism', considering the term 'actual' too 'reticent' and 'timid'; Irving Louis

The designation of education as a fundamentally important sphere of the spiritual life of the state is consistently derived by Gentile from the above-mentioned work, *The Reform of Education. Lectures to the Teachers of Trieste*, as well as from his own practical experience as a Fascist minister. The specific historical character of Fascism proclaimed by Gentile is a reference to his dialectical conception of history as detailed in *The Theory of Mind*. The statement on the religious nature of the doctrine also refers to the same work.

The total statism asserted in the theses seven to thirteen of Fundamental Ideas is a concise expression of the actualist practical philosophy laid out in *The Genesis and Structure of Society*. This philosophy rejects any understanding of the individual outside the state, since it is the latter which has a sacred character, which can give meaning, values, and content to life. The State anticipates not only the individual, but the nation, being both the primordial source and the threshold of social life. According to actualist idealism, the state cannot find itself in a situation of oppressing the individual because, if it is just and genuine, its aspirations are fully identical with those of the individual (a return to the synthesis of the one and the many). Hence, the actualist system of thought leads to the paradoxical thesis that true freedom is only possible in a positively totalitarian state, that is, a state that is fully identical with the individual citizen. Such a complete convergence is the ultimate, ideal case.

This is the vector Gentile sought to give the Fascist regime through his intense scientific and social work—to build a model of a 'caring' ethical state in which the entire plurality of human souls would receive full individual creative expression, without being detached from the whole, and all would strive towards the heights of the human spirit. In spite of the obvious success of the educational system constructed by Gentile, whose elements remain in educational practice in Italy in

---

Horowitz is one such example. Irving Louis Horowitz, 'On the Social Theories of Giovanni Gentile', *Philosophy and Phenomenological Research*, 23, No. 2 (Dec., 1962), p. 264.

the twenty-first century, political practice has taken a different course. Gentile — who sincerely criticised utopias and sought the unity of theory and practice, and, to his credit, succeeded in realising many of his ideas, even during the regime — despite his status as the 'chief philosopher of Fascism', was significantly less influential politically than some party functionaries with ideas less bright and sincere.

The second part of the Fascists' programme text, 'Political and Social Doctrine', symbolises the transition from political ontology to direct political philosophy; from abstract theory to the concrete. The second part of the Doctrine is replete with references to specific historical events and dates, as well as quotations from Benito Mussolini's speeches of various years. At the beginning of this chapter, Mussolini writes that in the pre-war years 'his doctrine was the doctrine of action'[245] — socialism, which gave him the experience of a life of struggle, did not give him any doctrinal experience.[246] Fascism, which emerged after the end of the war, appears in the Duce's account as a doctrine of action, born out of the fervent aspirations of a generation of front-line soldiers for radical change. The aspirations were crystallised in concise statements, short talking points that were later developed doctrinally. All the energy of the Fascists in the period before the March on Rome was directed towards combat. Mussolini writes: 'A doctrine well-formed and substantiated, divided into chapters and paragraphs, might have been lacking; in its place there was something more definite: faith'.[247] However, he argues that in the heat of the struggle the

245 Mussolini, *La dottrina del Fascismo*, Dottrina politica e sociale. I.

246 Moreover, Mussolini presents socialism as something outdated, irrelevant, a thing of the past. However, he notes that 'in the powerful torrent of Fascism you will find currents originating from Sorel, Lagardelle, the *Mouvement Socialiste*, which were picked up by Italian Syndicalists: Oliviero Olivetti, Orano, and Leone. Mussolini refers to one of his speeches from the formative years of the Fascist movement, in which he asserted the necessity of 'adopting the demands of National Syndicalism from an economic point of view', which were in turn reflected in Fascist corporatism. Ibid., Dottrina politica e sociale. I.

247 Ibid., Dottrina politica e sociale. II.

basic theses on key philosophical issues were already articulated, out of which the doctrine subsequently evolved. 'Fascism now has its own point of view',[248] the Duce claims.

What is behind this perspective? Mussolini's first thesis is that Fascism does not believe in perpetual peace and rejects pacifism, celebrating war and sacrifice. Because of this belief Fascism also rejects international political organisations. The rationale of Fascist militarism is that war brings out the full potential of the human being and develops courage and character. It is the education of man in constant struggle and maximum risk, where his life is at stake, that Mussolini attributes to the stoic virtues. 'The Fascist accepts and loves life, rejects and regards suicide as cowardice; he understands life as a duty, an exaltation, a conquest. Life must be lofty and full; experienced for oneself, but most importantly for others, near and far, present and future'.[249] The love for one's neighbour that Mussolini writes about must be a love that is concrete, nurturing, active, but at the same time stern and rigorous.

The Duce goes on to define the three main negative principles of the political doctrine of Fascism: anti-Marxism, anti-democracy, and anti-liberalism. Fascism is opposed to Marxism: it believes in sanctity and heroism (*santità e nell'eroismo*) rather than historical materialism. Economic factors are not sufficient to make history; economic motives are not always expressed in great historical achievements. On this basis, Fascism rejects both the class struggle and the economic understanding of happiness as well-being in contemporary socialism. Fascism also opposes democracy because it 'denies that a number, a simple number as such, can rule human society; it denies that a number can rule through periodic consultations'.[250] Fascism, on the other hand, claims that inequality is fruitful and beneficial (*feconda e benefica*) for those who do not succumb to a mechanical equation. Fascism also

248 Ibid., Dottrina politica e sociale. II.

249 Ibid., Dottrina politica e sociale. III.

250 Ibid., Dottrina politica e sociale. VI.

removes the false (in the opinion of the Doctrine's authors) opposition between monarchy and republic, believing both to be temporary historical forms with no conceptual value.[251] Mussolini dedicates one major thesis of the doctrine to the French philosopher and writer Ernest Renan, who, as the Duce writes, 'had pre-Fascist insights',[252] denying the possibility of arranging the reasonable existence of the people by consulting the whole of the people, rather than the best part of it. The statements of Renan quoted by Mussolini are aimed at justifying normative elitism, to which the Fascist leader adds the denial of collective responsibility and denunciation of the 'lie of progress'. The third major rejection of Fascism is aimed at liberalism, both in politics and economics. Mussolini presents liberalism as one of the many nineteenth-century ideologies that temporarily had great popularity, characterised by agnosticism in economics and indifferentism in politics and morality. Liberalism is presented in the Doctrine as the 'historical and logical antecedent of anarchy'. Mussolini's rejection of liberalism is so strong that he even claims that Mazzini and Garibaldi were not liberals.[253] Fascism thus appears as a denial of everything 'leftist', everything egalitarian, materialist, or mechanistic.

251 Mussolini uses this statement as an argument against democracy, with its traditional rejection of all monarchy and aristocracy, coupled with its adherence to the republic as a form of political organisation of power in the state.

252 Ibid., Dottrina politica e sociale. VII.

253 The claim is understandable within the ideological struggle, but more than questionable in terms of truth. Mazzini's liberal political aspirations were discussed in detail in Chapter 1 of this work. As for Garibaldi, he was also a member of Young Italy in his younger years, fought for the liberals in the Uruguayan Civil War during his South American exile, and supported Pope Pius IX, who was famous for liberal reforms.

Benito Mussolini was not only a successful politician, but also a distinctive intellectual. With no formal philosophical training, he was fascinated by the ideas of Nietzsche, Sorel, Pareto, and Machiavelli. The Duce also made his own philosophical attempts—not without the help of Giovanni Gentile.

Having finished with rejections, Mussolini moves on to assertions. The positive content of Fascism lies in the assertion of modernism, fundamental statism, a compromise with tradition and an imperial will to dominate. The modernist character of Fascism manifests itself in the fact that it does not seek to return the world to the pre-1789 order of things, but insists on a rapid movement forward, overcoming the doctrines of the nineteenth century. Mussolini writes that if the nineteenth century was the liberal age of individualism, the twentieth must become the Fascist age of the collective, and therefore of the state. 'The basic premise of the Fascist doctrine is the doctrine of the state, of its essence, tasks, and aims',[254] writes the Duce. He, following Gentile, asserts the absolute nature of the state, as well as its ethical and metaphysical character. Mussolini also reiterates the thesis of its spirituality, adding that the state is 'the guarantor of internal and external security, as well as the guardian and transmitter of the popular

254 Mussolini, La dottrina del Fascismo, Dottrina politica e sociale. X.

spirit, for centuries evolved through language, customs and faith'.[255] In the *Doctrine of Fascism*, the state is presented as a single consciousness of the nation, balancing the aspirations, desires, and interests of its constituent individuals. From this, it deduces both its organising role in the economy, manifested in the principles of corporatism, and its harmonious attitude to religion as 'one of the deepest manifestations of the spirit'.[256] With regard to religion, Mussolini claims that 'Fascism did not create its "God"',[257] but 'honors the God of ascetics, saints and heroes, and God as he is seen and glorified by the simple and primitive heart of the people'.[258] Finally, Mussolini, true to the Nietzschean aspirations of his youth, writes that 'the Fascist state is the will to power and domination'.[259] He uses vitalist rhetoric: 'For Fascism, the desire for empire, for national expansion, is a manifestation of life',[260] and also makes a direct link between the health of the people and their imperial ambitions. The doctrine of Fascism, proclaimed by Mussolini as 'the doctrine of life in the twentieth century',[261] is described as universal, ushering in a new era in human history.

---

255 Ibid., Dottrina politica e sociale. X.

256 Ibid., Dottrina politica e sociale. XII.

257 Ibid., Dottrina politica e sociale. XII.

258 Ibid., Dottrina politica e sociale. XII.

259 Ibid., Dottrina politica e sociale. XIII.

260Ibid., Dottrina politica e sociale. XIII.

261 Ibid., Dottrina politica e sociale. XIII.

Benito Mussolini, leader of Italian Fascism

If 'Fundamental Ideas' can still be interpreted as a philosophical text, 'Political and Social Doctrine' is a model of a purely ideological narrative. While declaring a commitment to 'right-wing values' — idealism, elitism, tradition — Mussolini at the same time enters into certain contradictions with a coherent actualist system. In particular, freedom, extolled by Gentile in *The Theory of Mind as Pure Act* and appearing in the 'Fundamental Ideas' in a positive sense (as 'freedom for' as opposed to the negative liberal 'freedom from'), is hardly mentioned in the second part of the Doctrine: the fundamental points of political philosophy are contained exclusively in the concepts of the individual's duty to the State, a militant attitude towards life, and total self-sacrifice. The philosophical origins that inspired the author of 'Political and Social Doctrine' are not so much Mazzini and Hegel, but Sorel and Nietzsche.

Nevertheless, the overall content of *The Doctrine of Fascism* as an entire text could well be characterised as actualist. The totalitarian statism derived from an idealist political ontology, the activism, the modernist spirit of the work, and its intolerance of materialist and positivist attitudes are striking evidence of one dominant source — the actual idealism of Giovanni Gentile. The Italian philosopher's line of thought was unwavering, and his intellectual intuition in a sense anticipated the coming inter-war period, finding practical expression in *The Doctrine of Fascism*.[262]

262 To a certain extent we can agree with A. James Gregor, who put forward the thesis that 'long before Fascism came into being, Giovanni Gentile was its philosopher'. Gregor, *Giovanni Gentile: Philosopher of Fascism*, p. 95.

CHAPTER THREE

DEVELOPMENT OF THE DOCTRINE

§1. A Time of Ideologues

1.1. *The Political Doctrine of Fascism* by Alfredo Rocco

As shown in the previous chapter, Giovanni Gentile's actual idealism was the foundation of the political philosophy of Fascism, justifying key ideological aspects of the Mussolini regime, as evidenced by the Doctrine published under the Duce's name in 1932. However, it is incorrect to reduce all Fascist political thought to one dominant current — actualism. Over the years, there have been many attempts to understand Fascism and to define its fundamental bases. This chapter briefly examines the ideas of the regime's most influential ideologists, as well as those of the 'intellectuals in power'. Some attention is also paid to the internal doctrinal debates among the various intellectuals.

The first thinker we must examine as part of a consideration of the key ideological variations on the theme of *ventennio* Fascism is Alfredo Rocco (1875- 1935). A native of Naples, Rocco achieved early academic success in the fields of commercial and financial law. He was made professor of law at the University of Urbino at the age of twenty-four, and at the University of Padua at thirty-eight. Already an illustrious jurist, Rocco associated himself with Marxists for some time and was even a member of the Italian Radical Party. In 1914, this infatuation finally passed, as the thinker joined the Association of Italian Nationalists (ANI) headed by Enrico Corradini. By this time, as A. James Gregor notes, Rocco 'not only adopted the main tenets of Corradini's view of the modern world, but also articulated a full-fledged program of national economic revival'.[1]

In agreement with Corradini, Rocco was convinced that the late unification of Italy was one of the main factors behind its economic backwardness compared to the developed countries — Britain, Germany, and France. By the time the Risorgimento succeeded, these states were already colonial empires. Italy's productive power was no more than 20 percent of that of Britain; there were no effective factors to accelerate economic development — only the emigration of workers to the hated 'plutocracies' in the hope of finding better fortunes there. In addition, the developed countries imposed cultural hegemony on Italy, manifested primarily in the promotion of political individualism that undermined the fragile Italian national identity, and the doctrine of 'human rights', which also fostered individualistic sentiments. This state of affairs condemned Italy to a 'secondary role' in world politics and, according to Rocco, threatened the existence of the Italian nation.

Rocco saw the significant strengthening of the role the state had within the economy as a solution to Italy's difficult situation. Rocco saw improvement in the difficult situation in Italy in the significant strengthening of the role of the state in the economy. Thinking in the same vein as the German Historical School (Friedrich List, Bruno Hildebrand, Gustav von Schmoller), the Italian jurist argued that in Italy, and other developing nations, state economic policy must be based exclusively on long-term collective interests — otherwise the strategic future of the country is betrayed for the short-term enrichment of the living.[2] Directing most of the resources of an unsustain-

1 Gregor, *Mussolini's Intellectuals. Fascist Social and Political Thought*, p. 42.

2 At the same time, Rocco stipulates that countries that have reached a high level of industrial development can afford a liberal economic policy, up to complete laissez-faire. However, in order to afford such a luxury, the economy must be

able, underdeveloped economy to present-day consumption, and thus diluting national wealth, risks preventing the nation from ever moving from the 'backward' to the 'developed' category. Rocco insisted on the need to limit consumption to a 'reasonable level' and direct all the resources thus saved to accelerating catch-up development in all sectors of the economy (especially the infrastructure sectors with a strong multiplier effect) in order to maximise national expansion and enter into competition with the developed countries.

Alfredo Rocco, Minister of Justice of Fascist Italy
and influential Fascist ideologue

Rocco's economic beliefs, like those of his colleague Corradini, were largely based on the notion that economic power, expressed in the

sustainable in the long term. When reviewing Rocco's economic thought, one must not lose sight of the geopolitical notions that define it — in particular, Rocco believed that developed countries were justified in imposing free trade models on other countries because in such conditions they gained a tangible advantage over unprepared competitors, while for the 'backward' (including Italy) playing by the rules of the 'developed' would be detrimental to the national future. All of Rocco's concrete economic proposals must be understood from the perspective of an Italian nationalist who cares about his country's future, and not as an 'abstractly correct' model.

development of productive capacity, is one of the most important driving forces of history. The more developed countries impose their hegemony on the laggards. To move from the category of 'backward' to 'developed' requires a national effort inspired by a belief in the promise and future of the homeland. To accomplish such a feat, to sacrifice the present for the future, the nation had to be well disciplined and united by a strong collective solidarity. It seemed obvious to the nationalists that the liberal Italian government was not up to this task. At this time Italy was displaying the exact opposite tendencies: the few rich wanted to become even richer as soon as possible, the national aims were unfocused, and Marxist sentiment was gaining strength.

Another dimension of Rocco's thought needs to be touched upon here. Well aware of the Marxist threat (as mentioned above, Rocco was briefly a member of the Radical Party), the thinker pointed out that a nation can never achieve a high level of solidarity if workers are alienated. Economic expansion is possible only if everyone in society realises the importance of their own role within the whole. It is therefore in the interest of the nation to protect the corporate interests of the workers. Such thinking (already evident in the pre-war years) prompted Rocco to formulate the first principles of integral corporatism — an original Fascist economic doctrine, which received its most mature expression in the works of the philosopher Ugo Spirito, a disciple of Giovanni Gentile. Rocco wrote that all corporate interests must be taken into account in the legal field — this is the only way to create a solid foundation for the social harmony needed to build a Great Italy.[3] As A. James Gregor rightly points out, in Rocco's understanding 'a strong state must keep all associations of trade union, church, academic, educational, political, labour, and entrepreneurial

3 As a contemporary notes, Rocco 'wrote as early as 1914 about the revival of medieval "corporations", and in 1920 he outlined the theory of syndicalism, adopted by the Fascists with some amendments…'. Moreover, he 'led the passage of syndicalist laws in Parliament'. Herman Hausheer, 'Fascism in Italy', *Social Science*, 8, no. 4 (October 1933), p. 400.

nature firmly within its bounds'.[4] The renaissance of Italy, imagined by Italian nationalists in the form of a productive upsurge which would inevitably entail a cultural regeneration of the nation's spiritual forces, is only possible through the construction of such a corporate state — powerful, pervasive and independent.

Alfredo Rocco hoped that conditions for the formation of such a state would be created after Italy's victory in the First World War.[5] In the early post-war years, however, all the crises of the early twentieth century were exacerbated.[6] At the same time, the young Fascist movement that took power in October 1922 with the March on Rome was also gaining strength. Rocco, a member of the lower house of the Italian Parliament since 1921, was among those who actively supported Mussolini. This generally reflected the mood of the nationalists — in 1923 the ANI had merged with the Italian Fascist Party. Rocco, who saw in Fascism an opportunity to put his own statist ideals into practice, was given numerous opportunities to realise his vision in the following years; during the second half of 1924 he served as Speaker of the Lower House of Parliament, and on 5 January, 1925, he was appointed Minister of Justice by Mussolini, a post he held for seven years, until 1932.[7] Two years after his resignation as minister, Rocco was

4 Gregor, *Mussolini's Intellectuals. Fascist Social and Political Thought*, p. 60.

5 At the early stage of the war Rocco, like many Italian nationalists, was in favor of his country's alliance with the Central Powers, but later changed his mind — joining the Entente looked more logical from the nationalists' geopolitical point of view (the possible collapse of the Austro-Hungarian Empire, according to the nationalists, offered Italy very attractive prospects for new territories). A. J. de Grand, 'The Italian Nationalist Association in the Period of Italian Neutrality, August 1914-May 1915', *The Journal of Modern History*, 43, no. 3 (Sep., 1971), pp. 394–412.

6 In 1920 Rocco stated: 'The state is in crisis... It is rapidly losing all the attributes of sovereignty'. Cited in: Luisa Mangoni, 'La crisi dello Stato liberale e i giuristi italiani' [The Crisis of the Liberal State and Italian Jurists], *Studi Storici* [Historical Studies], 23, no. 1 (Jan.-Mar., 1982), p. 75.

7 Rocco initiated many legal reforms as Minister of Justice, such as the reform of trial by jury, which was passed by royal decree on 23 March 1931. See: Morris

appointed senator for life, but sat in the upper house of parliament for only one year — he died in 1935 at the age of sixty-nine.

Italian Prime Minister Benito Mussolini, 1928. The Roman numeral VI next to the date stands for 'The Sixth Year of the Fascist Era'. The new calendar was taken from the success of the March on Rome and the Fascists' rise to power.

Rocco's most prominent ideological work from the *ventennio* period, *The Political Doctrine of Fascism*, is in fact an abstract from a lecture he delivered in Perugia on August 30, 1925, six months after his appointment as Fascist Italy's Minister of Justice. Given that Rocco's lecture

Ploscowe, 'Jury Reform in Italy', *Journal of Criminal Law and Criminology (1931–1951)*, 25, no. 4 (Nov.–Dec., 1934), pp. 576–585. Another very important act by Rocco as Minister was the adoption of a new Penal Code (in force since July 1, 1931), which toughened penalties for 'crimes against the state' and 'crimes against the family' (for example, for adultery, under Article 559 of the Code, a Fascist state citizen could be imprisoned for two years). For more details, see: Giulio Battaglini, 'The Fascist Reform of the Penal Law in Italy', *Journal of Criminal Law and Criminology (1931–1951)*, 24, no. 1, Century of Progress Number: The Development of Criminology in the State of Illinois during the Past Century, in the United States of America at Large and in Other Nations of the World during the Past Quarter-Century (May-June, 1933), pp. 278–289.

was delivered seven years before the publication of *The Doctrine of Fascism* and was approved by Mussolini, it seems appropriate to consider its main theses.[8]

'First of all, let us ask ourselves whether there is a political doctrine of Fascism as such; whether there is any ideal content in the Fascist state',[9] Rocco asks. 'The truth is that Fascism is, first and foremost, an action and a feeling, and so it must remain. If it were otherwise, it would not be able to maintain its gigantic impulsive power, the renewing power it now possesses, and would move into the secluded reflections of a select few',[10] the thinker continues. However, Rocco argues that Fascism has a unique intellectual and theoretical content which is 'an integral part of this historical phenomenon'.[11] According to Rocco, Fascism's theoretical principles are autonomous and unique in their own way. He proves this thesis by comparing Fascism with the major contemporary political doctrines: liberalism, socialism, and Bolshevism.

Rocco argues that all modern political thought comes from one source — the Protestant Reformation, whose ideas, reinforced by the adherents of the doctrine of 'natural law' and based on the post-revolutionary practices of England, America, and France, had a significant influence on all political processes up to the advent of Fascism. The single fundamental basis of all modern political doctrines, according

8 Post-war and contemporary scholars agree on the importance of Rocco in the self-awareness of Fascism in the early years of the regime. For example, Emiliana Noether states that Rocco 'shared with Gentile the role of official theorist of the Fascist party'. Emiliana p. Noether, 'Italian Intellectuals under Fascism', *The Journal of Modern History*, 43, no. 4 (Dec., 1971), p. 640. A contemporary noted Rocco's importance even more, putting him on a par with the Duce: 'Mussolini, Gentile, Rocco, and Panunzio constitute the legal-philosophical quadruplet of Fascism'. H. Arthur Steiner, 'The Fascist Conception of Law', *Columbia Law Review*, 36, no. 8 (Dec., 1936), p. 1269.

9 Alfredo Rocco, 'The Political Doctrine of Fascism', *International Conciliation*, no. 223, (October 1926), p. 394.

10 Ibid., p. 394.

11 Ibid., p. 394.

to Rocco, is 'a mechanical or atomistic conception of the state'.[12] The key to such systems of political thought is the notion of society as the sum of separate individuals; a unity which mechanically disintegrates into isolated, unconnected parts. The consequence of this belief, according to Rocco, is fundamental anti-historicism, since for a society understood in this way, the temporal aspect has no meaning (due to social atomism, strategic state thinking makes no sense — what matters is the social life of a given generation 'now living'). Of course, such an approach is ontologically reduced to materialism — in such a worldview, spiritual and cultural heritage cannot denote anything concrete.

Liberalism, socialism, and Bolshevism all work towards the same goal: the happiness of living individuals in the form of a rapid increase in their prosperity. Their technical methods differ. In the liberal doctrine, for example, the greatest good is achieved through the least amount of state intervention in the affairs of citizens. 'Kant, who was undoubtedly the most powerful and profound philosopher of liberalism, said that "man, who is the end, cannot be seen as the means"',[13] writes Rocco. The liberal doctrine, by 'reducing' the state to a minimum, prevents it from interfering in any way in the affairs of citizens. This is further expressed in the system of checks and balances characteristic of the liberal approach to the organisation of power, greatly limiting the possibilities of the ruler.

The liberal political impulse was developed by socialists who questioned inequality and injustice. Indeed, the ideal liberal system, concentrating power in the hands of a few 'competent' elites and removing the state from the economic life of society, lacks any mechanisms for redistributing wealth. The first question posed by the Left is that of democracy. If the state is there for everyone, why is not everyone involved in its management? Adding the ideal of equality to the ideal

12 Ibid., p. 395.

13 Ibid., p. 396.

of 'freedom from', we get the Rousseauist conception of the sovereign people as bearers of a common will — a prerequisite for a democratic and republican form of power organisation. The next step 'to the left', as Rocco notes, came during the industrial revolution, which brought to the fore the question of economic inequality. He highlights the contradiction of initial liberal aspirations which comes out in the demand for state intervention in order to establish economic justice and eliminate the economic domination of the 'capitalists'. At the same time, he notes that socialism represents a further development of the concept of social atomism, in which the economic well-being of specific, presently living individuals demanded new sacrifices.

According to Rocco, socialism, understood radically, leads to Bolshevism, which calls for violence against 'capitalists' right up to their total annihilation and the establishment of a 'dictatorship of the proletariat' as the fairest system of government, eliminating any inequality and saving the 'working class' from exploitation by 'capitalists'. Thus, the idea of 'natural right' finds its final, complete embodiment precisely in Bolshevism, having passed through liberal, democratic, and socialist stages.[14] The key political aspiration of all these doctrines is the maximisation of material wealth and the well-being of living individuals.

The innovative nature of Fascism, according to Rocco, lies in the fact that Fascism is an integrative doctrine of the social, the opposite of both liberal and socialist atomism. Fascism's strength is that it is indifferent to methods: 'In its political praxis it uses liberal ways,

14 Here, too, a parallel can be drawn between Fascist thought and the political aspirations of the German 'conservative revolutionaries'. Oswald Spengler, to whose work *Prussianism and Socialism* we have already referred, in another, later book, *The Years of Decision* (1933), argued that 'active liberalism progresses successively from Jacobinism to Bolshevism' and the liberal differs from the Bolshevik only in the methods of struggle — their aspirations are similar. Oswald Spengler, *Years of Decisions*, (Yekaterinburg: U-Factoria, 2007), p. 107. It should be noted that Rocco voiced this idea eight years earlier than Spengler.

democratic means, and even socialist practices'.[15] All this is profoundly secondary, since Fascism, according to Rocco, proceeds from premises that are fundamentally different from the doctrine of 'natural rights'. In elaborating this thesis, the Italian jurist notes that 'man is not mere matter; and the real purposes of human beings are far from the materialistic ones that we share with other animals — they are of a spiritual nature, peculiar only to men; these purposes every society tries to achieve in one way or another as far as its level of development allows'.[16] Rocco argues that the unity of language, culture, religion, customs, and traditions is as important for any human society as a common understanding of material interests: economic aspirations, territory, and living conditions. Such an understanding of the social gives a different idea of temporality, lends significance to the past and the future. Fascism understood in this way is an organic and historical doctrine. A consequence of this understanding, as Rocco writes, is the change of the liberal formula 'society for the individual' to 'the individual for society'. According to Rocco, this understanding of the link between society and the individual does not destroy the latter but, on the contrary, allows him to develop as part of the whole. As the thinker writes, 'the life of society embraces the existence of individuals and projects itself into succeeding generations through centuries and millennia'.[17] The sum of the social does not change in time: individual citizens are born, live and die, but society continues to exist through the centuries.

Rocco elaborates on Fascism's understanding of key issues of political theory — issues of freedom, social justice and governance. In his discussion of freedom, he returns to the thesis of Fascism's indifference to methods: Fascism regards neither the pursuit of economic

---

15 Rocco, 'The Political Doctrine of Fascism', p. 400.

16 Ibid., p. 401.

17 Ibid., p. 403.

freedom nor the protection of 'natural rights' as dogma.[18] The Fascist state regards the individual as 'an economic tool for the development of society',[19] subordinating the interests of the individual to the interests of the whole and guaranteeing the individual freedom to the extent that this coincides with the strategic aspirations of society as an integrated organism. Turning to the discourse of government, Rocco argues that unlike other contemporary political theories, Fascism recognises the sovereignty not of an individual people but of a society as a whole legally organised in a state.[20] The state, in turn, is led by a political elite — a few special people who are set apart from the masses by virtue of their special qualities. Considering the problem of social justice, Rocco points out that Fascism undoubtedly recognises the right of private property, but for a different motivation than liberal doctrines indicate, namely because of the social utility of this institution. Fascism addresses the protection of various classes' interests (primarily economic ones) through the creation of corporatist institutions, involving trade union associations in the unified state organism.

In the concluding section of *The Political Doctrine of Fascism*, Rocco examines Fascism's historical value by referring to the history of social thought. He returns to the claim that all the other political doctrines, which he lumps together under the general term 'natural law doctrines', are a consequence of the Reformation and the French

18 However, Rocco recognises that individual ambition is the most effective motivator of economic development. Thus, conceptually, he acknowledges the effectiveness of market economic relations, but he opposes their absolutisation as the principle governing social life. In this sense, Rocco is very close to Gentile, who strongly rejects economic determinism (or more broadly 'economic imperialism', to use the notion of modern economic theory, such as the concept of G. Becker), but recognises the value of private initiative and its importance for economic development.

19 Ibid., p. 404.

20 Rocco's fundamental etatism is the reason for his suspicion of the Catholic Church and his negative attitude towards Freemasonry, which he regarded as 'internationalist and pacifist' institutions. Edward R. Tannenbaum, 'The Goals of Italian Fascism', *The American Historical Review*, 74, no. 4 (Apr., 1969), p. 1197.

Revolution. They are all individualistic, anti-social, and destructive of the state. Rocco notes that among the creators of the doctrines of 'natural law', who developed anti-state political aspirations, there were no Italians: 'Grotius and Spinoza were Dutch; Locke was an Englishman; St Pierre, Montesquieu, d'Argenson, Voltaire, Diderot, and the Encyclopedists were French; Althusius, Pufendorf, Kant, and Fichte were Germans'.[21] From this the Italian jurist deduces that the doctrines of 'natural law' are alien to 'Latin reason', the proper representation of state authority. Drawing a line of continuity from the Roman state tradition to the medieval scholastics (Rocco singles out St. Thomas Aquinas), and from them to the creator of modern political theory Niccolò Machiavelli, who 'liberated political science from the formalism of the scholastics and moved it into the sphere of concrete reality', Rocco traces the development of political thought parallel to that of the Enlightenment-liberal. Like other ideologues of Fascism, Rocco attaches great importance to Giambattista Vico and his 'strong resistance to the doctrines of natural law'.[22] Just like Gentile, Rocco calls the Risorgimento philosophers (first and foremost, of course, Mazzini, in whose thought the Fascist minister highlights the reflection on the duty of man) direct precursors of Fascism, who, in turn, took much from Vico. Thus, Rocco portrays Fascism as a typically Italian, 'Latin' political phenomenon, the prerequisites of which were political thought opposed to the doctrines of 'natural law'. According to Rocco, thanks to Fascism 'Italy once again speaks to the world and the world listens to Italy'.[23]

When analysing the doctrine of Fascism as portrayed by Rocco, it should be noted that, despite the recognition of common historical and philosophical preconditions of Fascism with the actualists (primarily the values of Vico and Mazzini), the Italian jurist emphasises the more practical aspects of the doctrine. In particular, while Gentile's practical

21 Rocco, 'The Political Doctrine of Fascism', p. 410.

22 Ibid., p. 412.

23 Ibid., p. 415.

philosophy is logically derived from his ontology and anthropology, Rocco does not delve into philosophical issues, operating mainly with economic and legal notions and referring mainly to the history of political thought. This is understandable, as Rocco was not a philosopher, but the absence of an underlying philosophical foundation as a basis for any practical insights in his doctrinal political thought leads to the conclusion that his intellectual constructions should be considered ideological rather than philosophical. A significant influence of his senior nationalist comrade Corradini is evident in Rocco's doctrine — the Italian jurist pays much more attention to economic questions than did Gentile and Mussolini. At the same time, much of what Rocco said coincided with what would be formalised in the *Doctrine of Fascism* seven years later (most of all, fundamental statism: the recognition of the state as the only legitimate sovereign, the total primacy of the whole over the individual, and the rejection of liberalism, democracy, and socialism).

1.2. Intellectuals in Power. Syndicalists and the Labour Charter. The Anti-Gentilean Approach of Carlo Costamagna. Giuseppe Bottai and Fascist Critique. Julius Evola's *Pagan Imperialism*

Turning to an analysis of the various approaches in the development of Fascist doctrine during the *ventennio* years, it is necessary to outline their multidirectional nature. Within this section we will briefly examine the main aspects of the leftist, Syndicalist variations of Fascism; the conservative political teaching of Carlo Costamagna — one of the main opponent of Gentile and the actualists; the key ideas of Giuseppe Bottai — perhaps the most prominent Fascist hierarch on the intellectual front; and the radical doctrine of pagan renaissance proposed by the traditionalist Julius Evola.

As shown in the first chapter of this work, revolutionary and National Syndicalism is one of the key sources of the political philosophy of Fascism. Many radical Syndicalists joined the Fascist movement in the early post-war years. Some of them (e.g. Sergio Panunzio and Angelo Oliviero Olivetti) reached significant career heights in the years after the war, became integrated into various governing bodies of the new Fascist state, and gained a platform for expressing and publishing their ideas. This raises the question of what issues they were concerned with between 1925 and 1943 and what contribution they made to the development of Fascist doctrine.

The most famous episode of Syndicalist participation in the debate which arose during the Fascist era is the dispute between Sergio Panunzio and Carlo Costamagna over the nature of the state and the role of Fascism. The dispute between the two intellectuals continued throughout 1926 and had several angles: whether Fascism was a genuinely revolutionary movement or a conservative one; what the socio-economic aspirations of Fascism were; what links would be established between trade unions, society, and the state. Panunzio expressed his position as early as November 1922, during a lecture he delivered in Ferrara. In it he argued that, contrary to the position of conservatives and nationalists who see trade unions as a manifestation of unhealthy social divisions, the union movement was in fact a reflection of a healthy, vibrant, and genuinely renewed popular spirit. According to Panunzio, the institutions of the liberal state die out because they are too abstract and incapable of perceiving the real life of society. The new, Fascist state must be based on a clearly structured interaction of economic unions.

For Costamagna, on the other hand, the syndicates are a typically liberal (left-wing in the classical sense) social trend that is destructive to the state. There is nothing creative in them; they are pure protest. To master this power, Fascism must build hierarchically organised corporations controlled from above. Panunzio rejected such a vision as 'unnecessarily static'. He asserted: 'For me, the underlying principle is society. The State is a form of social being. Sociology is a fundamental science of state theory'.[24] By this time, Panunzio, like Costamagna, was inclined to think that trade unions should be integrated into the state, but his logic was different from that of his colleague: the integration of syndicates must contribute to the development of the state, its positive transformation. For Costamagna, it was just a question of controlling potentially dangerous natural forces.

In April 1926 Fascist Italy passed the so-called 'Syndicate Law'. On the one hand it provided a legal framework for the presence of unions in the social and economic life of Italy, giving the syndicates some real powers (such as bargaining with industrialists over minimum wages for workers in particular sectors of the economy). On the other hand, it imposed a number of restrictions — there could only be one union in each industrial sector and strikes were banned, as were non-Fascist unions. This showcased, among other things, the regime's desire for institutional innovation of the collectivist sort, unanimously endorsed by most public intellectuals and key intellectuals in power: the nationalists Rocco and Corradini, the Syndicalists Panunzio and Oliviero Olivetti, and the Fascist party leaders Grandi and Bottai.[25]

The Fascist state continued its course towards institutional reforms — on 21 April, 1927, the Labour Charter[26] was issued, legislating the principles of corporatism. In particular, the Charter stated that 'work, in all its intellectual, technical and manual forms, is a social obligation' (Article 2); 'freedom of trade unions is declared in the State; however, only one trade union in each branch is recognised by the State and has the right to represent the workers and employers

24 Cited from: Roberts, *Syndicalist Tradition and Italian Fascism*, p. 243.

25 As Carmen Haider, a contemporary of these events, notes, 'there are three main differences between Fascist syndicalism and all other "doctrines of labour": the acceptance of the capitalist class as socially useful; the shift from class enmity to class collaboration, and the incorporation of the manufacturers' associations into the nation state'. Carmen Haider, 'The Italian Corporate State', *Political Science Quarterly*, 46, no. 2 (Jun., 1931), p. 228.

26 *Carta del Lavoro*, 1927. 21 aprile [Electronic resource]. URL: http://www.historia.unimi.it/sezione/fonti/codificazione/cartalavoro.pdf.

of the branch concerned' (Article 3); 'legal trade unions are bound to maintain equality of workers and employers and to maintain discipline in work and production' (Article 6);[27] 'corporations are public bodies' (Article 6); 'State intervention in the economy is permissible only when private initiative is insufficient or the political interests of the State are at stake' (Article 9); and 'the sphere of employment is the sphere of corporate control' (Article 13). The main intention of the Charter's authors (Giuseppe Bottai is considered its author and inspiration) was an attempt to overcome class divisions and relieve social tensions brought about by the Bolshevik upheaval. The Charter was well received by Syndicalists — in particular at the Lausanne Congress of 1928, where Oliviero Olivetti exclaimed: 'Corporations are instruments of national self-government; even more, they are the nation itself, making itself a state'.[28] Italy was on the way to unifying the political and economic spheres of the State into a coherent whole, which was also positively perceived by Syndicalists.[29] The apotheosis of the institutional and spiritual fusion of Syndicalists and Fascists was the opening of the Fascist Faculty of Political Sciences at the University of Perugia in March 1928, whose main task was the conceptualisation of the Fascist doctrine and its teaching to the future elite of society and the state. The faculty was headed by Panunzio, later joined by Orano and Oliviero Olivetti. Having merged with Fascism, the Italian Syndicalists continued to work for the regime for the rest of their lives.

The aforementioned Carlo Costamagna (1881–1965) positioned himself as an opponent of Gentile and actual idealism. As A. James Gregor notes, 'Costamagna can be seen as a member of the nationalist-Catholic faction among Fascist intellectuals. Having been Gentile's

27 For the Syndicalists, this provision of the Charter was crucial. See: G. Paresce, 'Problems of Italian Syndicalism', *Journal of the Royal Institute of International Affairs*, 9, no. 3 (May, 1930), pp. 376–383.

28 Roberts, *Syndicalist Tradition and Italian Fascism*, p. 256.

29 Panunzio exclaimed in 1934 that 'politics and economics are now one'. See: Ibid., p. 257.

ally at an early stage, Costamagna later distanced himself considerably — first of all because Gentile proved to be more of a statist than a nationalist but also because the Roman Catholic Church considered actual idealism a heresy'.[30]

Costamagna and Gentile disagreed even in their historical approaches to the interpretation of the Fascist phenomenon — while Gentile insisted on the continuity between the idealism, the national-liberalism of the Risorgimento, and Fascism, Costamagna vehemently denied this, interpreting Fascism as a revolutionary phenomenon. For Costamagna, the philosophical content of the Risorgimento did not play a significant role in the interpretation of Fascism — for him, national independence was achieved through military resistance to Napoleonic conquest, which played an important role in awakening the political instinct of the Italian people. As A. Tarquini notes, the Risorgimento in Costamagna's understanding was the result of 'military and statist factors, which have nothing to do with liberal political ideologies'.[31] Disagreeing on the underlying causes, Costamagna and Gentile also diverge on the consequences — from denying the role of Risorgimento intellectuals as precursors of Fascism, Costamagna comes to deny the influence of Giuseppe Mazzini (who is for Gentile one of the main intellectual reference points) and more generally to criticising the actualist understanding of Fascism as the next step towards 'true liberalism'.

Costamagna argues that Fascism was born of a totalitarian Roman Catholic state whose foundation is the 'Mediterranean-Latin tradition'. Whereas for Gentile the state is the essence of ethics, inseparable from the true freedom of the individual, for Costamagna it is domineering, completely subordinating the individual. In the doctrine of Fascism,

30 Gregor, *Mussolini's Intellectuals. Fascist Social and Political Thought*, p. 188.

31 Alessandra Tarquini, 'The Anti-Gentilians during the Fascist Regime', *Journal of Contemporary History*, 40, no. 4 (Oct., 2005), p. 659.

according to Costamagna, 'the state is a reality-in-itself ... it is a reality of the spirit and not a material mass or an intellectual construction'.[32]

Costamagna, continuing the thought of the German jurist and 'conservative revolutionary' Carl Schmitt (1888–1985), argued about 'large spaces', whose basis is the 'kinship of peoples'. According to him, a 'large space' can be governed from a single centre if the people living in it are organically related to one another. The 'organic cooperation' of the peoples, according to Costamagna, can be traced throughout Italian history — from the Roman Empire to the creation of the Roman Catholic Church. His concept has features that are similar to the main political aspirations of Italy's German allies: in particular, he argued that the peoples of the 'Aryan race', united by common ethno-cultural traits, are capable of 'organic cooperation' in 'large spaces'. A. James Gregor draws a direct parallel between Costamagna's 'spiritual forces that maintain national identity' and the 'homogeneity of the population' according to Schmitt, highlighting the biologically racist nature of the latter definition.[33] However, Costamagna himself noted that his discourse on 'Aryan' peoples is not limited to biology, calling for a more spiritual interpretation, which is generally consistent with his key aspiration to the principles of 'Roman Catholic civilisation'. In 1942, in *Large Spaces and Imperial Ethnarchy*, Costamagna asserts the need for an 'ethnarchical empire', highlighting the importance of the ethnic factor. This is an aspect completely absent from actual idealism, which does not recognise any biological determinism (or, as Gentile called it, 'naturalism') in matters of practical philosophy.

32 Carlo Costamagna, *Dottrina del Fascismo* [Doctrine of Fascism], (Rome, 1938). Cited from: Tarquini, 'The Anti-Gentilians during the Fascist Regime', p. 660.

33 It should be noted here that, despite this analogy, first drawn by James Gregor, it is by no means possible to equate Schmitt's discourse on 'large spaces' with the official political line of the Nazi party. Schmitt had a complicated relationship with the Nazis — having joined the NSDAP in May 1933 he was already in disgrace in December 1936 after being accused of being a 'Hegelian and a Catholic' and of being insincere in his anti-Semitism.

Costamagna is also one of the few Fascist intellectuals who in any way supported the anti-Semitic attitude of his German intellectual and political allies. In particular, he argued in his writings at the end of the *ventennio* era that 'the Jews are a significant threat to the spiritual integrity of the peoples of Europe'.[34] This was also unacceptable to the actualists (Gentile, Spirito, and Pellizzi), who never reduced political issues to a base biological level.

However, some Fascist hierarchs were no strangers to anti-Semitism — for example, Giuseppe Bottai (1895–1959), who had a brilliant political career[35] and is remembered as a notable *ventennio* intellectual.[36] The journal *Critica Fascista*, founded by Bottai, established itself as one of the largest venues for public debate during the Fascist period.

---

34 Costamagna, *Dottrina del Fascismo* in Gregor, *Mussolini's Intellectuals*, p. 189.

35 In 1921 he was first elected as a Member of Parliament for the Fascist Party. Bottai was a member of the twenty-sixth, twenty-seventh, twenty-eighth, and twenty-ninth parliament, and in 1939 he was elected a member of the Chamber of Fascists and Corporations, which replaced the lower house of the Italian parliament, a body formed on the basis of party representation, for the period spanning 1939–1943. In 1929 Mussolini relinquished to Bottai the post of Minister for Corporations that he had previously held personally. Bottai remained in office until 1932. From January 1935 to November 1936, Bottai served as mayor of Rome. The Italian lawyer left this high office to take on a more demanding job at national level when he returned to government to head the Ministry of Education. Bottai worked in that position until February 1943, leaving it a few months before Mussolini was overthrown by the Fascist Grand Council.

36 Historians of Fascism have a split opinion of Bottai. Some perceive the Italian jurist as an intelligent and educated man, a supporter of a plurality of opinions in public discussions about Fascism, and an opponent of the repressive imposition of the 'only correct' official point of view — as a technocratic minister who promoted the idea of Fascism (especially Fascist corporatism) as a 'third way' of state-building beyond liberalism and socialism. For example, see: Jeffrey Thompson Schnapp, *A Primer of Italian Fascism*, (Lincoln, Nebraska: University of Nebraska Press, 2000), p. 185. For others, Bottai is a fanatical Fascist and anti-Semite who has done his utmost to promote Nazi-type racial laws. Bottai wrote that Fascist anti-Semitism has a 'spiritual character', following on from 3,000 years of Italian history, thought and culture. However, as Minister of Education, Bottai completely unspiritualised the new racist legislation of 1938, as a result of which Italian Jews were denied access to schools and libraries.

Almost immediately after the March on Rome, Bottai began to advocate a vision of Fascism not as a state system or political force, but as a kind of receptacle of the 'national spirit', a guardian of Italian tradition, thought, culture and art. He insists on the need for the 'intellectual indoctrination' of Italians, which in his eyes was the mission of *Critica Fascista*.[37]

In 1928, a year before he took office as Minister of Corporations, in his introductory lecture to a course on corporate law at the University of Pisa, Bottai stated: 'Fascism-as-culture, into which, as we have seen, Fascism-as-action is integrated, is the foundation of Fascism-as-state. In our type of state, which is not a dry bureaucracy (which applies to the old bureaucracy as well as to the new one emerging from Syndicalism), the professional skills rooted in the mentality of the accountant are insufficient. Our state engages the spirit and consciousness of its citizens; it is in their spirit and consciousness that they must act to serve it'.[38] Justifying the need for a new understanding of higher education in line with the articulated paradigm of nation-building, he asserts: 'The role of the university in the Fascist state is to lay the foundation for a living culture capable of creating a class of people who can become leaders in politics, science, and the arts'.[39] Here Bottai sees Fascism as

The discriminatory treatment of Jews also affected higher education. For more details see: Duggan, *Fascist Voices: An Intimate History of Mussolini's Italy*, pp. 307–313. In 1933 Bottai and Gentile were also involved in setting up public schools to educate the children of Jews expelled from Germany. See Franklin H. Adler, 'Jew as Bourgeois, Jew as Enemy, Jew as Victim of Fascism', *Modern Judaism*, 28, no. 3 (Oct., 2008), pp. 306–326. For a discussion of the wisdom of the various historical accounts of Bottai as a 'tragic hero' of Italian Fascism, see: Vito Zagarrio, 'Bottai: Un Fascista critico?' [A Critical Fascist], *Studi Storici [Historical Studies]*, 17, no. 4 (Oct.–Dec., 1976), pp. 267–271.

37 For more detail, see: Alexandra de Luise, 'Le Arti and Intervention in the Arts', *RACAR: revue d'art canadienne / Canadian Art Review*, 19, no. 1/2, 'Art as Propaganda / Art et propaganda' (1992), pp. 123–132.

38 Giuseppe Bottai, 'Culture and Action' in Griffin, *Fascism*, p. 62.

39 Ibid., p. 62.

a life-giving principle that spiritualises all the higher spheres of human activity.

Young party functionary Giuseppe Bottai—founder of *Critica Fascista*

Shortly afterwards, in 1932, Bottai enthusiastically welcomed the publication of *The Doctrine of Fascism* by Mussolini. In an article with the pathos-filled title 'The Age of Mussolini', published in *Critica Fascista* on 15 August, 1932, Bottai describes the profound intuition of the great Duce, who undertook the theoretical effort to understand and conceptualise Fascism as a 'great whole' and to justify its place in human and spiritual history. The thinker claims that 'Mussolini felt the need to declare that Fascism has a universal value, reflecting a new phase in the history of the human spirit'.[40] According to Bottai, '*The Doctrine of Fascism*, which incorporates both democratic and socialist expertise, comprehends the state as a system of rights and duties of individuals organised to achieve the highest ethical goals of the human being in its particular national manifestation'.[41] Thus, *The Doctrine of Fascism*,

40 Bottai, 'The Century of Mussolini' in Griffin, *Fascism*, p. 70.

41 Ibid., p. 70.

according to Bottai, should be understood as 'a manifesto for the revolution of ideas that will conquer the world'.[42]

Bottai actively supported the propaganda tendency of Fascism which aimed to maintain the 'myth of Romanness' (*romanita*) that prevailed in the 1930s. In Bottai's interpretation, 'Romanness' was not reduced to a mere historical continuity between the Roman Empire and Fascist Italy—the fascination with Rome came 'not from books, not from a so-called "dead history", but above all from its capacity and possibility to inspire action in the present'.[43] Fascism, according to the Italian thinker, does not aspire to a restoration of the Roman Empire, but 'to a renewal, to a revolution in the Roman idea'.[44] Thus, Bottai's approach to the myth of *romanita* can be described as quite modernist.

Giuseppe Bottai, 1924

42 Ibid., p. 71.

43 Giuseppe Bottai, *Roma e Fascismo* (1937), cited from: Griffin, *Modernism and Fascism. The Sense of a Beginning under Mussolini and Hitler*, p. 222.

44 Ibid., p. 222.

In addition to cultural policy, Bottai actively supported youth work, which the Fascist Party intensified in the second half of the 1930s. In 1937 a single youth organisation, the *Gioventù Italiana del Littorio* (Italian Youth of the Littorio), was founded. Commenting on this event, Bottai noted that 'participation in the GIL must be perceived as a "service" in which young people can prepare for collective life in the Fascist state and service in the Fascist army; ultimately, the task of the GIL is to create a whole person: a Fascist'.[45] After assuming the post of Minister of Education, Bottai implemented his own school reform — in 1939 the Charter of Schools (*La Carta della scuola*) was adopted, dividing schoolchildren along both social and gender lines. School, according to Bottai, was more about 'teaching life' than giving knowledge. There were mandatory 'lessons in labour education' (an obvious Nazi influence) and separate 'schools for girls', who — according to Bottai and his followers — simply did not need certain subjects, since the social role of the Fascist woman was first and foremost that of motherhood and the family home.[46]

45 Cited from: Michel Ostenc, 'La jeunesse italienne et le Fascisme a la veille de la Seconde guerre mondiale' [Italian Youth and Fascism on the Eve of the Second World War], *Revue d'histoire de la Deuxième Guerre Mondiale* [Review of the history of the Second World War], 24, no. 94 (April 1974), p. 49.

46 For more information on Bottai's educational reforms, see: Tracy H. Koon, *Believe, Obey, Fight. Political Socialization of Youth in Fascist Italy, 1922–1943*, (Chapel Hill, NC: University of North Carolina Press, 2012); Michel Ostenc, 'Les étudiants Fascistes italiens des années 1930' [Italian Fascist Students of the 1930s], *Le Mouvement social* [The Social Movement], no. 120, Entre Socialisme et Nationalisme: Les Mouvements Étudiants Européens (Jul. — Sep., 1982), pp. 95–106.

Giuseppe Bottai during the Second Italo-Ethiopian War (1935–1936). Bottai left his post as mayor of Rome, joined the army with the rank of major and entered the Ethiopian capital Addis Ababa on 5 May 1936 with Italian troops led by Marshal Pietro Badoglio, after which he was briefly appointed mayor of that city.

Despite a seemingly spotless and brilliant political career, Bottai was out of Mussolini's favour from the late 1920s to the early 1930s[47] and was among the Fascist hierarchs who voted to dismiss the Duce during the historic meeting of the Great Fascist Council on 24 July, 1943.[48] He was not involved in the events of the Salò period.

47 Mussolini, gripped by a typically dictatorial megalomania and suspicions of disloyalty from his inner circle, gradually retired all members of the so-called 'Government of All Talents' formed in 1929. Alfredo Rocco, Luigi Federzoni, Edmondo Rossoni, Augusto Turati, Dino Grandi, and Giuseppe Bottai had left the Fascist government by 1932.

48 A few months before the 'Grandi Mutiny' Bottai would write in *Critica Fascista*: 'A revolution cannot overcome obstacles and avoid fatal mistakes if it rejects the critical forces that gave rise to it and continue to drive it forward.' Giuseppe Bottai, 'Twenty years of Critica Fascista' in Schnapp, *A Primer of Italian Fascism*, p. 192. The entry in Bottai's diary of 24 July, 1943, begins with the following lines: 'A dramatic and exciting day awaits us... A fork in the road. Our duty calls for a choice: country or party, Italy or regime, king or leader...'. Bottai, *Diario 1935–1944*, p. 404. Understanding the situation in this way, Bottai obviously opted for the country and the King.

Giuseppe Bottai at work

Finally, when considering non-actualist influence on the development of Fascist ideology, it is necessary to mention the project of pagan revival proposed by the traditionalist Julius Evola (1898–1974).[49] In terms of the practical realisation of his own socio-political philosophy, Baron Evola had certain hopes for the Italian Fascist regime, which he expressed in his book *Pagan Imperialism*.[50] In this work, he creates an idealistic image of an authoritarian state with 'an active immanent spirit' standing in the background as a guarantor of a just hierarchy.[51]

49 See: Dmitry Moiseev, 'Социально-политическая философия Юлиуса Эволы и фашистский режим' [The Social and Political Philosophy of Julius Evola and the Fascist Regime], *Материалы Международного молодежного научного форума «Ломоносов-2014»* [Proceedings of the Lomonosov-2014 International Youth Scientific Forum], ed. A. I. Andreev and E. A. Antipov (Moscow: Max Press, 2014). [Electronic Resource]

50 Julius Evola, *Pagan Imperialism*, (Gornahoor Press, 2017).

51 In this respect, the restructuring of the state implemented by the Fascists did not suit Evola because it preserved the parliamentary and constitutional order of Italian statehood. Moreover, in his socio-political writings, Evola is a consistent opponent of the suppression of political opponents by force, a practice that Mussolini used without any regard for morality.

In the synthesis of the material and the spiritual, the *Imperium*, an embodiment of political power, is born. The radical change which Baron Evola called for could only be realised through the spiritual authority of the elite, through a 'revolution from above'. In *Pagan Imperialism*, Evola, by insisting on the idea of a pagan revival in Italy, sought to give the Fascist regime a strategic vector for the restoration of ancient traditions from which only fragmentary memories remained in the mass consciousness. His radical, idealist approach was not understood or supported in the circles of the Fascist elite.[52] The ideas of *Pagan Imperialism*, despite giving Mussolini's book some attention, were not put into practice, leading to Evola's deep disillusionment with Fascism. In 1930 he severely criticised Mussolini's regime from a right-wing perspective in his own magazine, *La Torre*, after which the publication was closed and the Italian intellectual himself withdrew into 'internal exile', retreating from active political life. In the post-war years, the Italian intellectual remained apolitical, but actively commented on both the crisis state of the modern world[53] and the failed experience of Fascism.[54]

---

52 Philosophically, Evola is certainly an idealist. However, his idealism is of a completely different kind than Gentile's actual idealism. Devoted to antiquity, Évola insists on the need to separate 'science' from 'wisdom' and opposes all academicism. For example, in *Pagan Imperialism* he writes: 'Wisdom gives rise to freedom, provides an open space for action, lets you breathe. In socialised knowledge there is instead always a hidden "you must", a secret, uncompromising, moral obligation: what is "scientific" or "philosophical" truth must be — insofar as it is truth — recognised by everyone. Ibid., p. 97. Evola eschews all academic philosophising and openly opposes the Italian Neo-Hegelians, regarding their philosophy as lifeless.

53 Julius Evola, Men Among the Ruins, (Rochester, Vermont: Inner Traditions, 2002).

54 Julius Evola, Fascism Viewed from the Right, (London: Arktos Media Ltd., 2013).

Julius Evola—aristocrat, traditionalist, and author of *Pagan Imperialism* (1928)

Summarising this discussion, the following crucial fact should be noted: the ideological resistance to Gentile's actual idealism both 'from within' the Fascist party and in general from the right flank of contemporary Italian thought was not voiced by philosophers, but by ideologists, lawyers, and mystics. At the same time, Gentile and his opponents shared many of the doctrinal aspirations characteristic of right-wing ideologies, especially the 'negative' aspirations (opposing Fascism to left-wing ideologies and their values). However, it should be stressed that among Gentile's opponents 'from within' there was not a single philosopher of academic character with competence comparable to his, not one competent enough to impose any meaningful public dialogue.[55] Thus, despite the presence of other viewpoints in the public space of Fascist Italy, if we talk about Fascist philosophy, we are referring first and foremost to actualism.

55 The question of the optimal organisation of a meaningful and productive public dialogue remains relevant even today. For more details, see: A. B. Zakharov and Dmitry Moiseev, 'Эффективность публичных коммуникаций как необходимое условие развития государства' [Public Communication Effectiveness as a Necessary Condition for State Development], *Ценности и смыслы* [Values and Meanings], 32, no. 4 (2012), pp. 66– 69.

§2. The Gentile School

2.1. Ugo Spirito's Integral Corporatism

Giovanni Gentile's influence on the formation and development of the political philosophy of Fascism was not limited to his personal intellectual contribution. As a professional philosopher rather than an ideologue, he influenced many intellectuals whose formative years fell within the *ventennio* era. Of these, the philosopher Ugo Spirito (1896–1979) and the jurist Camillo Pellizzi (1896–1979) made the greatest contributions to social and political discourse.

Ugo Spirito was born in 1896 in Arezzo, Tuscany. Spirito spent his childhood and youth in the backward southern regions of the country, in Caserta and Chieti. He went to university in 1914, at the age of eighteen, and became fascinated by positivism. In 1918, continuing his studies at La Sapienza University in Rome, Spirito was strongly influenced by Gentile and adopted the positions of actual idealism. Following in the footsteps of his teacher, the young philosopher supported Fascism and joined the ranks of Fascist intellectuals. In his first major work, *Pragmatism in Modern Philosophy*,[56] Spirito criticised pragmatism from an actualist position. By 1923 the philosopher was a devout follower of Gentile. Like his teacher, Spirito defended an idealist epistemology and ontology, claiming the impossibility of any reality independent of the consciousness of the mind. Moreover, Spirito drew similar conclusions to Gentile's thought from ontology to social

56 Ugo Spirito, *Il pragmatismo nella filosofia contemporanea* [Pragmatism in Contemporary Philosophy], (Florence: Vallecchi, 1921). In this epistemological work Spirito observes that pragmatism 'froze halfway' to idealism as understood by Gentile, and accuses pragmatism of intellectualism. As discussed in detail in the second chapter of my book, Gentile singled out the issue of the transition from the ideal to the positive as the main problem of intellectualist philosophical doctrines, contrasting them with actual idealism as a philosophy that presupposes a unity of thought and action. Spirito agreed with Gentile that any intellectualism is abstract and therefore incomplete.

philosophy: since the self cannot exist without the non-self, the collective 'we', a transcendental society (due to the actualist understanding of the spirit as a synthesis of unity and multiplicity), Spirito suggests that ethics should be at the centre of philosophical problems in actuality. Since ethics, according to an actualist social philosophy, is an attribute of the state, and the state, which is the embodiment of the national spirit, at the same time embodies the national morality, then ethical problems inevitably lead the philosopher to the conceptualisation of the social order. Sharing Gentile's belief that work is a vital spiritual activity which contributes to the true formation and development of the individual, Spirito develops his theory of corporatism.

Spirito's corporatism, as A. James Gregor rightly points out, combines the aspirations of actualists, nationalists, and Syndicalists.[57]

Before we tackle the question of Fascist economic policy and its philosophical foundations, it is necessary to address political history. When Mussolini came to power at the end of 1922, he could not forgo an alliance with the existing parliamentary forces. The right-wing liberals were the closest to the Fascists in their aspirations, sharing the anti-socialist, anti-egalitarian, and anti-Marxist aspects of Fascism.[58] Taking this into account, as well as Fascism's opposition to left-wing socialist radicals, the early years of Mussolini's rule in terms of economic policy were extremely liberal and market-oriented, in the spirit of the *laissez-faire* doctrine and Manchester free-trade. This largely ensured that Mussolini had the support of the economically active sections of the population, and, against the background of the complete economic collapse of Soviet 'War Communism', his policies looked attractive to the general population as well. Moreover, between 1922 and 1925 many Italian Syndicalists (e.g. Sergio Panunzio and Filippo Corridoni) supported the Italian government's drive towards a market economy. Having finally secured the stability of the new regime in

57 Gregor, *Mussolini's Intellectuals*, p. 99.

58 Moreover, the first Fascist government had three liberal ministers.

1925, Mussolini was interested in the stable development of the young Fascist state under his leadership and thus in a sustainable political-economic model that would accommodate the interests of both industrialists and workers, landowners and peasants alike, and which could be sufficiently well administered to be potentially oriented towards the political super-power, the 'new empire'. The classical market model was not suitable for this — it became necessary to develop, create and implement the principles of an authentically Fascist political economy. Speaking before the Grand Council of Fascism on January 23, 1925, Mussolini proclaimed the task of integrating all economic forces of the nation into the life of the state. During the course of 1925 he spoke with increasing frequency, in various speeches, of the need to subordinate state institutions to the will of the leader, expressing the will of the state. The market would not survive the establishment of a personal dictatorship, or, as Evola aptly put it, Mussolini's 'Caesarism'. Unlike the Bolsheviks, however, the Fascists were unwilling to sacrifice the economy to politics. Thus, the new economic model required a combination of elements of an efficient market order, Fascist state control, and the solidaristic aspirations of Italians.

Ugo Spirito's corporatist theory is a reflection of Giovanni Gentile's actual idealism in the field of economic relations. From 1927 he became, together with another follower of Gentile, Arnaldo Volpicelli (1892–1968), editor of the journal *New Studies in Law, Economics, and Politics* (*Nuovi studi di diritto, economica e politica*). Spirito's main works from the Fascist corporatist period are: 'Critique of Liberal Economics' (*La critica dell'economia liberale*, 1930), 'Foundations of Corporativist Economics' (*I fondamenti dell'economia corporative*, 1932), 'Capitalism and Corporativism' (*Capitalismo e corporativismo*, 1932), and 'From Liberal Economics to Corporativism' (*Dall'economia liberale al corporativismo*, 1939). Corporativism implies 'the subsumption of all the productive elements of the national economy under the dominance of a single-party state'.[59] As A. James Gregor rightly points out, such an approach is not possible without a systematic critique of the foundations of Western political thought, first and foremost of liberal thought. As Gentile's practical philosophy suggests, actual idealism rejects both the idea of the human being as an atomic individual and the idea of the state as a 'night watchman'. Spirito, as a follower of Gentile, emphasised the fact that the individual can only be complete in being part of the state. The individual who is human in the full sense is inseparable from the community in which he lives. This understanding of the existential importance of the link between the individual and the community is the first major clash between corporatism and liberalism.

The state in the actualist model allows the individual to rise to a higher level of morality in which the self exists insofar as it is contingent on the non-self. This imposes its limitations on the model of rational choice, which is a necessary component of the marginalist approach. Whereas in the conventional 'liberal' frame of reference an individual is free insofar as he follows his own rational economic interest, in the corporatist model the condition for his freedom is the choice in favour of goals shared by the community — 'free from bias, egoism, and empirical and logical errors'.[60]

Corporatist political economy asserts the need for the economic interest to be guided by the public interest. According to Spirito, the Labour Charter (1927), discussed above, legislated actualist ideas about the individual and his rights and freedoms — in particular the notion that labour is a social responsibility and that economic activity should be under the guardianship of the state. Both Spirito and Volpicelli believed that changing the economic system in the spirit of the Labour Charter would change attitudes towards property, which should be seen not as an individual but as a collective value. Although

59 Ibid., p. 112.

60 Ibid., p. 116.

property rights were not de jure restricted in Fascist Italy, corporatists insisted that property should be perceived as a historical and social product, since it took the strength of many generations to create it. Thus, the corporatist economic ideal can be characterised as a communalist ideal, an important characteristic of which is the treatment of property as a collective value.

The Fascist government was in no hurry to put this Communist ideal into practice — it was primarily guided by pragmatic considerations of political consolidation of the various social forces under a single centre of power. It actively promoted the creation of numerous associations, social organisations, and youth and trade unions. From a practical point of view, this was convenient for the Fascists, as the boundary between the private and the public was almost imperceptible. Moreover, given the corporate nature of representative power in Italy in the 1930s, it was possible for different social groups to participate in government.

Ugo Spirito, one of the most important philosophers of the Gentile school

Spirito, speaking as an actualist, provided a theoretical basis for the emerging social reality. The Gentilian-actualists developed the concept of a so-called 'totalitarian democracy' — 'totalitarian' because the individuals as individuals are totally 'fused' with the state as a whole, thus forming an entity with a single will; 'democracy' by virtue of the fact that the corporate system of representation enables each individual, each 'individual will', to influence the development of the state, which is thus to be perceived as the historical will of the community, integrating all the values of society. Without question, the notion of Fascism as the purest form of democracy goes back to Gentile (the first part of The Doctrine of Fascism). Such an actualist understanding leads to the perception of Fascist corporatism as a social doctrine that ensures the highest possible level of social harmony. According to Spirito and his associates, liberal forms of political representation essentially give no real choice to the citizens of the state, regularly exerting one manipulative influence on the masses or another. Fascism differs radically from them in that it produces an 'educator-state' that greatly expands the educational and cultural spheres. The Fascist state, represented by the party and its ideologists, scientists, intellectuals, and cultural figures, explains to citizens what they find difficult to understand on their own. The Fascist elite, these 'historical figures' in terms of actualist social philosophy, play a maximally active and responsible role in such a concept — that of leaders, of moral and intellectual reference points.[61]

Philosophically, the views of Spirito, Volpicelli, and other Fascist Gentilean actualists are rooted in the deep opposition between actualism and positivism. The refutation of positivist sociology with its pathos of 'empirical objective science' was an important aspiration of the actualists. Gentile had written as early as in *The Theory of Mind as*

61 For more detail, see: Giuseppe Bruguier, 'I fondamenti della economia corporativa' [The Foundations of Corporate Economics], *Giornale degli Economisti e Rivista di Statistica, Serie quarta* [Journal of Economists and Journal of Statistics, Series Four], 72, no. 7 (July 1932), pp. 502–514; Agostino Gemelli, 'Capitalismo e corporativisimo: a proposito della istituzione delle corporazioni di categoria' [Capitalism and Corporatism: On the Establishment of Trade Corporations], *Rivista Internazionale di Scienze Sociali e Discipline Ausiliarie* [International Journal of Social Sciences and Auxiliary Disciplines], Series III, Vol. 4, no. 6 (November 1933), pp. 731–734; Gianpasquale Santomassimo, 'Ugo Spirito e il corporativismo' [Ugo Spirito and Corporatism], *Studi Storici* [Historical Studies], 14, no. 1 (Jan. — Mar., 1973), pp. 61–113.

Pure Act that science, art, and religion are different kinds of activity of the spirit, none of which gives a representation of reality in its totality. Thus, to regard positivism as a metatheory of science is simply ridiculous. Let us translate the above into the language of political philosophy: liberalism, focusing only on the atomic-individual, is incapable of being the basis for the construction of a harmonious society. In the liberal system that Spirito harshly criticises, the individual is conceived in a strictly asocial context — viewed in classical liberal political economy as *homo economicus*, he strives to maximise his profitability function (in fact, his pleasure). With such a hedonistic interpretation, the utility of the community is left out of the picture, as is the public interest. Fascist corporatism must overcome this legacy of liberalism by creating a system capable of 'reconciling' the individual, society, and the state. By creating a harmonious system of representation and interaction, corporatism also solves another problem: overcoming the 'class conflicts' postulated by Marxists. Syndicates have a key role to play in this — there are both moral and technological advantages to the direct participation of workers in the management of enterprises. In that way, all working citizens are involved in achieving the productive aims of the nation. Moreover, they have a vested interest in the success of the whole. Corporatism must solve the problem of uniting labour and capital as the main productive forces, and remove the false opposition postulated by Marxists.

In the first half of the 1930s, Spirito began to write openly that the corporatist system spelled out in the *Labour Charter* and its derivatives should be seen as a transition from a liberal economic order to genuine corporatism. In particular, he saw the issue of property as unresolved. For Spirito, in true corporatism, property must be corporate; one must move away from the liberal understanding of private property. Workers should not just participate in the management of enterprises — they should be holders of its shares, its co-proprietors (in proportion to their contribution to the overall process, of course). According to Spirito, this would eliminate the opposition between employers and employees, between owners and workers. Since the enterprise, in a corporatist system, has its representation in the bodies of government, this whole construction, which can be called 'integral corporatism', will make it possible to put into practice the actualist dream of the fusion of the private and the common in a single synthesis, the complete unity of the individual and the state.[62]

When analysing Spirito's projected theory of integral corporatism, it is easy to see its socialist traits. An attack on private property and an economic planning system that, given human imperfection, easily becomes totalitarian in the worst sense of the word are characteristic aspects of the Bolshevik experiment. As a result, some Fascist intellectuals accused Spirito of a leftist turn—the philosopher's desire to bring the Fascist revolution to its logical conclusion was interpreted as a betrayal of its original principles (although the former socialist Mussolini was in general close to Spirito's pathos). At the same time, some of Spirito's ideas were realised—in particular, during the second half of the 1930s, the attitude towards private property in Fascist Italy changed[63] and the Great Fascist Council played an increasingly important role in economic policy. The role of the Duce as the 'chief spokesman of the nation's will' was also great.

As for Spirito himself, in 1937, when the rapprochement between Fascist Italy and Nazi Germany was taking shape, a year before the adoption of 'race laws' in Italy, he published *Life as a Quest* in which he criticised actual idealism.[64] During the war and post-war years,

62 These ideas were first voiced by Spirito at the Corporatist Congress in Ferrara in May 1932. Tannenbaum, 'The Goals of Italian Fascism'.

63 On the corporatist transformations in Italy against the backdrop of the Great Depression, see: Alberto Aquarone, 'Italy: The Crisis and Corporative Economy', *Journal of Contemporary History*, 4, no. 4, The Great Depression (Oct., 1969), pp. 37–58.

64 *Life as a Quest* was the first work of Spirito's post-actualist trilogy. After that he wrote *Life as Art* (1941) and *Life as Love* (1953). For more, see: Jean Pérès, 'Philosophie italienne contemporaine' [Contemporary Italian Philosophy], *Revue Philosophique de la France et de l'Etranger* [Philosophical Review of France

Spirito moved to problematicism altogether. In Spirito's post-war philosophy, which was totally immanentist and much more 'leftist' even than his actualist corporatism, he criticised Fascism, Communism, and Christianity. From problematicism (considering life as a problem and the current stage of human civilisation as deeply in crisis[65]) Spirito moves to scientistic omnicentrism (identifying the part and the whole, developing a 'scientific concept of man' and a 'concept of the total responsibility of the individual to society'). Spirito's post-war immanentist philosophy is even more totalitarian (in a negative sense) than his corporatist actualism — in fact, the Italian philosopher 'wants to create a world in which the dominant science and technology would so unify life that they would destroy all diversity, and with it individuals as unique individuals'.[66] Thus, in the post-war years Spirito departed quite far from the principles of actual idealism. He moved closer to Italian Communists, visited the Soviet Union in the 1950s and Communist China in 1961, before becoming disillusioned with Communism shortly afterwards. A year before he died in 1979, he wrote a work entitled *I Found God,* which was published posthumously.

2.2. Camillo Pellizzi's Actualist Imperialism

One of the most prominent proponents of Giovanni Gentile's actual idealism was Camillo Pellizzi (1896–1979). A native of Collegno in Piedmont, northern Italy, Pellizzi studied law at the University of Pisa. He served in the army during the First World War and was wounded at Caporetto. After moving to Milan in 1919, he met Mussolini and took

---

and Abroad], 124, No. 9/10 (Sept.–Oct. 1937), pp. 93–99; Patrick Romanell, 'Ugo Spirito's Philosophy of Love', *The Journal of Philosophy*, 54, no. 7 (Mar. 28, 1957), pp. 188–193.

65 For more on Spirito's problematism, see: Ugo Spirito and Dina Dreyfus, 'Itinéraire du problématisme' [Itinary of Problematism], *Les Études philosophiques* [Studies in Philosophy], Nouvelle Série, 8, no. 2 (April/June 1953), pp. 143–154.

66 Zorin, *Философско-этические взгляды кроческанцев и джентилеанцев* [Philosophical and Ethical Views of the Croceans and the Gentileans], p 70.

an active part in the formation of the Fascist movement but left for England in 1920 to continue his studies at the University of London. Between 1920 and 1939, Pellizzi spent most of his time in London, but remained actively involved in public life in Italy. He was fascinated by Mussolini as a person to whom one could pin his hopes for a revolutionary renewal of Italy. Pellizzi shared the main ideological goals of the young Fascist movement: to make Italy a powerful world power; to reject parliamentarism, democracy, and global institutions; and to fight against Marxism on every front (first of all on the ideological front).

Pellizzi began his career as a Fascist public figure in England, where in 1921 he created the first Fascist Federation. In 1922 he made his debut as a British correspondent for *Il Popolo d'Italia* and, following the success of the March on Rome, became a state delegate for the Fascist government in Britain and Ireland. He led active public work to popularise Fascism in England, establishing many Fascist federations in major British cities.[67] In 1926, in order to promote Italian culture, he set up a committee of the Dante Alighieri Society in London; in 1930 he became head of the Italian Institute of Culture in London. In 1939, the thinker returned to Italy at the invitation of Giuseppe Bottai to head the political science department at the University of Florence and then, in 1940, to head the National Institute of Fascist Culture founded by Gentile. Pellizzi remained in that position until 8 July 1943. After Mussolini was driven out of power by the Great Fascist Council, Pellizzi did not support the now-outlaw Duce and withdrew from political life. In the post-war years he devoted himself exclusively to scientific work, concentrating on sociology.[68]

---

67 For more details, see: T. p. Nesterova, 'Камилло Пеллицци. Интеллектуал в своей эпохе' [Camillo Pellizzi. The Intellectual in his Era], *Диалог со временем. Альманах интеллектуальной истории. 26* [Dialogue with Time. Almanac of Intellectual History. 26], (Moscow: Librokom Book House, 2009), pp. 311–325.

68 Pellizzi's attitude to Fascism in the post-war period was mixed. On the one hand, he did not hold anything against the generation of front-line soldiers who had followed Mussolini. On the other hand, he had become radically opposed to the

Camillo Pellizzi—jurist, publicist, and head of the National Institute of Fascist Culture (1940–1943)

As a philosopher, Pellizzi, like Spirito, was following in the footsteps of Gentile. The only point in which Pellizzi's views diverged from those of Gentile was the question of the interaction between Fascism and the Catholic Church. For all the idealist and spiritual orientation of actualist ontology, which claims that 'everything is in us and we are everything', no room is left for the personified God of the Roman church. Pellizzi, an actualist and Catholic, addressed this problem with a compromise—if the interests of the Roman church coincide with those of the totalitarian state, there is no ground for an essential

Duce himself. Pellizzi, who admired Mussolini at the start of Fascism, blamed the Duce for the failure of the Fascist dream after its collapse. According to Pellizzi, Mussolini had traded the dream of a technocratic revolution for his own dictatorship and personal caesarist aspirations. For more details, see: Emilio Gentile, 'L'héritage Fasciste entre mémoire et historiographie: Les origines du refoulement du totalitarisme dans l'analyse du Fascism' [The Fascist Heritage between Memory and Historiography: The Origins of the Repression of Totalitarianism in the Analysis of Fascism], *Vingtième Siècle. Revue d'histoire* [The Twentieth Century. History Review], no. 100, (Oct.–Dec., 2008), pp. 51–62; and Emiliana p. Noether, 'Italy Reviews Its Fascist Past: A Bibliographical Essay', *The American Historical Review*, 61, no. 4 (Jul., 1956), pp. 877–899.

conflict. Indeed, Pellizzi tended to see actualism as a spiritual current, as a 'bridge' to the 'true faith'.

The Italian thinker defined Fascism thus: 'Fascism is to be understood as a spiritual and historical reality that surpasses individual manifestations, accidental forms, and specific individuals'.[69] In Pellizzi's writings, it is not a concrete doctrine, but a 'way of life'.[70] Fascism requires every citizen to submit to a rigid hierarchy and directs individuals towards collective tasks; it hierarchises both individuals and various social groups.[71]

'Cinema is the most powerful weapon of all', Mussolini declared as early as 1922. In 1937, after the opening of the largest film studio in Europe, Cinecittà, the Duce changed his words into deeds—over the following six years at least 300 films were produced under his personal patronage.

69 Camillo Pellizzi, 'Fascism's Problems and Realities' in Schnapp, *A Primer of Italian Fascism*, p. 102.

70 For more detail, see: Schnapp, 'Fascinating Fascism', pp. 235–244.

71 Pellizzi's thesis echoes the key aspirations of Gentile's practical philosophy: the primacy and universality of the state will, the naturalness of the hierarchy, and the absurdity of contrasting the governed with the governing.

In Pellizzi's discourse on Fascism two major blocks have to be distinguished: his ideas on Fascist corporatism and his thoughts on the imperial mission of Fascism. Corporatism, according to Pellizzi, was 'a means of attracting the working and producing classes to the periphery of the totalitarian state, instilling in them an overpowering sense of participation in the fateful drama of national life'.[72] Thus, according to Pellizzi, Fascist corporatism is at best an advisory mechanism, but by no means an executive or legislative one, as the Syndicalists imagined it to be. The members of the corporations are not to be expected to show any initiative — in the final analysis they are subordinated to a single source of will, the will of the state, which is expressed by the Duce. Pellizzi thus interpreted Gentile's statist attitude to the creation of an ethical state united by a single consciousness in a very peculiar way. He showed himself to be more of an elitist than his teacher, giving a greater place in his social philosophy to the idea of a 'class of young heroes',[73] who would form Fascism as a phenomenon of a new era, opening another page in the history of human civilisation. The 'aristocracy of the trenches', the brotherhood of war veterans united by solidarity of a special kind, is to give Italy the real experience of comradeship from which a truly ethical state can be built.[74] Pellizzi defines squadrism as 'disciplined and militarised volunteering for direct

72 Gregor, *Mussolini's Intellectuals*, p. 171.

73 First and foremost, Pellizzi is referring to the veterans of the First World War, to whom he himself belongs.

74 A. James Gregor points out that this belief of Pellizzi's is in harmony with the perceptions of the National Syndicalists of the war period (Ibid., p. 172). However, it must be noted that Ernst Jünger (1895–1998), a representative of the 'conservative-revolutionary' current in Germany, followed an entirely similar logic in this time period. For example, in his article 'Distinctions and Connections' (*Die Standarte*, 1925), discussing the ideal of a man bringing the nationalist revolution closer, he writes: 'The figure of the lone fighter, the man in the steel helmet, the unknown warrior, bearing the heaviest burden on his shoulders, must become the ideal, the guiding star of the movement'. Ernst Jünger, Nationalist Revolution, (Moscow: Skymen, 2008), p. 21.

action'.[75] The thinker recognises that initially the Fascist movement was a highly chaotic one, bringing together a wide variety of passionate patriotic youth. Pellizzi responds very poetically to the accusation that most of the squadrists were scoundrels and mere bandits: 'Scoundrels of a type that will be monumented in the future, bandits like those who laid the foundation stone of Rome, pirates like those who founded the Republic of Venice and the British Empire, adventurers like the paladins from the chivalric ballads or noble men of the crusades'.[76] The Fascist ethical state predicted by Gentile was to be born 'out of their work, out of their discipline, out of their heroism'.[77]

In geopolitics, a key topic of intellectual discussion in Fascist circles at the end of the *ventennio* period due to the imminent Second World War, Pellizzi showed himself to be a convinced imperialist. Already in his work *Fascism — an Aristocracy* (1925) he claimed that the destiny of Fascism was not national, but global. Echoing Mussolini and Gentile's thesis in *The Doctrine of Fascism* that the pursuit of empire and national expansion is for Fascism a manifestation of life, Pellizzi predicted an imminent conflict between the major powers: 'the industrial and colonial empire of Great Britain, the monetary and financial empire of the United States, and Germany, which has taken an imperialist

75 Pellizzi, Fascism's Problems and Realities, p. 97.

76 Ibid., p. 97.

77 Ibid., p. 99. Pellizzi's consistency should be noted here: in the post-war years, in his work *The Failed Revolution* (1948), he would insist that Fascism was a regime that could only be built by a generation of front-line soldiers who had passed through the fire of the World War. However, it should also be borne in mind that in the post-war years he would no longer call for monuments to the squadrists, explaining the choice of the Italian people in favour of Fascism as a 'fatal predestination' laid down by the First World War. For further details see: Renato Treves, 'Idéologies politiques et jeunes generations' [Political Ideologies and Young Generations], *Revue européenne des sciences sociales* [European Social Science Journal], 17, no. 46, L'ubiquité de l'idéologie: Hommage à Raymond Polin [The Ubiquity of Ideology: A Tribute to Raymond Polin] (1979), pp. 227–233.

course'.[78] Italy, according to Pellizzi, must necessarily take part in this struggle and establish itself as a world power, as an empire. This conviction coincided with the idea of a 'healthy' State in actual idealist political philosophy, because according to Gentile the future-oriented State must always strive for expansion, growth, and enlargement. It is dynamic in its actuality and in virtue of its own transcendent character, and as an 'unfolding history' it transcends national, linguistic, and cultural boundaries.

According to Pellizzi, Italy's destiny is to restore the greatness of the Roman Empire, to update the ancient imperial tradition and bring it into the modern world. The thinker points out that the Roman Empire did not possess a 'nation' in the contemporary sense. Fascism, too, must disassociate itself from the national and create a revolutionary empire on the ruins of the outgoing liberal era. Italy must regain control of the Mediterranean, a task that requires territorial expansion. This can only be realised, according to Pellizzi, through Fascism, which is 'the first and unique meteoric force generated by Italian history'. 'Indifferent to regional and class differences, Fascism is unique because it includes people from all regions and all classes. Italy is its starting point, but its goal is the whole world',[79] Pellizzi asserts.

§3. The Collapse of the Doctrine. The Final Years of Fascism. The Manifesto of Verona. The Radicalism of Alessandro Pavolini. The Left-Wing Fascism of Nicola Bombacci. Ideology of the Salo Period

On 24 July, 1943, the *ventennio* era, Fascism's 'golden decades', came to an end. Following the defeat of the Axis forces on the Eastern Front, the Italians' loss of all African colonies, the landing of the anti-Hitler

78 Camillo Pellizzi, *Fascismo-aristocrazia* [Fascism-Aristocracy], (Milan, 1925). Cited from: Gregor, *Mussolini's Intellectuals*, p. 176.

79 Pellizzi, Fascism's Problems and Realities, p. 99.

coalition allies in Sicily, and the bombing of Rome, the Grand Fascist Council supported the initiative of Dino Grandi, President of the Chamber of Fascists and Corporations, and, with the approval of King Victor Emmanuel III of Italy, declared a vote of no confidence in the government of Benito Mussolini. The Italian government was headed by seventy-two year old Marshal Pietro Badoglio, who on 3 September, 1943, had signed the terms of Fascist Italy's unconditional surrender in World War II.[80]

At the same time the German Führer, Adolf Hitler, ordered Mussolini's release. Despite the fact that the arrested dictator was constantly being moved from one place of temporary detention to another, the Germans managed to locate him in the Gran Sasso Mountains

80 Before discussing the collapse of diarchical Fascism and the main aspects of the Fascist doctrine of the Salò period, which was much closer to German National Socialism than the Fascism of the golden age of the *ventennio*, we should briefly outline the twofold relationship between the Italian and German Right in the preceding period. In essence, the relationship between Fascism and Nazism, despite the military alliance, was never entirely seamless. Many Fascist thinkers and statesmen strongly disapproved of the biological racialism of the Nazis and generally looked down on the latter as representatives of a younger and less 'cultured' people. Nazism, despite its industrial and military might, which was relatively quickly re-established in Germany in the 1930s, was seen by many Fascists as a deeply peripheral phenomenon. The military alliance was largely forced by the foreign policy choices made by Mussolini, and many of those closest to him opposed the alliance. For example, Mussolini's son-in-law, Count Galeazzo Ciano, then Foreign Minister, recalls in his diary: 'The tragedy of Italy, in my opinion, began in August 1939 when, having gone on my own initiative to Salzburg, I was suddenly confronted by Germans determined to provoke a cynical conflict. The Treaty of Alliance was signed in May. I had always opposed it, and for a long time I managed to keep the German proposals hanging in the air. In my opinion, there was no reason for us to tie our fate to that of Nazi Germany for life and death'. Diary entry from Dicembre 23, Anno Era Fascista XXII (23 December 1943). Galeazzo Ciano, *Diary of a Fascist*, (Moscow: Platz, 2010), p. 645. By linking their fate to the Germans, Mussolini and the Fascists had to adopt a number of principles alien to the doctrine of Fascism (for example, the biological laws of race in 1938). The influence of Nazi principles will be evident when examining in this chapter the political aspirations of Alessandro Pavolini, one of the leading Fascist politicians of the Salò period.

in central Italy. On 12 September, 1943, the famous 'Operation Oak' took place, during which Mussolini was liberated and evacuated to Bavaria. A few days later, when he met Hitler in Rustenburg, Mussolini accepted the German leader's offer to return to Italy and proclaim a new Fascist state with a National Socialist agenda. On September 23rd, 1943, the Social Republic of Italy (*Repubblica Sociale Italiana*, R.S.I.), the second and final incarnation of Fascist Italy, was proclaimed. Rome was declared the official capital, but neither the deposed Mussolini nor the Germans backing him wanted him returning to a territory outside of Nazi military control. The real capital of the new regime was the small town of Salò on the western shore of Lake Garda, in Lombardy, northern Italy.

The proclamation of the Salò Republic was marked by Mussolini's fiery address to the Italians—over Munich radio. Backed by his German ally, the Duce proclaimed: 'It is not the regime that has betrayed the monarchy, but the monarchy has betrayed the regime, and so it has lost its prestige in the minds and hearts of the people, and it is simply absurd to suggest that this could in any small way undermine the unity of the Italian people. When the monarchy no longer serves its proper function, it loses its *raison d'être*. As for traditions, they are republican rather than monarchical; more than the monarchists, the republican movement, of which Giuseppe Mazzini was the pure and great apostle, fought for the unity and independence of Italy from all more or less foreign monarchies. The State we want to build will be national and social in the fullest sense of the word. It will be Fascist in the full sense of our original ideas.'[81]

81 From Mussolini's speech on Munich radio on 18 September, 1943. Cited in: A. G. Nesterov, *Итальянская социальная республика. Документы эпохи* [The Italian Social Republic. Documents from the Epoch], (Yekaterinburg: Urals University Publisher, 2002), p. 22.

Benito Mussolini and Alessandro Pavolini: The Salò years

The Salò period lasted less than two years[82] and was generally inglorious. Nevertheless, it is remembered for a very specific reinterpretation of the Fascist intellectual legacy. As many scholars have noted, during this period Fascism returned to its left-wing, Syndicalist, even socialist[83] roots.

On 14 November, 1943, the first and only congress of the Republican Fascist Party (*Partito Fascista Repubblicano*, P.F.R.) was held in Verona, resulting in the adoption of the Manifesto of Verona (*Manifesto di Verona*).[84]

82 The contemporary scholar, Emilio Gentile, called the period from 18 September, 1943, to 25 April, 1945, 'a new phase in the civil war between Fascism and anti-Fascism', a renewal of the struggle that Fascism had won in 1922, gaining 'a monopoly on patriotism'. As Gentile rightly points out, for the first time since the Risorgimento, Italians were killing each other in the name of liberating and saving the country, with each side convinced that they represented the 'best people of the nation'. See: Emilio Gentile, *La Grande Italia. The Myth of the Nation in the 20th Century*, (Madison: The University of Wisconsin Press, 2009), p. 215.

83 Socialist — when referring not to Fascism in general, but to Benito Mussolini personally.

84 Manifesto di Verona. [Electronic resource]. URL: http://www.storiologia.it/apricrono/storia/a1943u.htm.

Alessandro Pavolini—one of the most radical Fascist hierarchs

The Manifesto of Verona comprises eighteen clauses. It speaks of the overthrow of the Savoy monarchy and declares the king a traitor. A constituent assembly (*costituente*) of representatives of all the social groups and their syndicates is called in order to determine a new government. An Italian republic is established with a head (*Capo della Repubblica*) elected every five years. A one-party system is proclaimed, with the party seen as the 'guardian of the idea of revolution' (*custode dell'idea rivoluzionaria*). Roman Catholicism is proclaimed to be the state religion, while other religions are not forbidden. Jews are foreigners. The aims of the foreign policy of the Republic are proclaimed the unity of the homeland, the creation of a 'European community' as a federation of all nations (*una 'comunità europea' con la federazione di tutte le Nazioni*), the conquest of living space for forty-five million Italians, the eradication of British domination on the European continent, and the destruction of capitalism and world plutocracy (*abolizione del sistema capitalistico interno e lotta contro le plutocrazie mondiali*).

More than half of the declaration (ten out of eighteen points) is devoted to social policy issues. Work is proclaimed as a fundamental value. The state guarantees private property, but anything 'beyond the private interest' (*esce dall'interesse singolo*) is either declared state property or taken over by the state. Syndicates are required to participate in negotiating workers' wages. In agriculture, it is envisaged to transfer land not well managed by the relevant organisations to the workers in that area. The state recognises the private initiative of all workers, peasants, and craftsmen and does not intend to limit it. In addition, the manifesto proclaims a special housing programme, including the creation of a specialised National Housing Organisation (*Ente nazionale per la casa del popolo*), whose task is to provide housing for citizens. A single confederation of syndicates is created and the Labour Charter of 1927 is proclaimed the legal basis of the Syndicalist policy of the Republic. The document ends with a summons to fight the 'Anglo-American plutocracy' (*plutocrazie anglo-americane*) and a call to 'fight, work, win' (*combattere, lavorare, vincere*).

Benito Mussolini and Alessandro Pavolini, April 1945

The Manifesto of Verona was read out at the historic RFP congress by Alessandro Pavolini (1903–1945), one of the most radical Fascist hierarchs.[85] The founder of the infamous 'Black Brigades' and a staunch anti-Semite, he distinguished himself by a series of actions that fell well within the definition of 'War Crimes'. At the height of the *ventennio* (from 1939 to 1943) Pavolini was Fascist Italy's Minister of Popular Culture, and during the Salò years he essentially became the number two in the state.

Pavolini had been openly anti-Semitic and chauvinistic long before the 1938 racial laws were passed. As early as 1926, in an article for *Fascist Critique* entitled 'On Fascist Art', Pavolini wrote the following lines: 'Recluses in ivory towers, speaking to one another in their own jargon, constantly being "above the fray" and beyond any national boundaries... Critics speaking a mysterious language, editors of magazines that cannot be found and read, fraudsters and perverts, lazy intellectuals and idiotic businessmen, peddlers buying at five and selling at a thousand after the death of another "misunderstood artist"'.[86] This 'attack' by Pavolini, as one can easily guess, is directed against Jews and other 'cosmopolitans'. Anti-Semitism, which is not generally characteristic of Italian Fascism, was invariably inherent in Pavolini throughout his career. For example, in 1942, he wrote: 'The Axis war against the United States is a battle of "blood" against "gold" to save Europe from conquest by Anglo-Saxon plutocratic Judaism, led by the United States'.[87] Such a statement would be more 'befitting' a Nazi than an Italian Fascist.

---

85 F. W. Deakin, 'Le congrès de Vérone (14 Novembre 1943): Et le programme de la République de Salo' [The Verona Congress (14 November 1943): And the Programme of the Salo Republic], *Revue d'histoire de la Deuxième Guerre Mondiale* [Journal of World War II History], 7, no. 26 (April 1957), p. 65

86 Alessandro Pavolini, 'Dell'arte Fascista' [On Fascist Art], *Critica Fascista* [Fascist Critique], (Nov. 1, 1926). Cited from: Ruth Ben-Ghiat, *Fascist Modernities. Italy, 1922–1945*, (Oakland, California: University of California Press, 2004), p. 25.

87 Cited from: Emilio Gentile, 'Impending Modernity: Fascism and the Ambivalent Image of the United States', *Journal of Contemporary History*, 28, no. 1 (Jan., 1993), p. 23.

During the RFP congress in Verona Pavolini openly called for terror — he referred to a law 'passed during Badoglio, often useful, which we can safely follow. It is a law which authorises us to create within twenty-four hours, in urgent cases of popular unrest, tribunals which, immediately and under wartime law, can judge in such a way that the sentence is passed immediately and the guilty are sentenced to the only effective punishment — the death penalty'.[88] Pavolini also proposed that all Syndicalist organisations should be transformed into 'a single Confederation of Labour, Arts, Sciences and Technology'.[89] Pavolini argued that this clearly centralist and totalitarian proposal was necessary because 'the Syndicalist bureaucracy has grown unthinkably large'.[90] Openly expressing his racial beliefs, he insists on uncompromising anti-Semitism: 'All members of the Jewish race are foreigners and in this war they are an enemy race. For those who are familiar with the issue, the consequences of this statement, which is the total annihilation of the enemy, are clear'.[91] In addition, Pavolini outlines the geopolitical vector of the new republican government's aspirations: 'We are in favour of a community of European nations, which has always been our aspiration, possibly uniting in a federation based on the following principles: Europe for Europeans, the destruction of centuries of British domination of the continent, the dismantling of the intra-continental capitalist system, and the struggle against global plutocracy'.[92]

---

88 From Pavolini's speech at the First National Assembly of the RFP on November 14, 1943. Cited from Nesterov, *Итальянская социальная республика. Документы эпохи* [The Italian Social Republic. Documents from the Epoc], p. 26.

89 Ibid., p. 37.

90 Ibid., p. 37.

91 Ibid., p. 37. Pavolini would later become actively involved in the capture of Jews in northern Italy and their extradition to the Nazis, the result of which by then was already clear to all.

92 Ibid., p. 40.

One of the leading Fascist hierarchs, Roberto Farinacci, described Pavolini as a 'fanatic who understood nothing of politics'.[93] The latter remained with the Duce until the end — he was shot dead by partisans in April 1945 while trying to escape from the Lake Como area, after which his body was displayed in Milan's Piazzale Loreto along with the bodies of Mussolini, his mistress Clara Petacci, and his closest associates.[94]

Returning to the Manifesto of Verona, there were of course many authors, but the most passionate passages were written by a young man who few contemporaries would have expected to be so actively involved in the failed attempt at state-building — Nicola Bombacci (1879–1945).

Bombacci is the final significant figure in the intellectual history of Fascism. Born into a Catholic family in Forlì, in the Emilia-Romagna province, on 24 October, 1879, Bombacci was influenced by his father, a former papist soldier, to enter a Catholic seminary. When his father died, Bombacci abandoned his studies and became involved with socialist ideas. In 1903 he joined the Socialist Party of Italy and studied teaching. Bombacci became a teacher, dedicating part of his time to educating underprivileged children from poor families, and the other part to Party work, where he succeeded remarkably well. A talented organiser, Bombacci managed several socialist newspapers. In 1914 he was a member of the National Council of the Confederation of Labour, and in 1917 he was elected a member of the governing body of the Socialist Party of Italy. In 1918, Bombacci spent some time in prison, arrested for radical defeatist anti-national sentiments. The following year, 1919, he was elected to parliament. Bombacci's radical

93 Cited from: Eatwell, *Fascism, p.* 108.

94 Pavolini's last words were, 'Long live Italy! Long live Fascism!'. Duggan, *Fascist Voices: An Intimate History of Mussolini's Italy*, p. 415. For a detailed account of Pavolini's life, see Massimiliano Soldani, *L'ultimo poeta armato. Alessandro Pavolini segretario del P.F.R.* [The Last Armed Poet. Alessandro Pavolini Secretary of the P.F.R.], (Milan: Societa Editrice Barbarossa, 2012).

leftism reached its climax in 1920 when he attended the Second World Congress of the Comintern and declared himself one of the leading Italian Communists by signing the Italian Socialist radical faction's appeal. In 1921 Bombacci was elected to the Central Committee of the Italian Communist Party; the same year he was reelected to the Italian Parliament. By the time the March on Rome triumphed, Bombacci was as prominent a Communist leader as Amadeo Bordiga and Antonio Gramsci. The hatred of Bombacci in the Fascist camp was so great that the Blackshirts composed songs about him, mocking his famous beard.[95]

Nicola Bombacci (middle, with beard)—Communist turned Fascist

During the Fascist era, however, Bombacci's beliefs gradually began to change. First, he stopped insisting on internationalism, which automatically made him a heretic in the Communist camp. Then he actively supported the adoption of the Labour Charter and the introduction of a corporatist system. Finally, he spoke out against Stalin's USSR and the Communist International, accusing the Soviet Bolsheviks of betraying the interests of the proletariat. Bombacci greeted 1943 as a committed Fascist and welcomed the collapse of the Italian diarchy—the 'union

95 'We are not afraid of Bombacci // From his beard we will make brushes // To polish Mussolini's bald head to a shine'. Norling, *Revolutionary Fascism*, p. 27.

of king and leader', the Savoy monarchy and Fascism. Sympathetic to the Fascist ideals of the Salò Republic, he contributed in his own way to their formulation and further development.[96] Nicola Bombacci gave his life for his beliefs — like Mussolini, he was shot by the Bolshevik partisans on 28 April, 1945, near Lake Como. In the infamous footage from Piazzale Loreto in Milan, showing Benito Mussolini's corpse hanging upside down in public view, Bombacci's body hangs next to that of his friend and leader.[97]

96 After the events of July 1943, Bombacci wrote to Mussolini: 'I am now fully on your side. More than ever. The cowardly betrayal of the King and Badoglio has brought disgrace upon the whole of Italy, leaving it virtually in ruins, though it has freed it from the "plutomonarchical" compromises of 1922'. Cited in: Ibid., p. 34.

97 His personal relationship with Mussolini must have played a part in Bombacci's remarkable metamorphosis. Coming from the same province, they had known each other from a young age (attending the same high school), were comrades in the socialist movement, and kept in touch during the second half of the *ventennio*, which bore certain fruits. In particular, the socialist magazine *La Verità*, founded by Bombacci, was published between 1936 and 1943 with the support of the Fascist government. In 1936 the thinker wrote in a magazine article: 'Fascism has produced a grandiose social revolution. Mussolini and Lenin, the Soviet and Fascist corporate states, Rome and Moscow. Some ideas that have already been formed have to be clarified; we have nothing to be sorry for, because both in the past and in the present, we have been inspired by a single ideal: the triumph of labour'. Cited in: Ibid., p. 30.

'We are not afraid of Bombacci // From his beard we will make brushes // To polish Mussolini's bald head to a shine'—the Fascists had been writing songs about the formidable 'Red Pope' Nicola Bombacci since 1921. In 1943 Bombacci joined Mussolini in Salò and shared his fate in Milan's Piazzale Loreto.

How could a man with such a 'Red' (pre-1922) career end up as a staunch Fascist? Was he a traitor or did he gradually change his views during the *ventennio* years? It seems that neither of the above scenarios holds true in Bombacci's case. He undoubtedly underwent a certain intellectual evolution, but, on the whole, Bombacci was very consistent. Let us consider the main milestones of his evolution from Communism to Fascism.

The first significant matter is that of nationalism. Bombacci publicly supported the armed operation of Gabriele D'Annunzio and his *arditi* in Fiuma as early as 1919, at the height of his Comintern activities. According to Bombacci, D'Annunzio was first and foremost a revolutionary and only then a nationalist. In addition to the *arditi*, national-Syndicalists were also involved in the takeover of Fiume and Alceste De Ambris played an active role in writing the Fiume constitution, laying the foundations of corporatism within it. Bombacci, who actively collaborated with the Soviet Communists, advocated adopting the Russian revolutionary practices but based his rhetoric on the interests of Italians as a nation—an unprecedented turn of thought for a Communist. He proposed 'to overcome the nation without destroying it'—an idea that is incomprehensible to internationalist logic, as for them the national is of no value whatsoever. Moreover, the Italian thinker viewed the Communist revolution in Russia as an inherently national uprising, which also raised questions from his comrades on the Left.

Another major, specific feature of Bombacci's thought is his attitude towards socialism. Socialism was for him the unconditional ideal to aspire to, but a certain evolution can also be traced in Bombacci's interpretation of the socialist. In particular, while the early Bombacci, a Communist activist and deputy, was a supporter of the Soviet model, in the 1930s he accused the Soviet government of betraying the interests of the proletariat.[98] Bombacci came to admire the corporatist processes of the *ventennio* period that were contemporary to him. Fascist corporatism appeared to him to be the real practical embodiment of genuine socialism. Soviet Bolshevism, on the other hand, degenerated under Stalin to the level of an Asian despotism. Thus by 1943 Bombacci concluded that the defence of the Fascist corporate order was the real task of the proletariat, for whose benefit many institutional transformations had been implemented. Moreover, in the closing years of Fascism, the thinker wrote increasingly about the 'spiritual rise' of the Italian proletariat, resorting to terminology close to that of Sorel. Apart from a specific assessment of the domestic political and domestic economic situation, Bombacci also returned to the geopolitical notions

98 In 1943, Bombacci would write the following lines about Stalin's USSR: 'The materialistic, semi-barbaric Moscow, the embodiment of totalitarian state capitalism, wants to force through its five-year plans, driving its own people into total poverty, an industrialisation which other countries passed in the nineteenth century, Moscow completes the capitalist phase... Moscow after Stalin's reforms is institutionally no different from the bourgeois parliamentary states. Economically, however, there is an important difference: while bourgeois states are ruled by capitalist delegates, here the power belongs to the Bolshevik bureaucracy, a new class that is, in fact, much worse than the capitalists, because it has no control over the disposal of labor, production, or the lives of its own citizens'. Nicola Bombacci, 'I contadini nell'Italia di Mussolini' [Peasants in Mussolini's Italy]. Cited in: Norling, *Revolutionary Fascism*, p. 33.

characteristic of pre-war Italian nationalists (in particular Corradini). In Bombacci's picture of the world, Italy presents itself as a 'proletarian country' struggling against the 'plutocratic world' (Britain, France, the USA). In this clash he fully endorses a 'revolutionary' Fascist Italy — finding 'socialist' arguments even in favour of the colonial war in Ethiopia, seeing it as a prologue to a larger clash between countries that would provoke a global revolution capable of 'restoring the balance of the world'.

Thus, in Bombacci's new vision of the world, the military alliance between the Stalinist USSR and the Western 'plutocrats' seemed logical and consistent. In this case, for Bombacci, both the former and the latter regime represented the embodiment of everything negative and unjust — a faceless force of international capitalist despotism which should be resisted to the last breath. Bombacci maintained this belief until the end. The *Manifesto of Verona*, inspired by his work and abundant in socialist these, was the last literary monument to this extraordinary thinker.

It should be noted, however, that the ideology the brief and tragic Salò Fascist period is not exhausted by Bombacci's contribution alone. Alessandro Pavolini and Benito Mussolini himself also played an active role. The Duce's position is clearly expressed in his speech of 14 October 1944: 'Some people still ask us: what do you want? Our answer is in three words, expressing our whole program. Here they are: Italy, the Republic, Socialisation... Socialisation is nothing other than the realisation of Italian socialism, which is humane, ours and possible; I say "ours" because it proclaims work as the cornerstone of the economy, rejecting mechanical forces that do not exist in nature and are impossible in history'.[99]

99 From Mussolini's speech to the Milan Fascists and the 'Black Brigades' on 14 October, 1944. Norling, *Revolutionary Fascism*, p. 43.

Benedetto Croce (foreground left) and Enrico De Nicola (foreground right), author of the 'Manifesto of Anti-Fascist Intellectuals' and first president of the Italian Republic, 1948

Compared to the Fascist regime of the *ventennio* era, which, despite its totalitarian nature, was constructed by Mussolini and his associates with some concessions to other right-wing forces (conservatives, the Catholic Church, nationalists), the Fascism of the Salò period appears to be a much more radical ideological phenomenon. At a time when 'almost everything [was] lost', Mussolini, Pavolini, and Bombacci were proclaiming slogans which would have seemed completely unacceptable to the Fascist allies of the 1922 model (liberals and conservatives), but which were able to attract the radical Left. Even though the *Manifesto of Verona* had declared a special role for Catholicism, Mussolini's proclamation of 'socialisation' led Fascism to lose the support of the Catholic Church, which had traditionally resisted 'leftist' aspirations.

Despite attempts to revive the ideological intensity lost amidst military and political defeats, the fate of the Republic of Salò was sealed. As A.G. Nesterov rightly points out, 'rather quickly the Italian Social

Republic — while retaining formal independence — went from being a German-dependent state to a "puppet state".[100] From the summer of 1944 the government of the new Fascist state held practically no meetings — the Republic was placed under the external rule of the German ally. On 14 March, 1945, the last Council of Ministers of the Italian Social Republic met. On 25 April, 1945, the final incarnation of the Italian Fascist State ceased to exist. On the same day, one of Mussolini's most radical supporters, Roberto Farinacci, was shot by partisans. Soon afterwards Mussolini, Bombacci, and Starace were caught and shot by the anti-Fascist resistance. Their half-dressed corpses were displayed for all to see in Piazzale Loreto in Milan. This marked the final historical collapse of Italian Fascism — and the beginning of a reflection upon it.

100 Nesterov, *Итальянская социальная республика. Документы эпохи* [The Italian Social Republic. Documents from the Epoch], p. 13.

CONCLUSION

TO SUMMARISE this investigation — which has reconstructed the political philosophy of Italian Fascism in historical and philosophical terms from its origins, beginning in the Risorgimento period and tracking it right up to its collapse in 1945 — the following should be highlighted.

Italian Fascism is an independent political phenomenon with its own ideological and philosophical content. At the same time, Fascism is deeply diverse — it united Italian Syndicalists and monarchists, nationalists and liberals, creating the basis for a short-term (just over twenty years) political consensus within Italy. Fascism's political philosophy is as heterogeneous as is the phenomenon of Fascism itself — absorbing many different strata (from Neo-Hegelian idealism and modernist nationalism to Syndicalism and elitism), it can be seen as a confrontation between different groups of intellectuals, stretching over decades. While in the early years were dominated by the liberal spirit of actualism (Gentile), in the second decade the imperial-Roman trend prevailed (Bottai), and, shortly before its collapse, socialist (Pavolini, Bombacci) and openly racist (Costamagna) tendencies became more tangible.[1]

The genesis of Italian Fascism can be traced back to the unification era (Risorgimento) in which the young Italian nation's self-awareness was fostered by a specifically Italian idealism. The intellectual quest of the idealists Antonio Rosmini and Vincenzo Gioberti focused on the

1 In many respects, because of this diversity of thought, it is difficult to nail down a single and consistent Weberian 'ideal type' of Fascism.

search for a national Italian identity, on the need to define the grounds for a national consensus. Giuseppe Mazzini, an idealist Republican and one of the leaders of the Risorgimento, not only inspired the Italian Fascists' revolutionary struggle through the example of his life, but also formulated key ethical principles in *On the Duty of Man* (1860), which were then laid down as the foundation of the philosophy of actual idealism. In particular, Mazzini proposed to replace the 'theory of rights' with a 'theory of duty'—he analysed the relationship between the individual and society from the perspective of the duty which the individual owes to the whole, the service of the individual to humanity, of the citizen to the nation. Mazzini gave a definition of freedom that was also reflected in the practical philosophy of actual idealism: 'Freedom is not the negation of all authority; it is the negation of any authority that does not express the collective purpose of the nation or that seeks to establish itself contrary to social consensus'.[2]

In addition, the formation of Italian Fascism was also influenced by the Left—by Revolutionary Syndicalism. Mussolini regarded Georges Sorel as one of his teachers, adopting some of Sorel's ideas from *Reflections on Violence* (1906). In particular, Sorel's principles of the rejection of humanism, irreconcilable opposition to parliamentarianism, and the justification of the ethical value of violence and the instrumental value of myth formed the ideological basis of Fascism. Sergio Panunzio and Angelo Oliviero Olivetti, who combined Sorel's Syndicalism with the nationalism of Mazzini, popularised and creatively interpreted Sorel's ideas in Italy. Both Panunzio and Oliviero Olivetti subsequently occupied high positions in the Fascist state.

Despite its left-wing influences, Fascism positioned itself as a right-wing movement in opposition to both socialism and liberalism. We have also explored its right-wing origins—primarily the elitist sociology of Gaetano Mosca, Robert Michels, and Vilfredo Pareto. The elitist element in Fascism was very pronounced—most Fascist ideologues

2 Giuseppe Mazzini, *I doveri dell'uomo* [The Duties of Man], (Stabilimento tipografico Richiedei, 1872), p. 73.

would later write about natural inequality, elite groups and 'individual heroes' expressing the will of the nation (a prime example is Camillo Pellizzi). Fascism was also strongly influenced by the pre-war Italian nationalism of Enrico Corradini — the nationalists not only subsequently dissolved into the Fascist movement, but also gave it their best cadres (a prime example being Alfredo Rocco). The Fascist doctrine reflects many of the geopolitical aspirations of the nationalists. The *arditi* of Gabriele D'Annunzio can be considered the prototype of the *fasci di combattimento* — it was this Italian poet who first mobilised the energy of the young fighters, directing it towards revolutionary tasks. After capturing Fiume, D'Annunzio and the Syndicalist Alceste De Ambris wrote *The Charter of Carnaro*, the first legal document to reflect the principle of corporatism, which was then essential to Fascism. Finally, attention has also been given to one of the co-authors of the *Fascist Manifesto* (1919), Filippo Tommaso Marinetti, leader of the Futurist movement, who imbued Fascism with the militarist, revolutionary impulse of Futurism.

Having completed our consideration of the key intellectual origins of Fascism, we considered the main influences that shaped the worldview of Italian Fascist leader Benito Mussolini. We have identified the impact of the theories of Friedrich Nietzsche (primarily the doctrine of the reassessment of all values and the doctrine of the will to power), Georges Sorel (the doctrine of the instrumental value of myth), Vilfredo Pareto (a departure from the economic determinism characteristic of the young socialist Mussolini; elitist sociology), and Niccolò Machiavelli (political pragmatism) as major influences. With reference to the words of Mussolini himself, we can say that the Duce was somewhat influenced by William James and Alfredo Oriani.

Turning directly to the political philosophy of Fascism, we have reconstructed its fundamental philosophical concept, the actual idealism of Giovanni Gentile. Gentile's political philosophy is deeply rooted in the ontology of actual idealist philosophy, as detailed by the philosopher in *The Theory of Mind as Pure Act* (1916), discussed in the second chapter of this work. In that text, Gentile presents what he saw as the main philosophical problems.

The philosopher begins with the problem of knowledge. According to Gentile's actualism, spirit is an infinitely dynamic creative process, it represents the reality of becoming. Nature should not be compared to spirit — by doing so we only limit the universality of the latter. Yet spirit cannot exist outside its manifestations — thus Gentile removes the opposition between the spiritual and the material. Thought is real only when it is manifested in an act, in action. All judgements are acts of the thinking 'I'.

Turning to ontology, Gentile presents the world as a harmonious whole, unified with the horizon of the consciousness of individuals, which we denote spatially. The philosopher claims that 'everything is in us' — both space and time — which are expressions of the activity of the spirit. Spirit, according to Gentile, is timeless and immortal; immortality is a property of the spirit that transcends the natural. From this the philosopher also draws a conclusion about the immortality of our transcendental individuality ('that part of us which can die is the material which has never been alive'), the immortality of the individual as a spiritual act. In addition to this, Gentile argues that the spirit is history because it is a dialectical development. The historicity of the spirit manifests itself in the naturalisation of spiritual events, from which we are separated by space and time. Reality is eternal and historical at the same time — this is how Gentile formulates the 'historical antinomy of the spirit'. It is history that plays the role of reality in its concreteness, which is the basis of the absolute freedom of the spirit. Thus, in his ontology, the philosopher deduces all other conditions, the limits of space and time, from spirit. Spirit as an act supposes everything.

Moving on to anthropology, the Italian philosopher describes the 'realm of man' as the self-realisation of the creative spirit. Individuals, conceiving of themselves in acts, actions, and deeds, constitute the self-fulfillment of the universal, manifesting itself in a constant triumph over the natural and the material. Gentile develops the anthropological implications of his ontological doctrine in his writings on practical philosophy, the most complete of which is *The Genesis and Structure of Society*. As an ethicist, Gentile argues that all our actions have an inherent moral character. We need to talk about them in terms of duty and responsibility. Gentile's ethics is closely linked to the social dimension of the individual — a person is only fully human when he interacts with other people. Emphasising the uniqueness of the spiritual life of the individual, Gentile notes that where there is an 'I', there is always a 'We'. The ego-in-itself, without the world around it, is an emptiness, devoid of any capacity to create. Moreover, in the anthropology of Gentile, it is characteristic of a person to strive for the ideal and universal, to which he advances by performing appropriate acts. These acts are the condition of the spiritual life of the individual. The latter is impossible without freedom, which Gentile extols in all his works of practical philosophy.

As a social philosopher, Gentile was a convinced statist. In his philosophy, the state is a general and universal manifestation of the national will. The nation is primarily a 'form', the state is its concrete expression. The will of the State is expressed in law, which, as Gentile sees it, does not limit individual freedom, but confirms it. In reasoning about the state, Gentile is not attached to concrete political forms, he argues that forms must respond to the challenges of the times — they are in fact historical. Furthermore, the result that emerges from the affirmation of the plurality of citizens in the spiritual unity of the state is unimportant. The state, according to Gentile, bears an intrinsic ethical dimension in that it is the manifestation of the will of the individuals who feel a sense of belonging to it. When it comes to international politics, Gentile expresses the interaction of states with each other as identical to the interaction of individuals — states realise themselves in the world as unique entities, manifest their creative relevance in the eternal flow of history and interact with their 'Others' (with other states).

Finally, touching on the political, Gentile argues that politics is the activity of the spirit as expressed by the state. The experience of the political act and the experience of the ethical act are identical in actual idealism; the ethical is immanent in the political. The political seeks the fullness of the self-consciousness of the spirit, which is the ethical task. It is the ethical that drives political action — detachment from political life, according to Gentile, is immoral. By participating in the life of the State, the individual 'absorbs' the latter; by acting freely and creatively, he contributes to the formation of the universal, inseparable from himself.

Throughout the Fascist era, Gentile was active in Italian political life, holding a number of public offices and serving as a senator. Between 1922 and 1924, the philosopher served as Minister of Education. Gentile succeeded in carrying out an educational reform by introducing school and university standards. In particular he focused on teaching philosophy and significantly strengthened the humanistic component of education, introducing the compulsory teaching of the Law of God at primary school and philosophy at secondary school. As author of *The Doctrine of Fascism* and many other ideological pro-Fascist works of the 1920s, Gentile contributed significantly to the formation of Fascist doctrine. In a work of the same name, published in 1932 under the name of Mussolini, the influence of Gentile's actual idealism is visible. In particular, the first part of the Doctrine outlines the main ideas of his philosophy: statism derived from an idealist political ontology, activism, a modernist spirit, and intolerance towards a materialist and positivist worldview.

Having completed a detailed examination of the actualist 'core' of the official Fascist doctrine from the pens of Gentile and Mussolini, we turned to other interpretations of Fascism, also espoused during the *ventennio* years. Alfredo Rocco, in *The Political Doctrine of Fascism* (1925), defined Fascism as a feeling and action, and also as a historical phenomenon essentially opposed to the ideals of the Reformation and Enlightenment and their political expressions: liberalism, socialism, and Bolshevism. Carlo Costamagna, a Catholic conservative and staunch opponent of Gentile, defined Fascism as a Roman Catholic totalitarian state, which must completely subordinate the free expression of the will of its citizens to its imperial task. Guiseppe Bottai, Minister of Education of Fascist Italy and one of the most educated Fascist hierarchs, popularised the perception of Fascism as a 'spiritual state' that spiritualises all the higher spheres of human activity, contributed to maintaining the 'myth of Romanness', and carried out a reform aimed at the 'Fascisation' of Italian schools. Sergio Panunzio and Angelo Oliviero Olivetti contributed to the development of the Syndicalist aspect of Fascism: the adoption of the 'law of syndicates', the *Labour Charter* (1927). Julius Evola urged the Fascist regime to revive Roman paganism, insisting on the need to follow the hierarchical and imperial components of the political ideology of Fascism.

Returning to the actualism of the 1930s, we considered the socio-political theories of Gentile's followers, Ugo Spirito and Camillo Pellizzi. Spirito became one of the main ideologists of Fascist corporatism, a politico-economic doctrine aimed at realising the actualist principle of 'the unity of the individual and the state'. In his theory of 'integral corporatism', Spirito proposed the transition from private property to corporate ownership and the transfer of corporate shares to employees. Another Gentile follower, Pellizzi attempted to combine actual idealism and the teachings of the Catholic Church. Pellizzi saw Fascism as a spiritual reality and contributed to the formation of the doctrine of corporatism and to a conceptualisation of Italy's 'imperial mission'. Finally we turned to the collapse of Fascism and the beginning of our reflection upon it. Fascism of the Salò period, having discarded actualist philosophy, focused on its Syndicalist legacy as its ideological locus. Having proclaimed a course towards 'socialisation', Benito Mussolini, Alessandro Pavolini, and Nicola Bombacci retained in Salò Fascism only a few features characteristic of diarchical *ventennio* Fascism: nationalism, leaderism, statism, and the rejection of Communism. Much more radical was Mussolini's socialist, anti-capitalist outlook.

On the basis of the above, the following should be noted. Despite the manifold nature of Fascist philosophy, which was acknowledged by the Fascists themselves, one cannot interpret it as being irrationalist, based on a poetics of violence and a cult of blood. The first two aspects were present in the ideological propaganda of Fascism, while the latter was not characteristic of Fascism at all until the late 1930s when the military alliance with Germany was concluded. Moreover, it would be incorrect to reduce Fascism to mythology and deprive it of what appears to be its quite obvious intellectual content. At various stages of its doctrinal evolution, opposing forces often dominated. The most striking example of this is the economic doctrine of Fascism — liberal in nature in the 1920s, Syndicalist-corporate in the 1930s, and practically socialist in the Salò period.[3]

The actualist idealism of Giovanni Gentile is, from our perspective, the undoubted philosophical core of *The Doctrine of Fascism.* In this paper, a great deal of attention is paid to the importance of actualism as the intellectual basis of Fascism, largely because this fact has been underestimated in previous accounts, and the available and published Russian-language works have not addressed this topic at all. However, when discussing Fascism as a phenomenon, one should

3 Of course, we cannot talk about complete freedom of thought during the era of Italian Fascism — there was obviously no complete freedom. A certain 'orthodoxy' was present, one clearly articulated in *The Doctrine of Fascism.* There were, however, also different points of view on certain issues 'within' this concept (Gentile, for instance, took a more liberal view of the corporate economy, while Ugo Spirito took a more socialist view), as well as disputes with actualism itself (Carlo Costamagna's rejection of the line of continuity between the national liberalism of the Risorgimento and Fascism, which was typical of actualism). Moreover, the openly oppositional thoughts that Croce, for example, allowed himself to express were also voiced openly — and, it should be noted, Croce lived perfectly well throughout the Fascist era in Naples and was not persecuted. We can therefore say with certainty that the censorship and so-called 'totalitarian pressure' in Fascist Italy was much weaker than under Soviet Bolshevism and German Nazism — under those political regimes both Croce and Gramsci, who was convicted of openly revolutionary, anti-state activities and spent eleven years in prison, would surely have been shot.

not overestimate the importance of the Neo-Hegelian doctrine, since political reality is not reducible to a strict formulation of doctrinal statements. It is multi-factorial, multifaceted, and to a large extent historically, economically, and regionally dependent. Real historical Fascism was a far cry from the idealistic maxims of the actualist philosophy — as is often the case in political history, the movement that many believed in did not live up to expectations and degenerated in later years into a dictatorship conducted by a rather mediocre elite led by a leader who fancied himself the 'new Caesar', but who was, as history has shown, desperately distant from the highest Roman models of statesmanship.

At the same time, having completed the study of the political philosophy of Italian Fascism, we can draw a number of theoretical conclusions regarding its content. The following fundamental principles of Fascist political philosophy can be seen as common to all the currents found within it: idealist political ontology; fundamental statism; nationalism; modernism; corporatism; imperialism; normative elitism; and a self-identified opposition to liberalism, socialism, and the '1789 principles' in general. In addition to the above features characteristic of Italian Fascism as a whole, it is necessary to highlight a number of points of internal dispute between Fascist ideologues: the dispute over the primacy of nationalism and statism, the dispute over the fundamental importance of actualist philosophy and Catholic doctrine, and the dispute over the liberal and corporatist understanding of private property.

The history of Italian Fascism as a modernist political movement of the twentieth century ended in 1945.[4] Its political philosophy, based on the principles of actual idealism, also belongs to this era. At

4 However, it seems important to note that in 1946 the Italian Social Movement (*Movimento Sociale Italiano*) was founded, a political party which can be seen as the successor of the ideology of the Salò period. The M.S.I. existed until 1995 and ran for the Chamber of Deputies in all elections between 1948 and 1992, as well as in the European Parliament in 1979, 1984, and 1989. In 1995 M.S.I. joined the conservative National Alliance (*Alleanza Nazionale*) led by Gianfranco Fini.

the same time, the author of this work dares to hope that an appeal to this topic, not yet developed by domestic historians of philosophy, will make it possible to identify a number of principles relevant beyond time and to reconstruct and understand more objectively both the history of the twentieth century and some problematic aspects of our political and spiritual modernity.

BIBLIOGRAPHY

Moiseev, Dmitry. 'Этнос. Нация. Ценности' [Ethnos. Nation. Values]. *Вестник Российской нации* [Herald of the Russian Nation] 39, no. 1 (2015).

Moiseev, Dmitry. 'Политическая мысль Джузеппе Мадзини' [Giuseppe Mazzini's Political Thought]. *История философии* [History of Philosophy] 20. (Moscow: 2015).

Moiseev, Dmitry. 'Интеллектуальная история итальянского фашизма. Современные подходы' [An intellectual history of Italian Fascism. Contemporary approaches]. *Dialogue with Time* 55 (2016).

Moiseev, Dmitry. 'Ключевые особенности итальянского национализма конца XIX — начала XX вв. на примере литературных и философских работ Энрико Коррадини и его влияние на формирование доктрины фашизма' [Key features of Italian nationalism in the late nineteenth and early twentieth centuries as exemplified by Enrico Corradini's literary and philosophical works and his influence on the formation of Fascist doctrine]. *Материалы Международного молодежного научного форума «Ломоносов-2016»,* [Proceedings of the Lomonosov-2016 International Youth Scientific Forum]. Edited by I. A. Aleshkovsky, A. V. Andriyanov and E. A. Antipov. Moscow: Max Press, 2016. [Electronic resource]

Moiseev, Dmitry. 'Педагогическая наука в философии Джованни Джентиле' [Pedagogical Science in the Philosophy of Giovanni Gentile]. *Социальная философия науки. Российская перспектива. К юбилею В. С. Степина. Материалы конференции* [Social Philosophy of Science. Russian Perspective. For the Anniversary of V.S.Stepin. Conference papers]. Volume 5, section 4. STS — Epistemological Specifics of the Social Science. Edited by I.T.Kasavin, A.Y.Antonovski, and K.K.Momdzhyan. Moscow: Alpha-M, 2014.

Moiseev, Dmitry. 'Поэты и фашизм. Влияние Д'Аннунцио и Маринетти на становление и развитие итальянского фашизма' [Poets and Fascism. The Influence of D'Annunzio and Marinetti on the Formation and Development of Italian Fascism]. *Философия. Язык. Культура* [Philosophy. Language. Culture.], no. 5. St Petersburg, 2014.

Moiseev, Dmitry. 'Революционный синдикализм Жоржа Сореля и его влияние на становление фашизма в Италии' [Revolutionary Syndicalism of

Georges Sorel and its Impact on the Formation of Fascism in Italy]. *Материалы Международного молодежного научного форума «Ломоносов-2015»* [Proceedings of the International Youth Scientific Forum 'Lomonosov-2015']. Edited by A. I. Andreev, A. V. Andriyanov and E. A. Antipov. Moscow: Max Press, 2015. [Electronic Resource]

Moiseev, Dmitry. 'Социально-политическая философия Юлиуса Эволы и фашистский режим' [The Social and Political Philosophy of Julius Evola and the Fascist Regime]. *Материалы Международного молодежного научного форума «Ломоносов-2014»* [Proceedings of the Lomonosov-2014 International Youth Scientific Forum]. Edited by A. I. Andreev and E. A. Antipov. Moscow: Max Press, 2014. [Electronic Resource]

Zakharov, A. B. and Dmitry Moiseev. 'Эффективность публичных коммуникаций как необходимое условие развития государства' [Public Communication Effectiveness as a Necessary Condition for State Development]. *Ценности и смыслы* [Values and Meanings] 32, no. 4 (2012).

Adam, Michel. 'Actualité de Rosmini'. *Revue Philosophique de la France et de l'Etranger* 184, no. 2 (April-June 1994).

Adamson, Walter L. 'Gramsci's Interpretation of Fascism'. *Journal of the History of Ideas* 41: no. 4 (Oct. — Dec., 1980).

Adler, Franklin H. 'Jew as Bourgeois, Jew as Enemy, Jew as Victim of Fascism'. *Modern Judaism* 28, no. 3 (Oct., 2008).

Alfonso, N. D. 'Bertrando Spaventa'. *The Journal of Speculative Philosophy* 17, no. 4 (October, 1883).

Amendola, Giovanni. 'La philosophie italienne contemporaine' [Contemporary Italian Philosophy]. *Revue de Métaphysique et de Morale* 16, no. 5 (September 1908).

Antonov,Dmitry. *Очерки фашизма в Италии* [Essays on Fascism in Italy]. Moscow, 1923.

Aquarone, Alberto. 'Italy: The Crisis and Corporative Economy'. *Journal of Contemporary History* 4, no. 4, The Great Depression (Oct., 1969).

Arendt, Hannah. *Between Past and Future*. London: Penguin Books, 1993.

Arendt, Hannah. *The Origins of Totalitarianism*. San Diego: Harcourt, 1973.

Balabanoff, Angelica. *Моя жизнь — борьба. Мемуары русской социалистки 1897–1938* [My Life — the Struggle. Memoirs of a Russian Socialist 1897–1938]. Moscow: ZAO 'Tsentrpoligraf', 2007.

Barkley, Raymond. 'The Theory of the Elite and the Mythology of Power'. *Science & Society* 19, no. 2 (Spring, 1955).

Barzelloti, Giacomo. 'Philosophy in Italy'. *Mind* 3, no. 12 (Oct., 1878).

Battaglini, Giulio. 'The Fascist Reform of the Penal Law in Italy'. *Journal of Criminal Law and Criminology (1931–1951)* 24, no. 1, Century of Progress Number:

The Development of Criminology in the State of Illinois during the Past Century, in the United States of America at Large and in Other Nations of the World during the Past Quarter-Century (May-June, 1933).

Belousov, L. S. *Фашистский режим, рабочий класс и массовое сознание в Италии, конец 1920-х — 1943 гг* [The Fascist Regime, the Working Class and Mass Consciousness in Italy, late 1920s-1943]. Doctoral candidate in History. Moscow, 1999.

Belousov, L. S. *Муссолини. Диктатура и демагогия* [Mussolini. Dictatorship and Demagogy]. Moscow: Mashinostroenie, 1993.

Belousov, L. S. *Режим Муссолини и массы* [Mussolini's Regime and the Masses]. Moscow: Moscow State University Press, 2000.

Belousov, L. S and A. I. Patrushev. *Любовь диктаторов. Муссолини, Гитлер, Франко* [The Love of Dictators. Mussolini, Hitler, Franco]. Moscow: AST Press Book, 2001.

Ben-Ghiat, Ruth. *Fascist Modernities. Italy, 1922–1945*. Oakland, California: University of California Press, 2004.

Bernardini, Gene. 'The Origins and Development of Racial Anti-Semitism in Fascist Italy'. *The Journal of Modern History* 49, no. 3 (Sep., 1977).

Bertrand, Charles L. 'The Biennio Rosso: Anarchists and Revolutionary Syndicalists in Italy, 1919–1920'. *Réflexions Historiques* 9, no. 3 (Fall 1982).

Best, Heinrich. 'Marx or Mosca? An Inquiry into the Foundations of Ideocratic Regimes'. *Historical Social Research / Historische Sozialforschung* 37, no. 1 (139), Elite Foundations of Social Theory and Politics (2012).

Betti, Emilio. *Hermeneutics as a General Methodology of Sciences of the Spirit*. Oxfordshire: Routledge, 2021.

Bobbio, Norberto. 'Gaetano Mosca e la scienza politica' [Gaetano Mosca and Political Science]. *Giornale degli Economisti e Annali di Economia, Nuova Serie* [Journal of Economists and Annals of Economics, New Series] 18, No. 9/10 (Sept.-Oct. 1959).

Bowler, Anne. 'Politics as Art: Italian Futurism and Fascism'. *Theory and Society* 20, no. 6 (Dec., 1991).

Bruguier, Giuseppe. 'I fondamenti della economia corporativa' [The Foundations of Corporate Economics]. *Giornale degli Economisti e Rivista di Statistica, Serie quarta* [Journal of Economists and Journal of Statistics, Series Four] 72, no. 7 (July 1932).

Brzezinski, Zbigniew and Carl Joachim Friedrich. *Totalitarian Dictatorship and Autocracy*. Cambridge, Massachusetts: Harvard University Press, 1956.

Buissière, Evelyne. 'Éternité de l'esprit et actualité de la pensée de Hegel à gentile' [The Eternity of the Spirit and the Actuality of Thought from Hegel to Gentile]. Les *Études philosophiques*, no. 3, Emmanuel Lévinas (1996–2006) (July 2006).

Buissière, Evelyne. 'Giovanni gentile réformateur de la dialectique Hégélienne' [Giovanni Gentile, Reformer of the Hegelian Dialectic]. *Les Études philosophiques*, no. 4, Philosophie Italienne (Oct.-Dec. 1994).

Busino, Giovanni. 'La science sociale de Vilfredo Pareto' [The Social Science of Vilfredo Pareto]. *Revue européenne des sciences sociales* 46, no. 140, La sociologie en quête d'une théorie générale (2008).

Cammett, J.M. 'Communist Theories of Fascism, 1920–1935'. *Science & Society* 31.2 (Spring, 1967).

Campbell, Stuart L. 'The Four Paretos of Raymond Aron'. *Journal of the History of Ideas* 47, no. 2 (Apr.–Jun., 1986).

Carney, Larry. 'Sociology in the Throes of Fascism: Parsonian Meliorism and Myths of Triumphalism'. *International Journal of Politics, Culture, and Society* 7, no. 3 (Spring, 1994).

Chaix-Ruy, Jules. 'Philosophie et religion chez rosmini d'apres G. Rovea' [Philosophy and Religion in Rosmini after G. Rovea]. *Les Études philosophiques, New World Series* 10, no. 1 (January/March, 1955).

Ciano, Galeazzo. *Diary of a Fascist*. Moscow: Platz, 2010.

Ciccarelli, Andrea. 'Dante and Italian Culture from the Risorgimento to World War I'. *Dante Studies, with the Annual Report of the Dante Society* 119 (2001).

Cirillo, Renato. 'Was Vilfredo Pareto Really a "Precursor" of Fascism?' *The American Journal of Economics and Sociology* 42, no. 2 (Apr., 1983).

Clark, Martin. *The Italian Risorgimento*. Edinburgh: Pearson Education Limited, 2009.

Coli, Daniela. *Giovanni Gentile*. Bologna: Il Mulino, 2004.

Cook, Philip J. 'Robert Michels's Political Parties in Perspective'. *The Journal of Politics* 33, no. 3 (Aug., 1971).

Cook, Thomas I. 'Gaetano Mosca's "The Ruling Class"'. *Political Science Quarterly* 54, no. 3 (Sep., 1939).

Coppa, Frank J. '"Realpolitik" and Conviction in the Conflict between Piedmont and the Papacy during the "Risorgimento"'. *The Catholic Historical Review* 54, no. 4 (Jan., 1969).

Corradini, Enrico. *La guerra lontana* [The Distant War]. Milan: Editori Fratelli Treves, 1911.

Corradini, Enrico. *La Patria lontana* [A Distant Homeland]. Milan: Editori Fratelli Treves, 1911.

Croce, Benedetto. 'Manifesto degli intellettuali antiFascisti' [Manifesto of the AntiFascist Intellectuals] in E. P. Papa, *Fascismo e cultura* [Fascism and Culture]. Padua: Marsilio, 1974.

Cunsolo, Ronald. S. 'Italian Emigration and Its Effect on the Rise of Nationalism'. *Italian Americana* 12, no. 1 (Fall/Winter 1993).

Cunsolo, Ronald S. 'Libya, Italian Nationalism, and the Revolt against Giolitti'. *The Journal of Modern History* 37, no. 2 (Jun., 1965).

Curtis, Michael. *Three Against the Third Republic: Sorel, Barrès and Maurras*. New Brunswick, New Jersey: Transaction Publishers, 2010.

Davydova, G. E. *Философско-антропологические основания европейского фашизма* [Philosophical and Anthropological Foundations of European Fascism]. Dissertation candidate in philosophy. Rostov-on-Don, 2005.

Deakin, F. W. 'Le congrès de Vérone (14 Novembre 1943): Et le programme de la République de Salo' [The Verona Congress (14 November 1943): And the Programme of the Salo Republic]. *Revue d'histoire de la Deuxième Guerre Mondiale* [Journal of World War II History] 7, no. 26 (April 1957).

Degras, Jane. *The Communist International, 1919–1943: Documents*. London: Oxford University Press, 1956.

Diggins, John Patrick. *Mussolini and Fascism: The View from America*. Princeton, New Jersey: Princeton University Press, 2015.

Dilthey, Wilhelm. *Introduction to the Human Sciences*. Detroit: Wayne State University Press, 1988.

Dimitrov, Georgi. ' The Fascist Offensive and the Tasks of the Communist International in the Struggle of the Working Class against Fascism', in *Selected Works in Three Volumes* (Volume 2). Sofia Press, 1972.

Drake, Richard. 'The Theory and Practice of Italian Nationalism, 1900–1906'. *The Journal of Modern History* 53, no. 2 (Jun., 1981).

Duggan, Christopher. *Fascist Voices. An Intimate History of Mussolini's Italy*. Oxford: Oxford University Press, 2013.

Eatwell, Roger. *Fascism: a History*. New York: Penguin Books, 1997.

Evans, Valmai Burwood. 'Education in the Philosophy of Giovanni Gentile'. *International Journal of Ethics* 43, no. 2 (Jan., 1933).

Evans, Valmai Burdwood. 'The Ethics of Giovanni Gentile'. *International Journal of Ethics* 39, no. 2 (Jan., 1929).

Evola, Julius. *Fascism Viewed from the Right*. London: Arktos Media Ltd., 2013.

Evola, Julius. *Men Among the Ruins*. Rochester, Vermont: Inner Traditions, 2002.

Evola, Julius. *Pagan Imperialism*. Gornahoor Press, 2017.

Falasca-Zamponi, Simonetta. *Fascist Spectacle. The Aesthetics of Power in Mussolini's Italy*. Berkeley, CA: University of California Press, 2000.

de Felice, Renzo. *Il Fascismo. Le interpretazioni dei contemporanei e degli storici* [Fascism. The Interpretations of Contemporaries and Historians]. Bari: Editori Laterza, 2008.

de Felice, Renzo. *Le interpretazioni del Fascismo* [Interpretations of Fascism]. Bari: Editori Laterza, 2012.

de Felice, Renzo. *Mussolini il rivoluzionario. 1883–1920* [Mussolini the Revolutionary. 1883–1920]. Milan: Il Giornale — Biblioteca Storica, 2015.

de Felice, Renzo. *Mussolini il Fascista. La conquista del potere. 1921–1925* [Mussolini the Fascist. The Conquest of Power. 1921–1925]. Milan: Il Giornale — Biblioteca Storica, 2015.

de Felice, Renzo. *Mussolini il Fascista. L'organizzazione dello stato Fascista. 1925–1929* [Mussolini the Fascist. The Organisation of the Fascist State. 1925–1929]. Milan: Il Giornale — Biblioteca Storica, 2015.

de Felice, Renzo. *Mussolini il duce. Gli anni del consenso. 1929–1936* [Mussolini the Duce. The years of consensus. 1929–1936]. Milan: Il Giornale — Biblioteca Storica, 2015.

de Felice, Renzo. *Mussolini il duce. Lo Stato totalitario. 1936–1940* [Mussolini the Duce. The Totalitarian State. 1936–1940]. Milan: Il Giornale — Biblioteca Storica, 2015.

de Felice, Renzo. *Mussolini l'alleato. L'Italia in guerra. 1940–1943. Tomo primo. Dalla guerra "breve" alla guerra lunga* [Mussolini the Ally. Italy at war. 1940–1943. Tome I. From 'Short' to Long War]. Milan: Il Giornale — Biblioteca Storica, 2015.

de Felice, Renzo. *Mussolini l'alleato. L'Italia in guerra. 1940–1943. Tomo secondo. Crisi e agonia del regime* [Mussolini the Ally. Italy at war. 1940–1943. Tome Two: Crisis and Agony of the Regime]. Milan: Il Giornale — Biblioteca Storica, 2015.

de Felice, Renzo. *Mussolini l'alleato. La guerra civile. 1943–1945* [Mussolini the Ally. The Civil War. 1943–1945]. Milan: Il Giornale — Biblioteca Storica, 2015.

Femia, Joseph V. *Pareto and Political Theory*. Oxfordshire: Routledge, 2006.

Filatov, G. S. *Фашизм, неофашизм и антифашистская борьба в Италии* [Fascism, Neo-Fascism and the Anti-Fascist Struggle in Italy]. Moscow: Nauka, 1984.

Frandsen, Steen Bo and Adelaide Zocchi. 'Le città italiane fra tradizione municipalistica e gerarchia nazionale durante il Risorgimento' [Italian Cities Caught Between Municipalist Tradition and National Hierarchy During the Risorgimento]. *Meridiana* 33, Materiali'98 (November 1998).

Gemelli, Agostino. 'Capitalismo e corporativisimo: a proposito della istituzione delle corporazioni di categoria' [Capitalism and Corporatism: On the Establishment of Trade Corporations]. *Rivista Internazionale di Scienze Sociali e Discipline*

Ausiliarie [International Journal of Social Sciences and Auxiliary Disciplines], Series III, Vol. 4, no. 6 (November 1933).

Generalov, A. I. *Giovanni Gentile's 'Actual Idealism'*. Dissertation Candidate of Philosophy. Moscow, 1996.

Gentile, Emilio. 'Fascism as Political Religion'. *Journal of Contemporary History* 25, no. 2/3 (May-June, 1990).

Gentile, Emilio 'Fascism in Italian Historiography: In Search of an Individual Historical Identity'. *Journal of Contemporary History* 21, no. 2, Twentieth Anniversary Issue (Apr.,1986).

Gentile, Emilio. 'Fascism, Totalitarianism and Political Religion: Definitions and Critical Reflections on Criticism of and Interpretation' in *Fascism, Totalitarianism and Political Religion*. Edited by Roger Griffin. London and New York: Routledge, 2005.

Gentile, Emilio. *La Grande Italia. The Myth of the Nation in the 20th Century*. Madison: The University of Wisconsin Press, 2009.

Gentile, Emilio. 'L'héritage Fasciste entre mémoire et historiographie: Les origines du refoulement du totalitarisme dans l'analyse du Fascism' [The Fascist Heritage between Memory and Historiography: The Origins of the Repression of Totalitarianism in the Analysis of Fascism]. *Vingtième Siècle. Revue d'histoire* [The Twentieth Century. History Review], no. 100, (Oct.–Dec., 2008).

Gentile, Emilio. 'Impending Modernity: Fascism and the Ambivalent Image of the United States'. *Journal of Contemporary History* 28, no. 1 (Jan., 1993).

Gentile, Emilio. *Politics as Religion*. Princeton, New Jersey: Princeton University Press, 2006.

Gentile, Emilio. 'The Problem of the Party in Italian Fascism'. *Journal of Contemporary History* 19, no. 2 (Apr., 1984).

Gentile, Giovanni. 'Art et religion' [Art and Religion]. *Revue de Métaphysique et de Morale* 30, no. 4 (Oct.-Dec. 1923).

Gentile, Giovanni. *Genesi e struttura della società* [Genesis and Structure of Society]. Florence: Editore Arnoldo Mondadori, 1954.

Gentile, Giovanni. *Introduzione alla filosofia* [Introduction to Philosophy]. Florence: G. C. Sansoni, 1952.

Gentile, Giovanni. 'Manifesto degli intellettuali Fascisti agli intellettuali di tutte le Nazioni, dai giornali italiani del 21 aprile' [Fascist Intellectuals' Manifesto to Intellectuals of All Nations (*Manifesto of Italian Intellectuals* in English, from Italian newspapers of 21 April] in E. P. Papa, *Fascismo e cultura* [Fascism and Culture]. Padua: Marsilio, 1974.

Gentile, Giovanni. 'The Philosophic Basis of Fascism'. *Foreign Affairs* 6, no. 2 (Jan., 1928).

Gentile, Giovanni. 'Teoria generale dello spirito como atto puro' [The Theory of Mind as Pure Act] in *Works, Volume III*. Florence: Casa Editrice Le Lettere, 1987.

Germino, Dante. 'Italian Fascism in the History of Political Thought'. *Midwest Journal of Political Science* 8, no. 2 (May, 1964).

Gnoli, Gherardo. 'Giovanni Gentile Founder and President of ISMEO'. *East and West* 44, no. 2/4 (December 1994).

Gossett, Philip. 'Becoming a Citizen: The Chorus in "Risorgimento" Opera'. *Cambridge Opera Journal* 2, no. 1 (Mar., 1990).

de Grand, A. J. 'The Italian Nationalist Association in the Period of Italian Neutrality, August 1914-May 1915'. *The Journal of Modern History* 43, no. 3 (Sep., 1971).

Greenfield, Kent Roberts. 'Economic Ideas and Facts in the Early Period of the Risorgimento (1815–1848)'. *The American Historical Review* 36, no. 1 (Oct., 1930).

Gregor, A. James. *Giovanni Gentile: Philosopher of Fascism*. New Brunswick, New Jersey: Transaction Publishers, 2008.

Gregor, A. James. *Mussolini's Intellectuals. Fascist Social and Political Thought*. Princeton, New Jersey: Princeton University Press, 2005.

Gregor, A. James. *Sergio Panunzio — Il sindicalismo ed il fondamento razionale del Fascismo* [Sergio Panunzio — Syndicalism and the Rational Basis of Fascism]. Edizione Lulu.com, 2014.

Gregor, A. James. *Totalitarianism and Political Religion. An Intellectual History*. Redwood City, California: Stanford University Press, 2012.

Grew, Raymond. 'How Success Spoiled the Risorgimento'. *The Journal of Modern History* 34, no. 3 (Sep., 1962).

Griffin, Roger. *Fascism*. Oxford: Oxford University Press, 2009.

Griffin, Roger. *Modernism and Fascism. The Sense of a Beginning under Mussolini and Hitler*. London: Palgrave Macmillan, 2007.

Gullace, Giovanni. 'The Pragmatist Movement in Italy'. *Journal of the History of Ideas* 23, no. 1 (Jan.–Mar., 1962.

Haddock, Bruce. 'Political Union without Social Revolution: Vincenzo Gioberti's Primato'. *The Historical Journal* 41, no. 3 (Sep., 1998).

Haider, Carmen. 'The Italian Corporate State'. *Political Science Quarterly* 46, no. 2 (Jun., 1931).

Hausheer, Herman. 'Fascism in Italy'. *Social Science* 8, no. 4 (October 1933).

Hayek, Friedrich. *The Road to Serfdom*. Oxfordshire: Routledge Classics, 2001.

Hibbert, Christopher. *Benito Mussolini: The Rise and Fall of Il Duce*. London: Penguin, 1975.

Higley, John and Jan Pakulski. 'Elite Theory versus Marxism: The Twentieth Century's Verdict'. *Historical Social Research / Historische Sozialforschung* 37, no. 1 (139), Elite Foundations of Social Theory and Politics (2012).

Holmes, Roger W. *The Idealism of Giovanni Gentile*. New York: The Macmillan Company, 1937.

Horowitz, Irving Louis. 'On the Social Theories of Giovanni Gentile'. *Philosophy and Phenomenological Research* 23, No. 2 (Dec., 1962).

Hughes, Henry Stuart. 'The Aftermath of the Risorgimento in Four Successive Interpretations'. *The American Historical Review* 61, no. 1 (Oct., 1955).

Hutton, Patrick H. 'Vico's Theory of History and the French Revolutionary Tradition'. *Journal of the History of Ideas* 37, no. 2 (Apr.–Jun., 1976).

Ilyinsky, M. M. *Жизнь и смерть Бенито Муссолини* [The Life and Death of Benito Mussolini]. Moscow: Veche, 2000.

Jünger, Ernst. *Nationalist Revolution*. Moscow: Skymen, 2008.

Kahn, Paul. 'Mythe et Réalité Sociale chez Sorel' [Myth and Social Reality in Sorel]. *Cahiers Internationaux de Sociologie* 11 (1951).

Koon, Tracy H. *Believe, Obey, Fight. Political Socialisation of Youth in Fascist Italy, 1922–1943*. Chapel Hill, NC: University of North Carolina Press, 2012.

Kormiltsev, I. 'Три жизни Габриэле Д'Аннунцио' [The Three Lives of Gabriele D'Annunzio]. *Иностранная литература* [Foreign Literature], no. 11, 1999.

Kotov, S. V. *Европейский фашизм: социокультурные псевдоценности политического движения* [European Fascism: Social and Cultural Pseudo-Values of a Political Movement]. Dissertation candidate in Philosophy. Rostov-on-Don, 2005.

Kotov, S. V. *Неофашизм как политический феномен современности: философско-политические истоки и концептуальный генезис* [Neo-Fascism as a Political Phenomenon of Modernity: Philosophical and Political Origin and Conceptual Genesis]. Doctoral Dissertation in Political Science. Rostov-on-Don, 2011.

Krasin, Jurij Andreevič. 'О научном наследии Г. С. Филатова' [On the scientific legacy of G. S. Filatov] in G.S. Filatov, *Фашизм, неофашизм и антифашистская борьба в Италии* [Fascism, Neo-Fascism and the Anti-Fascist Struggle in Italy]. Moscow: Nauka,1984.

Labriola, Antonio. *Исторический материализм и философия: Письма к Жоржу Сорелю* [Historical materialism and philosophy: Letters to Georges Sorel]. Moscow: LKI Publishing, 2011.

Licata, Glauco. 'Il sindacalismo rivoluzionario italiano nel 1914' [Italian Revolutionary Trade Unionism in 1914]. *Aevum* 41, no. 3/4 (May-August 1967).

Lien, Arnold J. 'Machiavelli's Prince and Mussolini's Fascism'. *Social Science* 4, no. 4 (August, September, October, 1929).

Lopreato, Joseph and Robert C. Ness. 'Vilfredo Pareto: Sociologist or Ideologist?' *The Sociological Quarterly* 7, no. 1 (Winter, 1966).

Lopukhov, B. R. *Эволюция буржуазной власти в Италии* [The Evolution of Bourgeois Power in Italy]. Moscow, Science, 1986.

Lopukhov, B. R. *Фашизм и рабочее движение в Италии* [Fascism and the Labour Movement in Italy]. Moscow: Science, 1968.

Lopukhov, B. R. *История фашистского режима в Италии* [The History of the Fascist Regime in Italy]. Moscow: Science, 1977.

Lopukhov, B. R. *Борьба рабочего класса Италии против фашизма* [The Italian Working Class Struggle against Fascism]. Moscow: USSR Academy of Sciences Publishing, 1959.

Loria, Achille. 'Obituary: Robert Michels (1876–1936)'. *The Economic Journal* 46, no. 182 (Jun., 1936).

de Luise, Alexandra. 'Le Arti and Intervention in the Arts'. *RACAR: revue d'art canadienne / Canadian Art Review* 19, no. 1/2, 'Art as Propaganda / Art et propaganda' (1992).

Luzzatto, Sergio. *Padre Pio: Miracles and Politics in a Secular Age*. London: Picador, 2011.

Machiavelli, Niccolò. 'The Prince' in *Selected Works*. Moscow: Literatura Poetry, 1982.

Mangoni, Luisa. 'La crisi dello Stato liberale e i giuristi italiani' [The Crisis of the Liberal State and Italian Jurists]. *Studi Storici* [Historical Studies] 23, no. 1 (Jan.–Mar., 1982).

Marcello, Flavia. 'Mussolini and the idealisation of Empire: the Augustan Exhibition of Romanità'. *Modern Italy* 16, no. 3 (Aug. 2011).

Marinetti, Filippo Tommaso. *Manifesto del futurism* [The Futurist Manifesto]. Pubblicato dal 'Figaro' di Parigi il 20 febbraio, 1909.

Marinetti, Filippo Tommaso and Alceste De Ambris. 'Il manifesto dei fasci italiani di combattimento' [The Manifesto of the Italian Combat Fascists]. *Il Popolo d'Italia* [The People of Italy]. June 6, 1919.

May, John D. 'Democracy, Organization, Michels'. *The American Political Science Review* 59, no. 2 (Jun., 1965).

Mazzini, Giuseppe. *I doveri dell'uomo* [An Essay on the Duties of Man]. Stabilimento tipografico Richiedei, 1872.

Mazzini, Giuseppe. 'From a Revolutionary Alliance to the United States of Europe'. Edited by Stefano Recchia and Nadia Urbinati. *A Cosmopolitanism of Nations. Giuseppe Mazzini's Writings on Democracy, Nation Building and International Relations.* Princeton, New Jersey: Princeton University Press, 2009.

Mazzini, Giuseppe. 'Manifesto della Giovine Italia' [Manifesto of Young Italy] in *Mazzini G. Scritti editi e inediti. Vol. 1.* [Mazzini G. Published and Unpublished Works. Volume 1]. Edited by G. Daelli, 1861.

Mazzini, Giuseppe. 'I collaboratori della Giovine Italia ai loro concittadini' [The Collaborators of the Young Italy to their Fellow Citizens]. *La giovine Italia. Serie di scritti intorno alla condizione politica, morale e letteraria della Italia, tendenti alla sua rigenerazione* [The Young Italy. Series of Writings on the Political, Moral and Literary Condition of Italy, Tending Towards its Regeneration]. Marseille: Tipografia militare di Giulio Barile, 1832.

Meisel, James H. 'A Premature Fascist? Sorel and Mussolini'. *The Western Political Quarterly* 3, no. 1 (Mar., 1950).

Meisel, James H. 'Georges Sorel's Last Myth'. *The Journal of Politics* 12, no. 1 (Feb., 1950).

Michels, Robert. *Political Parties: A Sociological Study of the Oligarchical Tendencies of Modern Democracy.* Ontario: Batoche Books, 2001.

Mikhailenko, V. I. *Итальянский фашизм: основные вопросы историографии* [Italian Fascism: Main Issues of Historiography]. Sverdlovsk: Urals University Press, 1987.

Mikhailovsky. A. 'Германия' [Germany]. *Мыслящая Россия. История и теория интеллигенции и интеллектуалов* [Thinking Russia. History and Theory of the Intelligentsia and Intellectuals]. Moscow: Eurasia Heritage, 2009.

Mussolini, Benito. *La dottrina del Fascismo* [The Doctrine of Fascism]. Rome, 1941.

Mussolini, Benito. *My Autobiography.* New York: Scribner, 1928.

Mussolini, Benito. *Третий путь: без демократов и коммунистов* [The Third Way: Without Democrats and Communists]. Moscow: Algorithm, 2012.

Mussolini, Romano. *My Father, Il Duce.* Carlsbad, California: Kales Press, 2006.

Nesterov, A. G. *Итальянская социальная республика. Документы эпохи* [The Italian Social Republic. Documents from the Epoch]. Yekaterinburg: Urals University Publisher, 2002.

Nesterova, T. P. 'От реформы Джентиле к реформе Боттаи: образовательная политика Италии в 1920–1930-х гг.' [From the Gentile Reform to the Bottai Reform: Italian Educational Policy in 1920–1930s]. *Известия Уральского государственного университета. Сер. 2, Гуманитарные науки* [The Proceedings of the Ural State University. Series. 2 Humanities]. 2008.

Nesterova, T. P. 'Камилло Пеллицци. Интеллектуал в своей эпохе' [Camillo Pellizzi. The Intellectual in his Era]. *Диалог со временем. Альманах интеллектуальной истории. 26* [Dialogue with Time. Almanac of Intellectual History.]. Moscow: Librokom Book House, 2009.

Nietzsche, Friedrich. *Thus Spoke Zarathustra.* Originally published by Ernst Schmeitzner, 1883–1892.

Noether, Emiliana P. 'Italian Intellectuals under Fascism'. *The Journal of Modern History* 43, no. 4 (Dec., 1971).

Noether, Emiliana P. 'Italy Reviews Its Fascist Past: A Bibliographical Essay'. *The American Historical Review* 61, no. 4 (Jul., 1956).

Nohlen, Dieter and Philip Stöver. *Elections in Europe: A Data Handbook.* Baden-Baden: Nomos, 2010.

Nolte, Ernst. *Three Faces of Fascism: Action Francaise, Italian Fascism, National Socialism.* New York: Henry Holt & Company, 1966.

Norling, Erik. *Revolutionary Fascism.* Finis Mundi Press, 2011.

Osipova, E. V. *Социология Вильфредо Парето: политический аспект* [The Sociology of Vilfredo Pareto: A Political Aspect]. St Petersburg: Aletheia, 2004.

Ostenc, Michel. 'Les étudiants Fascistes italiens des années 1930' [Italian Fascist Students of the 1930s]. *Le Mouvement social* [The Social Movement], no. 120, Entre Socialisme et Nationalisme: Les Mouvements Étudiants Européens (Jul. — Sep., 1982).

Ostenc, Michel. 'La guerre et le mythe de la "résurrection" chez les intellectuels italiens: Réforme morale et révolution nationale (1902–1915)' [War and the Myth of 'Resurrection' among Italian Intellectuals: Moral Reform and National Revolution (1902–1915)]. *Guerres mondiales et conflits contemporains* [World Wars and Contemporary Conflicts], no. 227, Dossier: Artists and Intellectuals in War (July 2007).

Ostenc, Michel. 'La jeunesse italienne et le Fascisme a la veille de la Seconde guerre mondiale' [Italian Youth and Fascism on the Eve of the Second World War]. *Revue d'histoire de la Deuxième Guerre Mondiale* [Review of the history of the Second World War] 24, no. 94 (April 1974).

Pagano, Tullio. 'From Diaspora to Empire: Enrico Corradini's Nationalist Novels', *MLN* 119, no. 1, Italian Issue (Jan., 2004).

Paresce, G. 'Problems of Italian Syndicalism'. *Journal of the Royal Institute of International Affairs* 9, no. 3 (May, 1930).

Payne, Stanley G. *A History of Fascism 1914–1945.* Madison, Wisconsin: University of Wisconsin Press, 1996.

Pérès, Jean. 'Philosophie italienne contemporaine' [Contemporary Italian Philosophy]. *Revue Philosophique de la France et de l'Etranger* [Philosophical Review of France and Abroad] 124, No. 9/10 (Sept.–Oct. 1937).

Peters, Rik. 'Actes de présence: Presence in Fascist Political Culture'. *History and Theory* 45, no. 3 (Oct., 2006).

Peterson, Thomas E. 'Schismogenesis and National Character: The D'Annunzio-Mussolini Correspondence'. *Italica* 81, no. 1 (Spring, 2004).

Piraino, Marco and Stefano Fiorito. *Fascist Identity. Political Project and Doctrine of Fascism.* Lulu.com, 2011.

Ploscowe, Morris. 'Jury Reform in Italy'. *Journal of Criminal Law and Criminology (1931–1951)* 25, no. 4 (Nov.–Dec., 1934).

Porter, Clifford F. 'Eric Voegelin on Nazi Political Extremism'. *Journal of the History of Ideas* 63, no. 1 (Jan., 2002).

Renauld, J. F. 'Quelques Livres de Philosophie Italienne' [Some Titles of Italian Philosophy]. *Revue de Métaphysique et de Morale* 27, no. 4 (October 1920).

Riall, Lucy. *Risorgimento. The History of Italy from Napoleon to Nation State.* London: Palgrave Macmillan, 2009.

Ridley, Jasper. *Mussolini: A Biography.* Maryland: Cooper Square Press, 2000.

Ripepe, Eugenio. 'Après Karl Marx est-ce le temps de Gaetano Mosca?' [After Karl Marx is it Gaetano Mosca's Time?]. *Revue européenne des sciences sociales* [European Social Science Journal] 21, no. 65 (1983).

Roberts, David D. 'How Not to Think about Fascism and Ideology, Intellectual Antecedents and Historical Meaning'. *Journal of Contemporary History* 35, no. 2 (Apr., 2000).

Roberts, David D. *Syndicalist Tradition and Italian Fascism.* Chapel Hill, North Carolina: University of North Carolina Press, 1979.

Rocco, Alfredo. 'The Political Doctrine of Fascism'. *International Conciliation*, no. 223, (October 1926).

Romanell, Patrick. 'Ugo Spirito's Philosophy of Love'. *The Journal of Philosophy* 54, no. 7 (Mar. 28, 1957).

Romano, Sergio. 'Giovanni Gentile, philosophe du Fascisme' [Giovanni Gentile, Philosopher of Fascism]. *Vingtième Siècle. Revue d'histoire*, no. 21 (Jan.–Mar., 1989).

Roth, Jack J. 'Revolution and Morale in Modern French Thought: Sorel and the Sorelians'. *French Historical Studies* 3, no. 2 (Autumn, 1963).

Roth, Jack J. 'The Roots of Italian Fascism: Sorel and Sorelismo'. *The Journal of Modern History* 39, no. 1 (Mar., 1967).

Rouanet, S. P. 'Irrationalism and Myth in Georges Sorel'. *The Review of Politics* 26, no. 1 (Jan., 1964).

Rubini, Rocco. *The Other Renaissance. Italian Humanism Between Hegel and Heidegger.* Chicago, IL: The University of Chicago Press, 2014.

de Ruggiero, Guido and Constance M. Allen. 'Philosophy in Italy'. *Journal of Philosophical Studies* 3, no. 12 (Oct., 1928).

Sakhibgoryaev, V. K. *Фашизм как явление и концепция философии культуры* [Fascism as a Phenomenon and Concept of Philosophy of Culture]. Doctoral dissertation candidate in Philosophy. Rostov-on-Don, 2008.

Salomone, A. W. 'The Risorgimento between Ideology and History: The Political Myth of rivoluzione mancata'. *The American Historical Review* 68, no. 1 (Oct., 1962).

Salomone, A. W. 'Statecraft and Ideology in the Risorgimento. Reflections on the Italian National Revolution'. *Italica* 38, no. 3 (Sep., 1961).

Salvadori, Guglielmo. 'Positivism in Italy'. *The Journal of Philosophy, Psychology and Scientific Methods* 5, no. 17 (Aug. 13, 1908).

Sandomierski, Hershen Berkovich. *Закат фашизма* [Decline of Fascism]. Moscow, 1925.

Sandomierski, Hershen Berkovich. *Фашизм* [Fascism]. Moscow, 1923.

Sandomierski, Hershen Berkovich. *Фашизм и молодежь* [Fascism and Youth]. Moscow, 1925.

Santarelli, Enzo. 'Le socialisme national en Italie: Précédents et origines' [National Socialism in Italy: Precedents and Origins]. *Le Mouvement social* [The Social Movement], no. 50 (Jan.–Mar., 1965).

de Santillana, George. 'The Idealism of Giovanni Gentile'. *Isis* 29, no. 2 (Nov., 1938).

Santomassimo, Gianpasquale. 'Ugo Spirito e il corporativismo' [Ugo Spirito and Corporatism]. *Studi Storici* [Historical Studies] 14, no. 1 (Jan. — Mar., 1973).

Sarti, Roldan. 'Fascist Modernization in Italy: Traditional or Revolutionary'. *The American Historical Review* 75, no. 4 (Apr., 1970).

Sarti, Roland. *Mazzini: A Life for the Religion of Politics*. Westport, Connecticut: Greenwood Publishing Group, 1997.

Scaff, Lawrence A. 'Max Weber and Robert Michels'. *American Journal of Sociology* 86, no. 6 (May, 1981).

Scarangello, Anthony. 'Major Catholic-Liberal Educational Philosophers of the Italian Risorgimento'. *History of Education Quarterly* 4, no. 4 (Dec., 1964).

Schleiermacher, Friedrich. *Hermeneutics*. St. Petersburg: The European House, 2004.

Schnapp, Jeffrey Thompson. 'Fascinating Fascism'. *Journal of Contemporary History* 31, no. 2, Special Issue: The Aesthetics of Fascism (Apr., 1996).

Schnapp, Jeffrey Thompson. *A Primer of Italian Fascism*. Lincoln, Nebraska: University of Nebraska Press, 2000.

Schuwer, Camille. 'La pensée italienne contemporaine. L'idéalisme de Benedetto Croce et de Giovanni Gentile' [Contemporary Italian Thought. The Idealism of Benedetto Croce and Giovanni Gentile]. *Revue Philosophique de la France et de l'Etranger* 97 (January to June, 1924).

Sciacca, Michele Federico. 'Le problème de l'origine des idées et l'objectivité de la connaissance selon À. Rosmini' [The Problem of the Origin of Ideas and the Objectivity of Knowledge According to À. Rosmini]. *Revue de Métaphysique et de Morale* [Journal of Metaphysics and Morals] 60, no. 3 (July-September 1955).

Settembrini, Domenico. 'Mussolini and the Legacy of Revolutionary Socialism'. *Journal of Contemporary History* 11, no. 4, Special Issue: Theories of Fascism (Oct., 1976).

Skradol, Natalia. 'Carnival of Exception: Gabriele D'Annunzio's "Dialogues with the Crowd"'. *Rhetorica: A Journal of the History of Rhetoric* 30, no. 1 (Winter 2012).

Slobodskoj, S.M. *Итальянский фашизм и его крах* [Italian Fascism and its Collapse]. Moscow: Gospolitizdat, 1946.

Slobodskoj, S.M. *Социальная сущность фашизма* [The Social Nature of Fascism]. Moscow, 1928.

Smith, Denis Mack. 'Benedetto Croce: History and Politics'. *Journal of Contemporary History* 8, no. 1 (Jan., 1973).

Smith, Denis Mack. *Mussolini*. New York: Knopf, 1982.

Smith, J. A. 'The Philosophy of Giovanni Gentile'. *Proceedings of the Aristotelian Society, New Series*, 20 (1919–1920).

Soldani, Massimiliano. *L'ultimo poeta armato. Alessandro Pavolini segretario del P.F.R.* [The Last Armed Poet. Alessandro Pavolini Secretary of the P.F.R.]. Milan: Societa Editrice Barbarossa, 2012.

Solonevich, Ivan. *Диктатура сволочи* [Bastard Dictatorship]. Russkoye Slovo, 1995.

Sorel, Georges. *Introduction A L'Economie Moderne* [Introduction to the Study of Modern Economy]. Charleston, South Carolina: Nabu Press, 2013.

Sorel, Georges. *Социальные очерки современной экономики. Дегенерация капитализма и дегенерация социализма* [Social Essays on Modern Economics. The Degeneration of Capitalism and the Degeneration of Socialism]. Moscow: Krasand, 2011.

Sorel, Georges. *Reflections on Violence*. Cambridge: Cambridge University Press, 1999.

Sorel, Georges. (1847–1922). Supplement to the *Revue de Métaphysique et de Morale* 29, no. 4 (October-December 1922).

Spengler, Oswald. *Preußentum und Sozialismus* [Prussianism and Socialism]. London: Arktos, 2021.

Spengler, Oswald. *Years of Decisions*. Yekaterinburg: U-Factoria, 2007.

Spirito, Ugo and Dina Dreyfus. 'Itinéraire du problématisme' [Itinary of Problematism]. *Les Études philosophiques* [Studies in Philosophy], Nouvelle Série 8, no. 2 (April/June 1953).

Spirito, Ugo. *Il pragmatismo nella filosofia contemporanea* [Pragmatism in Contemporary Philosophy]. Florence: Vallecchi, 1921.

Steiner, H. Arthur. 'The Fascist Conception of Law'. *Columbia Law Review* 36, no. 8 (Dec., 1936).

Sternhell, Zeev. 'The "Anti-Materialist" Revision of Marxism as an Aspect of the Rise of Fascist Ideology'. *Journal of Contemporary History* 22, no. 3 (Jul., 1987).

Sternhell, Zeev. *The Birth of Fascist Ideology. From Cultural Rebellion to Political Revolution*. Princeton, New Jersey: Princeton University Press, 1995.

Stewart, L. W. 'The Mentors of Mussolini'. *The American Political Science Review* 22, no. 4 (Nov., 1928).

Tannenbaum, Edward R. *The Fascist Experience. Italian Society and Culture, 1922–1945*. London/New York: Basic Books, Inc., 1972.

Tannenbaum, Edward R. 'The Goals of Italian Fascism'. *The American Historical Review* 74, no. 4 (Apr., 1969).

Tarascio, Vincent J. 'Pareto: A View of the Present through the Past'. *Journal of Political Economy* 84, no. 1 (Feb., 1976).

Tarquini, Alessandra. 'The Anti-Gentilians during the Fascist Regime'. *Journal of Contemporary History* 40, no. 4 (Oct., 2005).

Tarquini, Alessandra. *Il Gentile dei Fascisti. Gentiliani e antigentiliani nel regime Fascista* [The Gentile of the Fascists. Gentilians and Anti-Gentilians in the Fascist Regime]. Bologna: Il Mulino, 2009.

Tashjean, John E. 'Mosca Revisited: Exegesis of an Elitist Argument'. *Revue européenne des sciences sociales* [European Social Science Journal] 10, no. 27 (1972).

Treves, Renato. 'Idéologies politiques et jeunes generations' [Political Ideologies and Young Generations]. *Revue européenne des sciences sociales* [European Social Science Journal] 17, no. 46, L'ubiquité de l'idéologie: Hommage à Raymond Polin [The Ubiquity of Ideology: A Tribute to Raymond Polin] (1979).

Turi, Gabriele. 'Giovanni Gentile: Oblivion, Remembrance, and Criticism'. *The Journal of Modern History* 70, no. 4 (December 1998).

Ustryalov, Nikolay. *Италия — колыбель фашизма* [Italy — the Cradle of Fascism]. Moscow: Algorithm, 2012.

Valeri, Nino. *Trent'anni di storia politica italiana, 1915–1945* [Thirty Years of Italian Political History, 1915–1945]. Turin: ERI, 1962.

Vittoria, Albertina. 'Giovanni Gentile e l'organizzazione della cultura' [Giovanni Gentile and the Organisation of Culture]. *Studi Storici* [Historical Studies] 25, no. 1, Louis Gernet e l'antropologia della Grecia antica (Jan.-Mar., 1984).

Vivarelli, Roberto. *Il dopoguerra in Italia e l'avvento del Fascismo* [Postwar Italy and the Formation of Fascism]. Naples: Istituto italiano per gli studi storici, 1967.

Voegelin, Eric. 'The Political Religions'. *The Collected Works of Eric Voegelin, Volume 5*. Columbia, Missouri: University of Missouri Press, 1999.

Weber, Max. *Science as a Vocation*. London: Unwin Hyman, 1989.

Winterton, Francis. 'The Papal Condemnation of Rosmini'. *Mind* 13, no. 52 (Oct., 1888).

Wistrich, Robert S. 'Leon Trotsky's Theory of Fascism'. *Journal of Contemporary History* 11, no. 4, Special Issue: Theories of Fascism (Oct., 1976).

Wynne, M. G. and L. F. T. Marinetti Barbi. 'Marinetti and Futurism'. *The Yale University Library Gazette* 57, no. 3/4 (April 1983).

Yarrow, Clarence H. 'The Forging of Fascist Doctrine'. *Journal of the History of Ideas* 3, no. 2 (Apr., 1942).

Zagarrio, Vito. 'Bottai: Un Fascista critico?' [A Critical Fascist]. *Studi Storici [*Historical Studies] 17, no. 4 (Oct.–Dec., 1976).

Zanden, James W. Vander. 'Pareto and Fascism Reconsidered'. *The American Journal of Economics and Sociology* 19, no. 4 (Jul., 1960).

Zorin, A. L. *Крочеанцы в поисках субъекта истории и морали* [Croceans in Search of the Subject of History and Morality]. Krasnodar: Krasnodar State University of Culture and Arts Press, 1998.

Zorin, A. L. *Этика итальянских неоидеалистов. Проблема обоснования морали и метода* [Ethics of Italian Neo-Idealists. The Problem of the Justification of Morality and Method]. Krasnodar: Krasnodar State University of Culture and Arts Press, 1999.

Zorin, A. L. *Моральная философия итальянского неоидеализма XX в.: проблема обоснования морали* [Moral Philosophy of Twentieth-Century Italian Neo-Idealism: The Problem of Moral Justification]. Doctoral dissertation in Philosophy. St. Petersburg, 1999.

Zorin, A.L. *Персонализм итальянских спиритуалистов XX в.* [Personalism of the Italian Spiritualists of the Twentieth Century]. Krasnodar: Krasnodar State University of Culture and Arts Press, 1998.

Zorin, A. L. *Философско-этические взгляды крочеанцев и джентилеанцев* [Philosophical and Ethical Views of the Croceans and the Gentileans]. Krasnodar: Krasnodar State University of Culture and Arts Press, 2001.

Zorin, A. L. *Философские искания левых джентилеанцев* [Philosophical Quests of the Left-Wing Gentileans]. Krasnodar: Krasnodar State University of Culture and Arts Press, 1999.

OTHER BOOKS PUBLISHED BY ARKTOS

Virginia Abernethy — *Born Abroad*

Sri Dharma Pravartaka Acharya — *The Dharma Manifesto*

Joakim Andersen — *Rising from the Ruins*

Winston C. Banks — *Excessive Immigration*

Alain de Benoist — *Beyond Human Rights*
Carl Schmitt Today
The Ideology of Sameness
The Indo-Europeans
Manifesto for a European Renaissance
On the Brink of the Abyss
The Problem of Democracy
Runes and the Origins of Writing
View from the Right (vol. 1–3)

Armand Berger — *Tolkien, Europe, and Tradition*

Arthur Moeller van den Bruck — *Germany's Third Empire*

Matt Battaglioli — *The Consequences of Equality*

Kerry Bolton — *The Perversion of Normality*
Revolution from Above
Yockey: A Fascist Odyssey

Isac Boman — *Money Power*

Charles William Dailey — *The Serpent Symbol in Tradition*

Ricardo Duchesne — *Faustian Man in a Multicultural Age*

Alexander Dugin — *Ethnos and Society*
Ethnosociology
Eurasian Mission
The Fourth Political Theory
The Great Awakening vs the Great Reset
Last War of the World-Island
Political Platonism
Putin vs Putin
The Rise of the Fourth Political Theory
The Theory of a Multipolar World

Edward Dutton — *Race Differences in Ethnocentrism*

Mark Dyal — *Hated and Proud*

Clare Ellis — *The Blackening of Europe*

Koenraad Elst — *Return of the Swastika*

Julius Evola — *The Bow and the Club*
Fascism Viewed from the Right
A Handbook for Right-Wing Youth
Metaphysics of Power
Metaphysics of War
The Myth of the Blood
Notes on the Third Reich
The Path of Cinnabar
Recognitions
A Traditionalist Confronts Fascism

OTHER BOOKS PUBLISHED BY ARKTOS

Guillaume Faye	*Archeofuturism* *Archeofuturism 2.0* *The Colonisation of Europe* *Convergence of Catastrophes* *Ethnic Apocalypse* *A Global Coup* *Prelude to War* *Sex and Deviance* *Understanding Islam* *Why We Fight*
Daniel S. Forrest	*Suprahumanism*
Andrew Fraser	*Dissident Dispatches* *Reinventing Aristocracy in the Age of Woke Capital* *The WASP Question*
Génération Identitaire	*We are Generation Identity*
Peter Goodchild	*The Taxi Driver from Baghdad* *The Western Path*
Paul Gottfried	*War and Democracy*
Petr Hampl	*Breached Enclosure*
Porus Homi Havewala	*The Saga of the Aryan Race*
Lars Holger Holm	*Hiding in Broad Daylight* *Homo Maximus* *Incidents of Travel in Latin America* *The Owls of Afrasiab*
Richard Houck	*Liberalism Unmasked*
Institut Iliade	*For a European Awakening*
A. J. Illingworth	*Political Justice*
Alexander Jacob	*De Naturae Natura*
Jason Reza Jorjani	*Artemis Unveiled* *Closer Encounters* *Faustian Futurist* *Iranian Leviathan* *Lovers of Sophia* *Novel Folklore* *Prometheism* *Promethean Pirate* *Prometheus and Atlas* *Psychotron* *Uber Man* *World State of Emergency*
Henrik Jonasson	*Sigmund*
Edgar Julius Jung	*The Significance of the German Revolution*
Ruuben Kaalep & August Meister	*Rebirth of Europe*
Roderick Kaine	*Smart and SeXy*

OTHER BOOKS PUBLISHED BY ARKTOS

Peter King	*Here and Now* *Keeping Things Close* *On Modern Manners*
James Kirkpatrick	*Conservatism Inc.*
Ludwig Klages	*The Biocentric Worldview* *Cosmogonic Reflections* *The Science of Character*
Andrew Korybko	*Hybrid Wars*
Pierre Krebs	*Guillaume Faye: Truths & Tributes* *Fighting for the Essence*
Julien Langella	*Catholic and Identitarian*
John Bruce Leonard	*The New Prometheans*
Stephen Pax Leonard	*The Ideology of Failure* *Travels in Cultural Nihilism*
William S. Lind	*Reforging Excalibur* *Retroculture*
Pentti Linkola	*Can Life Prevail?*
H. P. Lovecraft	*The Conservative*
Norman Lowell	*Imperium Europa*
Richard Lynn	*Sex Differences in Intelligence*
John MacLugash	*The Return of the Solar King*
Charles Maurras	*The Future of the Intelligentsia & For a French Awakening*
John Harmon McElroy	*Agitprop in America*
Michael O'Meara	*Guillaume Faye and the Battle of Europe* *New Culture, New Right*
Michael Millerman	*Beginning with Heidegger*
Maurice Muret	*The Greatness of Elites*
Brian Anse Patrick	*The NRA and the Media* *Rise of the Anti-Media* *The Ten Commandments of Propaganda* *Zombology*
Tito Perdue	*The Bent Pyramid* *Journey to a Location* *Lee* *Morning Crafts* *Philip* *The Sweet-Scented Manuscript* *William's House* (vol. 1–4)
John K. Press	*The True West vs the Zombie Apocalypse*
Raido	*A Handbook of Traditional Living* (vol. 1–2)
Claire Rae Randall	*The War on Gender*
P R Reddall	*Towards Awakening*
Steven J. Rosen	*The Agni and the Ecstasy* *The Jedi in the Lotus*

OTHER BOOKS PUBLISHED BY ARKTOS

Nicholas Rooney	*Talking to the Wolf*
Richard Rudgley	*Barbarians* *Essential Substances* *Wildest Dreams*
Ernst von Salomon	*It Cannot Be Stormed* *The Outlaws*
Werner Sombart	*Traders and Heroes*
Piero San Giorgio	*CBRN* *Giuseppe* *Survive the Economic Collapse*
Sri Sri Ravi Shankar	*Celebrating Silence* *Know Your Child* *Management Mantras* *Patanjali Yoga Sutras* *Secrets of Relationships*
George T. Shaw (ed.)	*A Fair Hearing*
Fenek Solère	*Kraal* *Reconquista*
Oswald Spengler	*The Decline of the West* *Man and Technics*
Richard Storey	*The Uniqueness of Western Law*
Tomislav Sunic	*Against Democracy and Equality* *Homo Americanus* *Postmortem Report* *Titans are in Town*
Askr Svarte	*Gods in the Abyss*
Hans-Jürgen Syberberg	*On the Fortunes and Misfortunes of Art in Post-War Germany*
Abir Taha	*Defining Terrorism* *The Epic of Arya* (2nd ed.) *Nietzsche's Coming God, or the Redemption of the Divine* *Verses of Light*
Jean Thiriart	*Europe: An Empire of 400 Million*
Bal Gangadhar Tilak	*The Arctic Home in the Vedas*
Dominique Venner	*For a Positive Critique* *The Shock of History*
Hans Vogel	*How Europe Became American*
Markus Willinger	*A Europe of Nations* *Generation Identity*
Alexander Wolfheze	*Alba Rosa* *Rupes Nigra*

Printed in Great Britain
by Amazon

54722703R00199